WIVES OF THE KINGS
OF ENGLAND

WIVES OF THE KINGS OF ENGLAND

From Normans to Stuarts

Mark Hichens

Book Guild Publishing
Sussex, England

First published in Great Britain in 2008 by
The Book Guild Ltd
Pavilion View
19 New Road
BN1 1UF

Typesetting in Times by
Keyboard Services, Luton, Bedfordshire

Printed and bound in Great Britain by
CPI Antony Rowe

A catalogue record for this book is available from
The British Library

ISBN 978 1 84624 300 4

CONTENTS

v

INTRODUCTION

The wives of England's kings have many a tale to tell – some heroic, some tragic, some nefarious. Certainly they are varied. On the one hand are the furies like Margaret of Anjou fomenting a bloody civil war, and Isabella, 'the she wolf of France', leading an invasion of the country which would depose her husband and put him to death. On the other are the gentle and compassionate like Matilda of Scotland, tending the sick and washing the feet of mendicants, and Philippa of Hainault, on her knees before her husband pleading for the lives of the burghers of Calais. And their fortunes have shifted treacherously: at times enthroned in splendour, gorgeously arrayed and fawned on by obsequious courtiers; at times hunted fugitives, crouching in a ditch or seeking shelter in the meanest hovel. Most on occasions have been in mortal danger, like Margaret of Anjou falling among thieves in a darkened forest or Eleanor of Provence escaping by river from an anarchic London pelted with rocks, ordure and carcasses amid cries of 'Drown the witch!' A few like Eleanor of Aquitaine spent years imprisoned or, like Elizabeth Woodville, were driven into sanctuary; and two, Anne Boleyn and Catherine Howard, ended on the executioner's block, although not on the orders of an enemy but of their husband.

There were not many who sought to be 'the power behind the throne', most being content with a subservient role, although some were to find themselves invested with authority while their husbands were with armies abroad. And there were some who, though humble and unambitious, nevertheless changed the course of history unintentionally. Catherine of Aragon would have been appalled to think she had had any part in the coming of the Reformation to England, but there can be no doubt that the uncompromising stand she took was one of the causes of it. Similarly at the time of the 'Glorious Revolution' Queen Mary II would have been unaware that by her loyalty to her husband, William

III, rather than to her father, James II, she was paving the way to a new political era.

Lasting happiness came to few English queens. Most of them had troubled and turbulent lives. Usually they would have had no say in the choice of their husbands which was decided by their parents whom they were bound to obey. They might be teenagers consigned to a husband twenty or even thirty years older, in a far distant land to whose alien culture they had to adapt. And always they were expected to be prolific bearers of children. Some like Catherine of Aragon and Catherine of Braganza suffered agonies from childlessness, while others brought forth abundantly but only to see many of their children dying in infancy (Anne of Denmark lost four out of seven, Mary of Modena five out of six).

Not least among the problems confronting the queens were the men they married, to whose ways, often quirky and libidinous, they had to adapt. They might be mighty warriors, feared throughout Europe, or ineffective weaklings (in some cases homoerotic) who had to be propped up; but all needed the support of wives. How vital this was, even to the strongest, became evident when they predeceased their husbands. After the death of Matilda of Flanders William I ('The Conqueror') went into a decline and became morose and introverted; and Edward III, once the most feared monarch in Europe, after the death of Philippa of Hainault, degenerated into a pathetic semblance of his former self.

All queens, then, including those who might seem to have been dim and of no account, had a fundamental role. And nearly all of them were a blessing both to their husbands and to their country. Their works of charity were many – religious houses endowed, schools and hospitals founded, poverty and suffering relieved, their piety in most cases exemplary. In an age of bloodshed and dark deeds their influence nearly always was benign and forbearing.

MATILDA OF FLANDERS (1031–1083)

Wife of William I

Matilda of Flanders has been given scant attention by history, the general opinion being that she was dim and colourless and completely overshadowed by her fearsome husband. But she deserves more notice than this: her influence, though inconspicuous, was significant and usually beneficial; her example of piety and charity gleamed in a dark world, and she was almost the only person to have had some restraining influence on the ferocity of her husband.

She was the daughter of a rich and renowned European ruler, Count Baldwin V of Flanders, and her ancestry was of the most exalted, with descent from both the Emperor Charlemagne and King Alfred. By comparison the origins of William, though romantic, were rough-hewn. He was descended from a line of Norsemen marauders who had occupied the part of France which became known as Normandy and who then spread southwards into Italy and Sicily and ultimately northwards into England.

William's father, Robert, was an impulsive, quixotic character who had been suddenly smitten in love by a woman of humble birth, the daughter of a tanner, while she was washing clothes in a river. He had straightaway borne her off, but not as his wife, as he already had one, but as a paramour by whom he had a son, William – the future 'Conqueror'. Concubinage was not unusual among Normans at that time, and before going off on a pilgrimage to Jerusalem, Robert had nominated William as his heir, and when he died soon afterwards on his way home, William at the age of seven became Duke of Normandy. It seemed unlikely that a child of that age, tainted as he was both by bastardy and being the grandson of a tanner, would survive, surrounded by power-hungry relatives and rebellious vassals. But survive he did, thanks mainly to support from the King of France.

William had set his sights on Matilda at an early age. At first the lady held back, as well she might from such an upstart, but

William was nothing if not resolute, and by 1051, when he was twenty-four, she had relented. Even then there were obstacles as their marriage was banned by Pope Leo IX. His reasons for doing so are not clear: officially it was because of consanguinity, but their relationship was not at all close (actually fifth cousins) and this should not have been an insuperable barrier. There were rumours that Matilda already had a husband from whom she was separated, but this has never been confirmed. In any case William was not to be put off and went ahead with the marriage, confident that in time the ban would be lifted as it was a few years later by Leo's successor, Pope Nicholas II, on condition that William and Matilda founded two religious houses, one for men and one for women.

William's success in encroaching on his neighbours in France led him to look further afield, and it seemed to him that the kingdom of England across the Channel was a fruit ready to be gathered. After a closely fought fight at Hastings William with his army of predatory warriors from all over Europe, numbering perhaps some twelve thousand, subjugated a country of one and a half million inhabitants. His methods were brutal and ruthless: anyone resisting was put to death or horribly dismembered while large areas were laid waste as a stark warning to anyone with thoughts of rebellion; and as a result many died from hunger in the ensuing famine. Vicious and tyrannical as was William's rule, it nevertheless brought some citizens a security they had not known before and were to miss sorely in years ahead under more propitiatory rulers. For William allowed no other despots but himself. A chronicler of the time wrote that he kept such good order that 'a man of any substance could travel unmolested throughout the country with his bosom full of gold' – which he certainly could not have done subsequently in the reign of King Stephen.

Little is known of the married life of this implacable tyrant, but it seems that he was a considerate and faithful husband. Unlike most warlords of that time he held puritanical views about the sanctity of marriage and disapproved strongly of moral laxity, particularly among the clergy. Perhaps his own illegitimate origins had some bearing on this. It does not seem that his love for Matilda was a passionate one, but he held her in great respect and trusted her completely, leaving her with confidence in charge of one part of his realm while he went off to wage war in another. Matilda was no warrior queen – a diminutive figure hardly more than four feet tall, she was not cut out for the part. Her authority rested rather on her calm and sensible judgement and her piety and works of charity. A monkish chronicler of the times praised her as a 'singular mirror of prudence' and another wrote of her as 'the perfection of virtue'.

Matilda was to bear William ten children – four sons and six daughters. The eldest son, Robert, was her special favourite, so much so that when a dispute broke out between him and his father about the granting of lands and titles to him in Normandy, she took his side, helping him out with money, even selling some of her jewellery to do so. Normally William would have been infuriated by such disloyalty and there would have been fearful consequences, but for once he showed forgiveness. When she died at the age of fifty-two, he was desolate, and during his last four years without her became ever more embittered and choleric. The people of England and Normandy could ill spare her.

Today we have most reason to be grateful to Matilda for the part she had in the creation of the Bayeux Tapestry, depicting the story of the Norman invasion of England. How great a part she played is questionable; the main design came from others but she is said to have joined in the needlework, and her patronage and encouragement must have been a stimulus.

MATILDA OF SCOTLAND (1080–1118)
and ADELIZA OF LORRAINE (1103–1151)

Wives of Henry I

On his deathbed William the Conqueror decided reluctantly that he had to divide his domains – they were beyond the capability of any one of his sons. And so to his eldest son, Robert, he bequeathed the dukedom of Normandy and to his second son, William, the kingdom of England. To his third son, Henry, he left only a sum of money but was said to have foretold that one day he would become a greater king than either of his brothers – a prophecy that was soon to be fulfilled.

William II was not a popular king. He was a strong ruler and enforced some sort of law and order, but he was harsh and capricious, provoked strong opposition from the Church by his disrespect for religion, and the moral tone of his court was depraved and known to be homoerotic. When in 1100 he was killed, allegedly by a stray arrow while hunting in the New Forest, few were sorry – certainly not his brother, Henry, who lost no time in gaining possession of the royal treasury and having himself crowned king, an action which he must have known would be disputatious as there were others with a stronger claim, notably his elder brother Robert who, a month after William's death, arrived back from the First Crusade where he had taken part in the capture of Jerusalem and had won great distinction. For the time being, however, he was immersed in the tangled affairs of Normandy and at first acknowledged Henry as King of England. But Henry's position was insecure and he needed to consolidate it by winning the support of the indigenous English population which he attempted to do by promising to abide by the laws and customs of the last Anglo-Saxon king, Edward the Confessor and by amending outstanding grievances.

He also gained favour by taking as his wife an English, or rather Anglo-Scottish, princess. Matilda of Scotland (or Edith as she was first known) was the daughter of the Scottish king, Malcolm

III[1] and his English wife, Margaret Atheling, who was a granddaughter of the English king, Edmund Ironside. At the age of twelve, following the deaths of her father and mother she was compelled to take refuge in England where she was placed in an aristocratic convent under the rule of her aunt, Christina. There for seven years she lived the life of a nun but she did not take a nun's vows. This was to be of great importance later. To Henry I she seemed the ideal wife not only because of her ancestry but because she was a lady of learning and taste which Henry appreciated because he himself had academic aspirations, unusual for a king, which had won for him the pseudonym of 'Beauclerc'. But first it was necessary that it should be shown beyond doubt that, as Matilda insisted, she had not taken the vows of a nun, as this would have precluded marriage. And so Archbishop Anselm set up a court of enquiry which after a close examination came to the conclusion that she was to be believed.

Once married Matilda soon fulfilled the main obligation expected of her, the begetting of children – in 1102 a daughter, Maud (later Matilda), and in 1103 a son, William. Although then only twenty-three and with twelve years of marriage ahead of her, she was to have no more children.

As queen, Matilda was to be called on to take part in government when Henry was out of England, and this became more frequent after 1106 when he invaded Normandy with a mainly English army and defeated his brother, Robert, at the battle of Tinchebrai. As a result Henry became Duke of Normandy with all the problems that that entailed, while Robert for the rest of his life, twenty-eight years, was to be a prisoner in England, fortunately in not very rigorous conditions.

Although Matilda performed her political duties with good judgement and grace, her main interests were always in works of charity and piety. Her convent upbringing had left its mark. Many religious houses were endowed by her and she saw to the establishment of hospitals, schools and even bath houses. And her religious observances were the strictest, extending even to the care of lepers and washing the feet of mendicants.

Matilda died in 1118 at the age of thirty-eight. Henry was in Normandy at the time but did not come to England for her funeral.

---

[1] Best known for overcoming the usurper and murderer Macbeth.

It seems that while he had respect for his wife and trusted her completely, he felt no passionate love for her. Certainly he was not a faithful husband, fathering perhaps as many as twenty bastards, but there is no record of Matilda taking him to task for his infidelity.

Matilda's death caused heartfelt grief in England where she was greatly beloved. Monkish chronicles were more than usually lavish in her praise. 'Her spirit showed by tokens more than ordinary that it inhabits heaven,' wrote one. And on her tombstone was inscribed: 'Here lies the renowned Queen Matilda the second, excelling both young and old of her day, she was for everyone the benchmark of morals, and the ornament of life.' By some she was regarded as a saint and pilgrims were to come to her tomb in the hope of a miraculous cure.

Two years after Matilda's death her son William, heir to the throne, was drowned when the White Ship sank in the English Channel, a tragedy which surely changed the course of English history. Certainly Henry thought so; he never recovered from it and was said not to have smiled again. In 1122 he married Adeliza, daughter of the Duke of Lorraine, aged eighteen and very beautiful; but for her it can hardly have been a joyous prospect – marriage to a man thirty-five years her senior and steeped in melancholia, but it survived for fourteen years, although there were no children. Henry, so prolific out of wedlock, could beget no more than two legitimate heirs. And Adeliza cannot be held responsible, for in her second marriage to an English nobleman she gave birth to seven children to become the founder of one of England's most illustrious families, that of the dukes of Norfolk. Unexpectedly, when still in her forties and surrounded by a large and loving family, she withdrew to a convent in Flanders.

MATILDA OF BOULOGNE (1104–1151)

Wife of Stephen

Most queens of England in the Middle Ages had rough rides, but few had such a sad and turbulent life as Matilda of Boulogne, who had the misfortune to be queen at the time of a particularly bloody civil war. In this she often had a crucial role and was, perhaps, the only leading figure to emerge with some honour, but she could do nothing to prevent the country from sinking into the darkest abyss in its history.

Matilda's father was Count Eustace III of Boulogne, a maritime state whose rulers at one time had been given to freebooting in the English Channel. But they had been diverted from this by the call of the Cross and had taken part in the First Crusade as a result of which two of their members had become, somewhat precariously, kings of Jerusalem. Matilda's mother, Mary, was a sister of Matilda of Scotland, wife of Henry I (see previous chapter) and so of Anglo-Scottish descent. She had married Stephen in 1125, five years after the tragedy of the White Ship, and she may well have been present in 1127 when Henry I assembled the leading magnates of England, including Stephen, and made them take an oath accepting his daughter, another Matilda but better known as Maud, as heir to the throne.

Maud had been married at the age of twelve to the Emperor of Germany, Henry V, some thirty years her elder, who had disappeared mysteriously in 1126 and was assumed to have died.[1] Henry I had then insisted that the Empress Maud should return to England as she was his only legitimate heir. He also ordered her to marry Geoffrey of Anjou, the thought of which appalled her. Was she, the daughter of a king and widow of an emperor, to marry the

---

[1] Later a legend arose that he had been discovered on his deathbed in a hospital where he had taken service to atone for his sins. Maud was said to have acknowledged him as her former husband.

son of a mere count, some eleven years younger than she and from a land reputed for its barbarous ways and believed to be descended from devils? Geoffrey too was dismayed. He found the Empress Maud insufferably arrogant and disagreeable and, despite her undoubted learning and good looks, life with her intolerable. But his father Count Fulk V (just off to be king of Jerusalem) was as adamant as Henry I, and so married they were for a lifetime of marital discord. Remarkably, after seven years, three sons were born to them of which the eldest, the future Henry II of England, was to change the face of Europe.

When Henry I died in 1135 the barons of England were deeply uneasy at the prospect of a queen regnant. There had never been one before in England and there was no confidence that a woman would be able to govern the country, even one of whom it was said that 'she had the nature of a man in the frame of a woman'. There were also fears that her husband, Geoffrey, who had a reputation for being scheming and ambitious, might be a dangerous power behind the throne. And so, in spite of the oaths they had taken, most of the barons upheld the claims of Henry's nephew, Stephen, son of his sister Adela. He had been brought up in the English court and had become close to his uncle Henry who had treated him like a son and was even rumoured on his deathbed to have named him as his successor. He was also on the spot and ready to be crowned and had the blessing not only of the Archbishop of Canterbury but also of the Pope who absolved the barons from their oaths.

At first the Empress Maud, who was far off in Anjou at the time, did not dispute Stephen's succession, but five years later she came to England with an armed force and plunged the country into civil war which was to last on and off for fifteen years. In this she did not at any time have help from her husband who had no interest in England and was concerned only in conquering Normandy, which in time he was to do successfully.

By the time the Empress Maud invaded the country Stephen had proved himself a weak and inept ruler. Charming, brave and full of good intentions, he was incapable of controlling the turbulent Norman barons who were set on breaking the central power of the monarch established by Henry I. Finding they could defy his authority with impunity, they robbed and imprisoned innocent citizens in the castles Stephen had been powerless to prevent them from building. A chronicler of the time wrote sadly: 'When the traitors perceived that King Stephen was a mild man and soft and good and did no justice, then did they all manner of horrors. They had done homage to him and sworn oaths, but they held no faith.'

There were, therefore, at first many who welcomed the Empress Maud as saviour of the country and joined forces with her; and initially they were victorious. At the battle of Lincoln in 1141 Stephen was defeated and taken prisoner, and for nearly a year the Empress Maud was in control of most of the country. But she soon made herself unpopular. Her manner was offensively haughty and overbearing and she grossly abused her powers. Her treatment of Stephen – incarcerated in chains in a 'filthy dungeon' – caused great offence, and when she was asked to release him (provided he were to go into a monastery abroad) she refused 'with harsh and insulting language'.

It was during Stephen's imprisonment that his wife, Matilda of Boulogne (hereafter referred to as Queen Matilda) came to the fore and kept the flag flying for him while others were deserting in droves. She was able to build up a sizeable fighting force in Kent and advanced on London where the Empress had deeply offended the citizens by her draconian ways and extortionate demands for money and with the approach of the Queen they rose in revolt, and the Empress was forced to flee from the city. For a time she was based in Winchester but was driven out of there after a battle in which the royalist forces of the Queen made an important captive.

The principal supporter of the Empress had always been Earl Robert of Gloucester, one of Henry I's numerous bastards and so the Empress's half-brother. With his capture the royalists had a strong bargaining counter in negotiating the release of Stephen. In this Queen Matilda had a leading role and after some hard bargaining an agreement was reached and on 1st November 1141 Stephen was set free. This was a notable triumph for the queen; without her Stephen's cause might well have lapsed; it was she who had rallied his supporters and prevailed on many who had deserted him to return to their allegiance. This was acknowledged by contemporaries, one of whom wrote: 'Forgetting the weakness of her sex and a woman's softness she bore herself with the valour of a man.'

By 1142 the forces of the Empress were in disarray and she found herself bottled up in Oxford Castle where she endured a siege of three months. Appeals were made for help from her

11

husband, but Geoffrey continued to withhold any support; he was still occupied with the conquest of Normandy, but possibly he was also not all that concerned with his wife's fate. But the Empress, arrogant and bad tempered though she might be, was not lacking in courage, and in mid-winter, clad in white to camouflage her in the snow, she contrived to escape from Oxford and make her way to nearby Wallingford where friends awaited her – a serious misfortune for Stephen as her capture might have ended the war.

But it was to continue for twelve more years with fluctuating fortunes as double-dealing barons changed sides according to the way the wind was blowing. In 1142 Stephen suffered a defeat at Wilton in Wiltshire and narrowly escaped recapture. From then on the war between him and the Empress became something of a stalemate, but there was still much fighting between over-powerful barons, vying for each other's lands. The lack of monarchical authority allowed them to take the law into their own hands as the country sank ever deeper into anarchy. There were piteous accounts of conditions in some parts of England at that time. In the Anglo-Saxon Chronicle a monk of Peterborough described graphically the sufferings of the fen country:

> Every powerful man made his castles and held them against the King ... and they filled them with devils and evil men. Then they seized those men who they supposed had any possessions, both by night and day, men and women, and put them to prison for their gold and silver, and tortured them with unspeakable tortures... Many thousands they killed with hunger. I neither can nor may tell all the horrors and all the tortures that they did to the wretched men of this land... When the wretched men had no more to give they robbed and burnt all the villages, so that you might go a whole day's journey and you would never find a man in a village or land being tilled...

How much Queen Matilda was aware of these anarchic conditions cannot be known, but they would have horrified her as she was reputed to be of a compassionate nature and given to works of charity. She tried too to bring peace between the warring parties but as long as Stephen was alive and king this was not possible. She died three years before him in 1151 at the age of forty-seven.

ELEANOR OF AQUITAINE (1122–1204)

Wife of Henry II

Eleanor of Aquitaine will always be unique among queens – the wife of a king of France then of a king of England, co-founder of an empire stretching from the Pyrenees to the borders of Scotland, a crusader and mother of ten children including two of the most famous kings of England (Richard I and John). At the age of fifteen Eleanor became Duchess of Aquitaine and Gascony and Countess of Poitou. Her realm was by far the largest in France, overshadowing the demesne of the King of France to whom in theory she paid homage. Aquitaine had been put on the map by her grandfather, Duke William IX. Raunchy, rash, charismatic and with an artistic flair, notably for the writing of poetry, he succeeded in making Aquitaine not only a great power but also the centre of Western European culture, attended by artists, troubadours and musicians. But he had also had his disasters, notably when an army he led on a crusade was annihilated; and because of his multiple infidelities both of his wives left him for religious houses.

His son, William X, father of Eleanor, was of a different hue. Weak willed and lacking political judgement, he struggled vainly to exercise some control over rebellious vassals and to keep his vast domain intact. During the eleven years of his reign Eleanor and her younger sister, Petronilla, received a liberal and not too demanding an education – a little Latin and Greek but not too much, plenty of reading and learning by heart of love songs and epics of the troubadours as well as proficiency in embroidery, music and the arts. In 1130, when Eleanor was eight years old, the family suffered a double blow with the deaths of her mother and younger brother so that she then became heiress to the domains of her father. A prominent figure in her childhood was her father's youngest brother, Raymond of Poitou, a man of tremendous physical strength and macho charms and, only eight years older than her, more like a brother than an uncle. For a time they were to be close but were to be parted when Raymond, a landless younger son, went to seek his fortune first at the court of Henry I of England and then in the city of Antioch in Syria where he and Eleanor were to be reunited years later in fateful circumstances.

In 1137 William X died while on a pilgrimage to the shrine of Saint James at Santiago de Compostela in Spain, leaving his domains to Eleanor and placing her in the guardianship of his overlord, the King of France who, he hoped, would preserve her realm intact and find her a suitable husband. Louis VI of France, a gross figure known as Louis the Fat, was delighted by the news of William's death and the terms of his will, and lost no time in ordering a marriage between Eleanor and his son and heir, the future Louis VII. Such a union would vastly increase the size of his kingdom. And so Prince Louis was despatched with all haste to Aquitaine to be married immediately. At the time he was sixteen and had only recently become heir to the throne following the death of his elder brother. Until then he had been destined for a life in the church which suited him ideally as he was by nature pious and chaste and unworldly. He had no wish for kingship nor for marriage, but he had to obey his father's instructions and within four months of William X's death he and Eleanor were married. On their way back to Paris news reached them of the death of Louis the Fat, and so in their mid-teens they found themselves king and queen of France.

Before they reached Paris the two of them must have been realising that they were mismatched. They were so very different: Louis, mild and reclusive; Eleanor, full-blooded and worldly. And their backgrounds had been totally dissimilar: Louis in a monastery at prayer and study; Eleanor in a court renowned for its free and easy ways and the pursuit of pleasure.

As might be expected Eleanor did not fit easily into court life in Paris which was more constrained, more ceremonial and more priest-ridden than she had been accustomed to. It was also more erudite: instead of the epics of troubadours and sensuous love poems there were learned discourses and scholarly debate. These were of a high calibre, the highest in Europe, but they were not to Eleanor's taste. She could not agree with the chronicler, John of Salisbury, that 'of all nations Paris was the sweetest and most civilised'. She found the Cité Palace cold and bleak and the streets noisy and filthy. And Parisians did not take to her: she was considered frivolous and lacking the dignity required of a queen. And there were no signs of her and Louis establishing closer rapport. Louis was not to be distracted from his religious practices – forever fasting, keeping vigils and singing in choirs; nor were children from the marriage forthcoming. Increasingly Eleanor became alienated from her husband who fell far short of the bold, virile, adventurous consort she had once envisaged. Well might she have lamented that she thought she had married a prince and found herself married to a monk. It was not until the eighth year of marriage that a child was born – a daughter, Marie, which was a disappointment.

Certainly Louis was not cut out to be a king: weak and indecisive, he was always taking wrong decisions – appeasing when he should have been firm and overreacting when he should have been conciliatory. Eleanor tried to put steel into him, usually with disastrous results, notably when she urged him into a war with the principality of Toulouse. In the course of this there occurred an incident which seared Louis traumatically. While his army was besieging the city of Vitry-sur-Marne the inhabitants took refuge in the cathedral which was set on fire by incendiary arrows, and the agonised screams of the inflamed men, women and children were to haunt him forever. He felt an overwhelming guilt for which he had to make some great atonement. It was perhaps the determining factor behind the most unfortunate decision of his life – to take part in the Second Crusade.

This had been called by Pope Eugenius III in 1145 following the capture by the Turks of the city of Edessa, thus posing a threat to Jerusalem. Urged on fiercely by St Bernard, Abbot of Clairvaux and founder of the Cistercian order of monks, Louis VII responded immediately as also later did Emperor Conrad of Germany. No one was more enthusiastic about the crusade than Eleanor and she was determined to be included in it. Her motives, however, were not primarily spiritual; she was more concerned in escaping from the boredom of life in Paris and had dreams of a far away land full of exotic wonders where the sun was always shining. She lost no time in drumming up support. Arrayed, so it was alleged, as Queen Penthesilea of the Amazons with lance and shield and sitting astride a richly caparisoned white horse, she toured the estates of her

15

vassals in Aquitaine, putting every pressure on them to take the Cross.[1]

By June 1147, after extensive preparations, the crusade was ready to set out. By then a crowd of 100,000 had been assembled of which not all were soldiers. Also included were a large number of miscellaneous hangers-on – grooms, cooks, falconers, troubadours and vagabonds of one kind or another. And there were many women. Eleanor was accompanied by ladies of noble birth, each of whom had a large retinue of female attendants. She travelled separately from Louis mainly in the company of adventurous types, looking out for excitement and ready to enjoy themselves. In contrast, Louis, clad in hair shirt and the simple black tunic of a crusader, was attended by the sober and the godfearing who looked with stern disapproval on any tendencies to treat the crusade lightheartedly.

And so this vast unwieldy mass set out eastwards, following the course of the river Danube and by the beginning of October it reached Constantinople. There the Byzantine emperor, Manuel Comnenus, wished the crusaders well but was glad to see them on their way. Soon afterwards they ran into serious trouble in Asia Minor. Beset by torrential rain and floods and under constant attack by the Turks, morale sank abysmally and many died or deserted. The crusade that had set out with such high hopes had become a nightmare. It was necessary to complete the journey by sea which meant leaving thousands behind.

In March 1148, however, Louis, Eleanor and what remained of their army reached Antioch with its hanging gardens, orange groves, marble-paved streets and a city wall with 360 towers. It had once been the third city of the Roman empire but was then under the rule of Eleanor's uncle, Raymond of Poitiers, whom she had loved as a child. He was to welcome them lavishly but it soon became apparent that he had ulterior motives. For Antioch was under threat from the Saracens and Raymond wanted Louis to campaign against them. Louis refused, insisting that his prime task was to press on to Jerusalem. The disagreement was to have serious consequences as Eleanor took the part of her uncle. It had been noticed that since arriving in Antioch she had been spending much time alone with him, and the suspicion had arisen that they were lovers.

---

[1] Penthesilea came to the siege of Troy to fight against the Greeks and was killed by Achilles who lamented her grievously.

16

Whether this was so or not she told Louis that if he proceeded to Jerusalem she would stay behind with Raymond and seek an annulment of their marriage. To Louis this came as a bombshell and he took drastic action; he arranged to leave Antioch at midnight and, just before, he ordered Eleanor to be abducted and taken with him. For this Eleanor never forgave him; their marriage was to last for a few years yet but there was never a genuine reconciliation.

In May 1148, almost a year after setting out, Louis, with what remained of the crusaders, arrived in Jerusalem where he was given an ecstatic welcome. This was a great emotional experience and he was to remain in the Holy City for nearly a year in spite of his presence being urgently needed back in France. While there Eleanor was not much in evidence; she seems to have been tucked away out of sight, perhaps in disgrace after her behaviour at Antioch, or perhaps under guard to prevent her from escaping and returning to her uncle.

Louis and Eleanor finally set sail for home in April 1149. They travelled in separate ships, for whatever reason, and in the course of the voyage through the Mediterranean they became separated and for two months Eleanor was lost; it has never become known what happened to her during this time; there were reports that she was washed up on the coast of Barbary, but these are unconfirmed. What is certain is that she arrived at the Sicilian port of Palermo in mid-July, exhausted and very ill. Louis too had been blown off course but turned up soon afterwards in Calabria. When they had been reunited and Eleanor was well enough to travel they set off up the Italian mainland. Eleanor by then was determined on a divorce and became even more so when news reached her of the death of her uncle Raymond in battle against the Turks; and for this she blamed Louis for not staying and giving him support. Raymond was perhaps the one man that Eleanor ever really loved.

On their way northwards Louis and Eleanor took in a visit to Pope Eugenius III who had been expelled from Saint Peter's and was residing at the time in the city of Tusculum to the south of Rome. Eleanor was full of hope that he would annul her marriage on the grounds of consanguinity – she and Louis were third cousins, but Eugenius proved adamant. He insisted that their marriage was valid and must remain intact; he also acted as marriage counsellor, listening to their woes and persuading them to overcome their differences; he even provided them with a magnificent double bed beautifully adorned and perfumed which he hoped might act as an aphrodisiac. And in this the old Pope was temporarily successful: conjugal rights were restored and Eleanor to her dismay became pregnant.

On 11 November 1149 after an absence of two and a half years Louis and Eleanor were back in Paris. The citizens put on a welcome for them but it could not but be somewhat muted as there was no disguising the fact that the Crusade had been a disastrous failure. The Christian principalities were no more secure than they had been before, if anything rather less so as the Crusade had united warring factions among the Turks while rivalries among the Christians had been exacerbated. Pious monkish chroniclers were at a loss to understand why God had withheld victory from the crusaders and could only conclude sadly that it was because they had 'abandoned themselves to open fornication and to adulteries hateful to God'.

Moreover the Crusade marked the coming of the separation of Louis and Eleanor. The return to Paris gave Eleanor no joy. The Cité Palace seemed as bleak and inhospitable as ever and the following winter was the coldest in memory. More than ever she was determined to end her marriage. In the spring of 1150 she gave birth to another daughter, Princess Alix, which caused general disappointment although not to her, as she realised that her failure to bear a son would bring support for an annulment. Even Louis was beginning to feel that if he was to have a son and heir it would have to be by another wife. There were, however, strong reasons against an annulment: Louis would have to give up all claims of suzerainty over Aquitaine. As things stood this would pass in time to his daughters, Marie and Alix; but if Eleanor were to marry again and have a son this inheritance would be lost to them. And the kingdom of France without Aquitaine would be a much less formidable proposition.

Eleanor was aware that if she did obtain an annulment and the governance of Aquitaine reverted to her, she would need a strong husband by her side, as Aquitaine had the reputation of being wild and almost ungovernable. And in casting around for a suitable candidate her thoughts turned towards the house of Anjou. The province of Anjou had once been held in contempt by its neighbours, its inhabitants being regarded as barbaric and descended from the devil. But a great change had come about following the accession of Count Geoffrey, known as Plantagenet because of the *planta genista* (wild broom) he wore in his crest. He was a man of great determination and ambition, also of striking good looks. He inherited his title at the age of sixteen when his father, Fulk V, went off to marry Melisende, the widowed queen of Jerusalem. Just before going, however, he compelled his son to marry Matilda, daughter of Henry I of England and widow of the emperor of Germany who was nine years his senior and oppressively haughty. She treated Geoffrey with contempt and their marriage was bitterly unhappy, but somehow it resulted in the birth of three children, the eldest of whom was to become Henry II of England.

Geoffrey did not go on the Second Crusade preferring to remain at home to consolidate the position of Anjou and of himself. Soon after the return of Louis and Eleanor, war between Anjou and France became imminent, but it was called off at the last minute and Geoffrey and his son Henry, then aged eighteen, came to Paris for peace talks in the course of which there were secret meetings between the young Henry and Eleanor. What happened at these meetings is not known, but later a monkish chronicler was to write prudishly that 'Henry cast lustful eyes on Eleanor who cast unchaste eyes on him.' She was eleven years older than he but still a beautiful woman with a vibrant personality and perhaps all the more attractive for a somewhat dubious past. And Henry – thick-set, bull-necked, bow-legged with cropped red hair – was hardly a beauty, but full-blooded, strong willed and bursting with energy and youthful masculinity, all the things Louis lacked.

If they did not then come to an understanding about marriage the way for this was soon to be opened up by events: on the way back to Anjou Geoffrey died suddenly so that Henry, already created Duke of Normandy, became also Count of Anjou and was soon to be declared heir to the throne of England. And a year later at a specially convened court of bishops and archbishops the marriage of Louis and Eleanor was formally annulled on the grounds of consanguinity. Three months later she and Henry were married. This caused shock and surprise throughout Europe. A chaste chronicler wrote: 'He presumed to sleep adulterously with the Queen of France, taking her from his own lord and marrying her himself. How could anything fortunate, I ask, emerge from such copulations?' Most shocked of all was Louis VII who could not imagine Eleanor, a sophisticated woman of thirty whom he still loved, wedded to a raw youth of nineteen, and one, moreover, who was just as closely related to her as he was. And the prospect of the creation of a state ten times larger than his own was seriously menacing. Certainly this low-key, shotgun wedding (a baby was born four months later) was to be of momentous importance. The histories of England and France would have been different without it.

In the following year Henry with ships from Aquitaine provided by Eleanor mounted an invasion of England and secured from King Stephen a promise that he would succeed him as king on his death which, fortunately for England, occurred soon afterwards, and in 1154 Henry and Eleanor found themselves with an empire stretching from the Scottish border to the Pyrenees. As well as King of England he was also Duke of Normandy, Lord of Aquitaine, Poitou, Anjou, Maine and Guienne. And before he died Brittany and Ireland were to be added to the list.

The inheritance of the throne of England at that time was hardly one to be envied. For sixteen years the country had been racked by civil war, robber barons held sway and law and order were virtually non-existent. A strong ruthless king was urgently needed and few could have filled this role better than Henry II. No more than twenty-one and by birth and upbringing a Frenchman, he soon realised what had to be done and threw himself into the task with tremendous verve: rebellious barons were subdued, made to pull down the castles they had built illegally and to submit to royal authority. For this alone Henry deserved the gratitude of the people of England, but he did more besides. He instituted an efficient civil service for administration and, more importantly, laid the foundations of English Common Law. Of course changes of such magnitude did not occur overnight, but it was Henry who initiated them and set them in motion. For a young foreigner his achievements were prodigious. Sir Winston Churchill has written of him that 'no man has left a deeper mark on the laws and institutions of the country'.

In his great work Eleanor for most of the time was at his side but hers was only ever a supporting role; even in her own domain of Aquitaine she was given no share of government; this was not considered a woman's realm. Besides, she was much occupied bearing children. During her fifteen-year marriage to Louis she could only bring forth two daughters; but married to

Henry she bore eight children in thirteen years, five sons and three daughters.[2]

Eleanor's life in England can hardly have been agreeable.[3] Compared with the charm and elegance of the court of Aquitaine, English castles were gaunt and comfortless. She had been accustomed to silken hangings, oriental carpets, tapestries and glazed windows, but these were not often to be found in England. And Henry's court was not noted for its style and grace; his own tastes were rough and ready and he seemed to enjoy the company of low characters – pimps, prostitutes, gamblers and buffoons. A contemporary described his court as 'a hotbed of scandal and frivolity' and compared it unfavourably to ancient Babylon. And certainly he made no pretence of being a faithful husband, grasping every opportunity that came his way.

To keep the country in order it was necessary for Henry to be constantly on the move, travelling from one part of his realm to another. These journeyings were often chaotic as Henry saw no need to adhere to a timetable and would move off or stay put as the spirit moved him. Eleanor would usually accompany him and would have to rough it with the rest of them. At times they might be put up in comparative comfort in a castle but at others they might find themselves in some hovel hardly fit for animals. And as Henry was indifferent to food it was often disgusting – stale fish and decaying meat – and wine so thick that to get it down 'a man had to close his eyes, clench his teeth, grimacing with horror'.

Henry's success in restoring law and order in England was due in the main to his own willpower and prodigious energy but also to his ability to choose the best people to work for him. Of these the most notable was Thomas Becket, the son of a well-to-do merchant of Norman origin, and soon after becoming king Henry appointed him chancellor. For years they worked together in harmony and there was a close friendship between them, but this came to an end when Henry insisted on appointing him Archbishop of Canterbury to cooperate with him in curbing the growing power of the Church, whereupon Becket underwent a character change.

---

[2] Three of the sons – William, Henry and Geoffrey – predeceased their father. The other two – Richard and John – became kings of England.

[3] Eleanor, in a letter to the Pope at the end of her life, signs herself, 'Eleanor by the wrath of God Queen of England'.

For he could not serve two masters. Gone was the splendid sybaritic minister and in its place came an austere prelate living a life of the greatest rigour and implacably determined to uphold the powers and privileges of the Church. Henry was dumbfounded. Instead of a collaborator he discovered an unbending opponent. Unwittingly he had provided the Church with its strongest defender. The story of their famous quarrel culminating in Becket's murder in Canterbury Cathedral by four knights is well known. It was a turning point in Henry's reign: until then it had been a success story. Afterward tragedy and failure crowded in.

Already relations with Eleanor had begun to deteriorate, especially as their sons grew older and jealousies among them emerged. There was too the affair of Rosamond – 'Rose of the World'. This famous legend (which did not emerge until many years later) told how Henry fell desperately in love with the great beauty, Rosamond Clifford (which is true) and hid her away in a 'wondrous bower the like was never seen' protected by a supposedly impenetrable maze, and how Queen Eleanor discovered its secret with the help of a silken thread and pressed on Rosamond the choice of a dagger or a cup of poison and how she chose the latter; but this cannot be sustained if only because at the time of Rosamond's death in 1178 Eleanor, as will be seen, was in close confinement. Nor was it likely that she would have been unduly upset by the affair; she had become accustomed by then to Henry's infidelities. The story, nevertheless, gripped the imagination of later historians and romancers and was to appear in many hyperbolical versions.

Henry's contention with Becket had for a time drawn him closer to Eleanor who had never had any love for the 'upstart priest'. But soon after the birth in 1166 of Prince John, her eighth child by Henry, she decided that she had had enough of life in England and took herself off to Aquitaine where she attempted to revive the court life of her grandfather, William IX, with poets, musicians and troubadours recounting epics and composing chansons – usually in praise of her. She seems to have had dreams too of a state where women were treated as goddesses free from harsh male dominance and she sat in courts set up to pontificate on the nature of true love and give judgement on disputes between lovers. It is likely that most of these ideas belonged to the world of fantasy but they afforded welcome temporary relief from her dour life in England and the even harder one that was soon to await her there.

She took with her to Aquitaine her third son, Richard, then aged eleven, for whom she had a special affection and whom in a splendid ceremony she had invested as the Duke of Aquitaine and Count of Poitou, to the marked exclusion of her husband.

It seems that Henry and Eleanor were fated for a turbulent and unhappy family life. A hermit had once told William IX, Eleanor's grandfather, that his descendants would never know happiness in children. And the Arthurian seer, Merlin, was said to have made a prophecy that 'the cubs shall awake and shall roar loud and, leaving the woods, shall seek their prey within the walls of the cities', and this was believed to apply to the sons of Henry. They too seemed to have felt that they were doomed to discord. Henry's fourth son Geoffrey, smooth-talking and avaricious, once opined that 'it is our proper nature, planted in us by inheritance from our ancestors, that none of us should love the other, but that always, brother against brother and son against father, we try our utmost to injure one another.' And these prophecies of doom were to be borne out; the last twenty years of Henry's reign were to be racked by family wrangles, jealousies and bloodshed.

In 1169 Henry, who had been spending much time lately subduing rebellious vassals in his French lands, made a move to come to terms with the King of France who, he knew, had been encouraging his enemies and causing him trouble wherever he could. They met in Montmirail in Maine where Henry offered to pay homage to Louis for his French domains and so too would his sons. He announced that the eldest, Henry, would receive England, Normandy and Anjou, Richard would have Aquitaine and Poitou and Geoffrey would be allowed to marry the heiress of Brittany, so ensuring a principality for him. Louis VII must have been well pleased with these provisions as it had always been his aim to break up the Plantagenet empire. He had been greatly gratified four years before when after twenty-eight years of marriage and three wives a son had at last been born to him, the future king Philip Augustus, and he had hopes that one day he would be king of a united France. So he readily agreed to these terms as he did also to the betrothal of Princess Alys, his daughter by his second marriage, to Henry's son Richard. It is not altogether clear why Henry should have made these arrangements for his sons who had not yet reached the age of knighthood, but the likelihood is that he had come to the conclusion that his vast domains were ungovernable by one man and had to be divided up with the concurrence of Louis. It seemed at the time that this had been achieved with amity, but this was to be shortlived.

Eleanor had been excluded from the Montmirail meeting. If she had been there she might have objected to Richard's betrothal to the French princess as this opened up the possibility of France and Aquitaine being reunited; but she made no protest about it; she might have felt that it could later be avoided – as indeed it was. During her five years in Aquitaine Eleanor did not only preside over Courts of Love and listen to troubadours. She made efforts to conciliate the many enemies Henry had made by his brutal strongarm methods, and in this she had some success. She also introduced Richard into the ways of government at which he showed some aptitude and at an early age acquired the reputation of a formidable warrior. But she also could not resist making trouble for her husband, whom she had come to detest, and the most effective way of doing this was through his sons, all of whom had or thought they had grievances. Henry, the eldest, was especially disgruntled because, although he had been designated his father's successor in England, Normandy and Anjou, and had even been crowned in advance, Henry was showing no readiness to surrender any of his powers to him. He was leading an idle and pointless life; his coronation had been a farce and 'the crown no more than a plaything signifying nothing'. His brothers, Richard and Geoffrey, also thought their father was keeping them on too tight a rein, especially in the matter of finance.

Henry's sons were not worthy of him. The young King Henry had charm and good looks and great skill in the martial arts but he was also shallow and feckless and entirely without his father's grit and determination. 'A restless youth born for many men's undoing' was how a contemporary chronicler described him. Richard was certainly gifted, combining beauty, knightly valour and a talent for music and poetry, but also brutal and ruthless and lacking in warmth. Of Geoffrey few people had anything good to say. 'Untrustworthy' was the word most commonly used of him or, more bluntly, 'a son of perdition'. And then there was John, as yet a mere child and because no domains had been assigned to him known as 'Lackland'.

A great crisis in Henry II's reign came in 1173. In that year his immense Plantagenet empire was nearly toppled by rebellion, and there can be little doubt that the main instigator was Eleanor. Certainly chroniclers of the time thought so. Not only did she spur her sons into action but also discontented Aquitainian noblemen and neighbouring rulers including the counts of Boulogne, Flanders and Champagne. Louis VII too was persuaded to join in the fray although as usual not very decisively. And the rebellion was not confined to France: in England too there were those who sought to shake off the rule of a despotic king, and William the Lyon King of Scotland took the opportunity to invade Northumbria. It seemed as if Henry's day of doom must have arrived, but he rose to the occasion. Gathering together such support as still remained loyal to him, particularly in Normandy and England and engaging a large force of mercenaries from Brabant, he took on all comers. As a military commander he far eclipsed his eldest son and Louis VII, and it was not long before he was gaining the upper hand; and when this became apparent opposition soon dwindled.

Down in Aquitaine Eleanor saw that she was about to be stranded and, disguised as a knight, attempted to make her way into the kingdom of France, but she left it too late and was captured and handed over to Henry who put her into tight security. In 1174 the war continued to go in Henry's favour and in July of that year he felt able to cross into England with Eleanor and other royal ladies. Once there Henry was clear what he had to do first. Barefoot and clad only in the rough tunic of a pilgrim, he proceeded to Canterbury where he prostrated himself before the tomb of Becket and remained there all night in prayer and then, after drinking a phial of what purported to be Becket's blood and submitting to being lashed by monks and other ecclesiastics, he took the road to London on which he was greeted with wondrous news: the King of Scotland had been defeated and made prisoner and the danger of a Scottish invasion removed. Such an event was immediately attributed to the intervention of the Holy and Blessed Martyr, and this had a profound effect. If Saint Thomas were on the side of Henry who could be against him? It marked the end of insurrection in England, and Henry returned to France to come to terms with his sons and King Louis and other rebel leaders. In a clearly dominant position he was inclined to be forgiving. No great retribution was inflicted. His sons' disloyalty was attributed to their youth and the evil influence of others, notably their mother. For Eleanor there was no clemency. Sixteen years of imprisonment awaited her.

25

Details of Eleanor's imprisonment are incomplete and uncertain. There was much secrecy about it. To confine her was necessary because at liberty she would have made trouble; but it was also necessary to keep her alive because without her Henry's claim to Aquitaine would lapse. And so she was kept in prison at first in a castle in Old Sarum (Salisbury), a windswept hilltop where there had once been an Iron Age fort. Life there must have been bleak but she was later moved to Winchester Castle where (judging from royal accounts) conditions of life were reasonably comfortable although certainly not luxurious. Nevertheless, for one as vital and intelligent as Eleanor life in any kind of prison must have been grim. In 1175 she might have escaped from it when at Henry's instigation she was given the chance of taking the veil and becoming abbess of the wealthy and prestigious abbey of Fontevrault, but she would not hear of this. She had no vocation for a religious life and did not want to commit herself to one, as she was always hoping for an early release from prison.

During her captivity Eleanor was denied nearly all contact with the outside world but she would have come to hear of the main events. In 1176 she no doubt heard with some satisfaction of the death of the fair Rosamond. But she would have been appalled at the rumours that followed, how Henry had taken as mistress Princess Alys, aged sixteen, some twenty-seven years younger than he and betrothed to his son Richard. It was even being spread abroad that he was thinking of annulling his marriage to Eleanor, marrying Alys and starting another family by her which would bastardise all his existing children. Certainly in middle age he was becoming malevolent and capricious, as when in 1177 he had his wayward youngest son John crowned King of Ireland with chaotic consequences.

A death which, maybe, caused Eleanor mixed feelings was that in 1180 of her former husband, Louis VII of France. For forty-three years he had grappled, often helplessly, with the problems of kingship. A death of greater significance was that in 1183 of her eldest son, Henry, at the age of twenty-eight. She had not been as close to him as to his younger brother, Richard, but she had loved him and lamented him despite his unworthiness.

The young prince's death had serious repercussions in that it upset the division of the Plantagenet empire which had been agreed at the treaty of Montmirail. Who was now to inherit England, Normandy and Anjou? By rights it should be Richard, but he already had Aquitaine and the object of the treaty had been to divide the empire into smaller parts. The twists and turns of Henry's intentions in the following years are hard to understand. At one time he seemed bent on disinheriting Richard when he ordered him to cede Aquitaine to his youngest brother, John, which he refused to do. Then he seemed to want to make his fourth son, Geoffrey, his principal heir, but Geoffrey died suddenly in 1186. Two years earlier he had released Eleanor from prison, not for compassionate reasons but because she had a role to play in the quarrel which had developed between himself and the young King of France, Philip Augustus, who was demanding that the lands belonging to the deceased young Henry should pass to his widow, Marguerite, who was his half-sister; and Henry wanted to display Eleanor as the rightful owner of these lands.

To Eleanor the matter of supreme importance was that Richard should remain Duke of Aquitaine which was the part of the Plantagenet empire for which she had the deepest feeling, and Richard was the son for whom she had the greatest love. In pursuit of this aim she acted deviously, ordering Richard to obey his father and cede Aquitaine to John, but this she did only because she saw it as a way of forcing Henry to acknowledge Richard as heir to the whole Angevin empire. And in this she was to be successful. For Richard then entered into a close even intimate relationship with the French king, Philip Augustus, living, eating and even sleeping with him which exposed him to comment but which did bring about the downfall of his father.

For one who had achieved great things and much of whose life had been admirable the last years of Henry II were stark tragedy. Alienated from all his family except his youngest son, John, and suffering from an agonising and debilitating disease, he was hunted down and captured and forced to agree to humiliating terms which included forgiveness to all who had fought against him and, reading through this list, he was aghast to see the name of John who, fickle as always, had sensed which way the wind was blowing and changed sides. After that Henry had no further interest in living. 'Say no more,' he uttered. 'Now let the rest go as it will. I care no more for myself nor for aught in this world.' His last words were said to have been: 'Shame, shame on a vanquished king.'

He died on 6 July at the age of fifty-six. By then the situation in France and England had taken further twists: the close friendship between Philip and Richard had turned into enmity partly because of a dispute about territory and partly because of Richard's refusal to honour his obligation to marry Philip's half-sister, Princess Alys. And then came fearful news from Palestine: the Turks under their great leader, Saladin, had captured Jerusalem, deposed the Christian king and were desecrating the holy shrines. The Pope immediately called for a crusade which both Philip and Richard bound themselves to join.

Before he died Henry ordered that Eleanor be returned to captivity, but on Richard becoming king she was immediately set free. At the time she was sixty-seven and it might have been expected that she would spend the rest of her life peacefully and at ease, but in fact she was about to embark on the most intense activity of her life. She set about at once doing all she could to bolster Richard's reputation in England which was not favourable; for although he had been born there he had spent nearly all his life in France, could speak little English and was ignorant of English customs and government. And so Eleanor took total charge, stirring up support for him wherever she could, arranging a splendid coronation for him and raising money to pay for his crusade.

There was a further matter which she took urgently in hand, that of Richard's marriage. She thought it vitally important that before going on the crusade in which he might be killed he should marry and provide an heir to the throne. He was, of course, betrothed to Princess Alys, but Eleanor had been outraged by her liaison with Henry and regarded her as 'soiled goods' and quite unfitted to be Queen of England, and Richard agreed with her. And so she cast around for another wife and her attention became focused on Princess Berengaria, daughter of the King of Navarre. Richard had once met her and been favourably impressed and, although not enthusiastic, was willing to have her as wife, but he was not willing to postpone the date of his departure on the crusade. So Eleanor had to be quick. Despite her years and the onset of winter she set off at once across France, over the Pyrenees and into Navarre where she inspected Berengaria, quickly decided that she was suitable and came to terms with her father on financial matters. Although it was by then mid-winter Eleanor would brook no delay as Richard had by then set sail, and so the unfortunate Berengaria was hustled off.

In Sicily Eleanor found a troubled scene. Relations between

Richard and Philip Augustus had reached breaking point. The French king could not forgive the treatment of his half-sister Alys which had, indeed, been shameful. Betrothed to Richard at the age of nine, she had gone at first to the court of Queen Eleanor in Aquitaine, but after this had been broken up following the war of 1173 she had been taken to England where at the age of sixteen she had been seduced by Henry II and had borne him a child. On the death of Henry she had been imprisoned, treated as a fallen woman and her engagement to Richard broken off. This Philip had regarded as a mortal insult to the French monarchy. 'If you put her aside and marry another woman,' he told Richard, 'I will be the enemy of you and yours for so long as I live.' And when Eleanor and Berengaria reached Sicily he sailed away in a fury.

Eleanor would have liked to see Richard and Berengaria wedded and bedded at once, but this was not possible as it was Lent; and Eleanor could not afford to wait. During her journey disturbing reports had reached her of events in France and England, and she felt that her presence there was urgently necessary. The security of the Plantaganet empire was of far greater importance to her than the success of any crusade (of which she had none too happy memories). And so after only four days the indefatigable old lady set out on the return journey.

At the time of proclaiming the crusade Pope Celestine III had issued a 'Truce of God' by which, under pain of excommunication, all Christian kings, princes and governors had been debarred from making wars on crusaders, but this had not been strictly observed. On arrival in Rouen, capital of Normandy, Eleanor found Richard's French lands under threat from neighbouring states and with characteristic energy and determination set about strengthening border posts and rallying forces loyal to Richard. In England she found a chaotic situation. Richard had left William Longchamp as ruler of the country, who combined among other offices those of Bishop of Ely, Papal Legate and Chancellor of England. It was an unfortunate choice. Longchamp was a Norman of humble origins who spoke little English and was noted for his avarice and arrogance.

It was not long before there was seething discontent of which Prince John took advantage to further his claims to the throne by courting popularity and making promises he would not be able to fulfil. Civil war then broke out between his forces and those of Longchamp and the latter was forced to flee abroad. John then became a serious threat to Richard's authority and this increased after the early return from the crusade of the French king, Philip Augustus, who, racked by disease and haunted by failure, was more than ever embittered against Richard and, despite the Truce of God, was ready for anything that would bring him down. And John was eager to collude with him and promise him anything he wanted – cession to him of Normandy, homage for all English lands in France, even marriage to the ill-fated Princess Alys. That these plots came to nothing was largely due to Eleanor who had some restraining influence on her youngest son and whose presence in England and strong personality did much to hold the fort for Richard.

In Palestine Richard, laid low by malaria and deserted by most of his fellow crusaders, had by the middle of 1192 been forced to the conclusion that he was not going to be able to capture Jerusalem and so made a treaty with Saladin and set out for home at the beginning of October. He was expected to arrive by Christmas but there was no sign of him which gave rise to anxiety. What could have happened to him? And then in January 1193 came a dreadful report by way of the court of France that on his way home he had been shipwrecked and in attempting to continue his journey overland had been captured and fallen into the hands first of Duke Leopold of Austria and then of the Holy Roman Emperor Henry VI, both great personal enemies. Henry would have been only too willing to put him to death, but he realised what an enormous ransom might be exacted for his release, and so for the time being was holding him in close, secret captivity while this was negotiated. Eleanor, by then over seventy, immediately became active both in raising the money for the ransom and in trying to discover where Richard was being held, and for this purpose despatched agents all over Germany who after a few months were able to track him down.

There was to be long wrangling about the ransom. The sum demanded was an exorbitant 100,000 silver marks, twice the English national revenue and by weight some 35 tons. It seemed an impossible amount to raise. Only two years before England had been taxed to the bone to pay for the Third Crusade, and now another vast sum was required; but Eleanor set about the task at once. Barons and all freemen had to contribute one quarter of their annual income; and churches were given a special dispensation to yield their valuables. Eleanor hardened her heart and excused no one, rich or poor. An even more pitiless task was finding the two hundred hostages, mostly young boys from noble households, to be held as surety for the full payment of the ransom. But Eleanor was ruthless, she was utterly determined that her favourite son should be set free.

Thanks mainly to Eleanor sufficient money was eventually raised for Richard's release and at the end of 1193 and in mid-winter she set out with it in a fleet of ships to the court of the German Emperor. On arrival there were still some delays, but on 4 February 1194 Richard was formally 'restored to his mother and freedom', and five weeks later he landed in England where he was given an enthusiastic welcome. English people had little reason to be grateful to him on whose behalf they had made tremendous sacrifices but they nevertheless felt great pride in their warrior king whose exploits on the battlefield had become legendary. But Richard did not stay for long. After one royal tour and a coronation in Winchester Cathedral, he and Eleanor left for France to wrest from the French king those parts of Normandy which had been ceded to him by John.

For the next five years there was to be intermittent warfare between Richard and Philip Augustus with no decisive results. In 1194 Eleanor retired to the abbey of Fontevrault, not as abbess as she once might have been nor did she take the veil, but she was an honoured guest. Fontevrault had long given refuge to high-born ladies but as well it also provided shelter for indigents including lepers, penitent harlots and monks and nuns in their death throes.

Before retiring there, however, Eleanor achieved one thing close to her heart – a reconciliation between her two surviving sons, Richard and John. No one could have behaved worse than the latter: during his brother's absence on the crusade, he had been flagrantly disloyal, conspiring openly with Philip Augustus to bring him down; and during his imprisonment had raised money for his ransom which he then kept for himself; in conjunction with the French king he had even tried to bribe the German emperor not to let Richard go or to hand him over to them. But since Richard's release, influenced by Eleanor, he had realised on which side his bread was buttered and meek, craven and in tears, he came to beg forgiveness which Richard, also prompted by Eleanor, freely gave. He seems to have regarded John as a wayward, irresponsible child

31

(albeit one of twenty-six) to be humoured and tolerated and all his misdeeds blamed on others. For the time being John was on good behaviour but this was not to last.

In 1199 at the age of forty-two Richard was still an imposing figure, a force to be reckoned with on the battlefield and dreaming of going on another crusade, but his death in that year came suddenly and unworthily. He had become involved in a dispute with one of his vassals about some gold coins of no great value which had been discovered on his land and to which as overlord he laid a claim, and in enforcing this he was besieging one of his castles. The castle of Chaluz was no great stronghold and could have been captured easily, and Richard in lighthearted mood was strolling about it unarmed and unprotected when he was sighted by a lone archer who loosed an arrow which found its mark in Richard's shoulder. At first the king did not take the matter too seriously, thinking that the arrow could be pulled out and the wound would heal; but this proved difficult and when the arrow was at last cut out the wound had festered and gangrene set in and the king's life despaired of. Word was sent at once to Eleanor who arrived just before Richard's death but in time once again to direct the course of English history by persuading him to nominate John as his successor rather than his nephew Arthur, son of his elder brother Geoffrey. Both knew that John would be an unreliable king but he was preferable to Arthur who was only twelve and had spent much time in the court of the King of France and was believed to be in thrall to him. Richard died on 6 April 1199.

Eleanor was devastated by Richard's death. 'He was the staff of my old age and the light of my eyes,' she wrote. But she was aware that he had not led a blameless life and she set up a number of charities to pray for the salvation of his soul. But her main immediate concern was to watch over John, prevent him from folly and strengthen his position. She knew how dangerous this was. In England he had been generally accepted as king, but in France Arthur had a considerable following. The French king at once declared in his favour as did some magnates in the Angevin empire who were seeking independence and thought they were more likely to obtain this from a boy of twelve than a man of thirty-two. Eleanor also knew John's weaknesses: he could be clever, even brilliant, but he was also capricious and indolent with a great capacity for making enemies. And so Eleanor did not return to

32

retirement in Fontevrault but, seventy-seven though she might be, set out on a long tour of Poitou and Aquitaine to rally support for John. And in the following year (1200) she embarked on another long journey to Spain to arrange a marriage between her granddaughter, Blanche, and a son of Philip Augustus. These journeys were always dangerous and on this one she was waylaid by an Aquitainian warlord who held her hostage until she assigned to him the county of La Marche. She persevered, however, over the Pyrenees to Castile where the marriage was soon agreed; but on the return journey, with Blanche in tow, she collapsed from exhaustion and had to retreat to Fontevrault before delivering Blanche to the French court.

In 1202, however, she was on her travels again as a result of war breaking out between John and Philip Augustus, determined as ever to rid France of all English rule. In the course of this he loosed Prince Arthur, then aged sixteen, with 200 knights to claim his inheritance and in particular to invade Poitou. It was this that brought Eleanor out of Fontevrault to stir up resistance. Travelling slowly because of her age (she was then into her eighties) she was staying in the castle of Mirabeau when she was surprised by her grandson and his knights who demanded her surrender, and when this was refused laid siege to her in the keep of the castle. It was unlikely that she could have held out for long, but it was then that John pulled off his most spectacular coup: marching at great speed (eighty miles in forty-eight hours) his army arrived in time to rescue his mother and to overwhelm the besiegers all of whom were killed or captured; and among the captives was Prince Arthur.

John's fortunes were then at their zenith, and if he had acted prudently he could have turned the tables decisively on Philip Augustus, but instead he behaved foolishly and brutally, having Arthur's knights dragged ignominiously at the end of ox wagons and then leaving them to starve to death in French or English dungeons, which caused outrage and led to many defectors from his cause. And then there was the fate of Arthur to be decided. Arthur was not the helpless child victim depicted in many history books. He was in early manhood, had rebelled against his anointed king and besieged his grandmother, for which in the Middle Ages death might well be inflicted. But many people, including Eleanor, had strongly urged John not to harm Arthur and he had undertaken not to do so. What did happen to Arthur remains a mystery. All

33

that is known is that he disappeared completely and was almost certainly killed on John's instructions, whether at the hands of a hired assassin or his own cannot be known. Ever since gruesome stories have been rife. Certain it is though, that following Arthur's disappearance the fortunes of war turned against John as more and more of his supporters deserted him and the cause of Philip Augustus gained impetus. By 1204 the Plantagenet Empire in France had come to an end. It seems likely that Eleanor was spared the agony of seeing this happen. In 1202 at Fontevrault she took the vows of a nun and from then her mind became clouded. Little is heard of her except that 'she only existed as one already dead to the world'. She died on 1 April 1204. It was not too soon: she was eighty-two and had outlived two husbands and eight of her ten children.

Predictably someone as dominant as Eleanor left behind a diverse reputation as well as many legends. To the nuns of Fontevrault 'she graced the nobility of her birth with the honesty of her life, enriched it with her moral excellence and adorned it with the flowers of her virtues.' But a later chronicler wrote that 'by reason of her excessive beauty she destroyed or injured nations'. And her son, John, is quoted as saying that she was 'an unhappy and shameless woman.' But her life was a phenomenon. In an age when most women were relegated to secondary, servile roles she became a pre-eminent figure in Europe with a position no other woman has achieved. And even more than Queen Victoria she could be called 'the grandmother of Europe'. Her descendants included kings of England and France, a Holy Roman Emperor, and kings of Castile and Jerusalem as well as two saints – Louis IX of France and Ferdinand III of Castile, a record which surely will always be unmatched.

BERENGARIA OF NAVARRE (1165–c.1230)

Wife of Richard I

Berengaria of Navarre, wife of the famous Coeur de Lion and wedded to him on his way to the Third Crusade, is sometimes imagined as a great beauty and romantic heroine. But this was hardly the case.

Rushed into marriage by Queen Eleanor to provide an heir to the throne, which she did not do, unloved by her husband and living apart from him for nearly all their married life, there was more tragedy in her life than romance.

Berengaria was the eldest daughter of Sancho VI of Navarre, a small kingdom in northern Spain. She had first met Richard in 1177 when he was twenty and she was twelve, and Richard was said to have been greatly impressed by her, a chronicler going so far as to write that he loved her very much and she had become his heart's desire. But if this was so he did not press his suit, as it was to be twelve years before he made any move to marry her, but he may have been inhibited because he was formally engaged to Princess Alys of France. In 1189, however, Richard, before setting out on the Third Crusade, was under pressure from his mother, Eleanor, to find a wife to provide for the succession to the throne in case he was killed. By then Princess Alys had been ruled out because of her adulterous liaison with Richard's father and, casting around for someone else, memories of Berengaria came back, and this was enough for Eleanor to set off at once to Navarre to finalise the matter.

Berengaria was then twenty-five, old in those days for marriage, and, it would seem, no great beauty. A chronicler described her somewhat guardedly as 'a prudent maid, a gentle lady, virtuous and fair, neither false nor double-tongued. She was the wisest lady in all truth that might anywhere be found.' Another was ready to call her 'a damsel famed for her beauty and eloquence'. But perhaps the most apt appraisal was that she was 'more accomplished than beautiful'. Certainly Eleanor took an immediate liking to her but this may have been not so much because of her accomplishments as because of her docility. She seemed ready to fall into line and had few ideas or initiatives of her own.

As soon as the formalities concerning her betrothal had been agreed, Berengaria was rushed off by Eleanor on a long and hazardous journey, mid-winter though it might be – across the Alps and the Plain of Lombardy and down to Naples to board a ship for Sicily where Richard awaited them and where they found a troubled situation. Richard had quarrelled violently both with King Tancred of Sicily and with Philip Augustus who, rather than encounter Queen Eleanor, his father's first wife and Berengaria who was supplanting his half-sister, Alys, as wife of Richard, had made an abrupt departure. Berengaria may have marvelled at the prospect of marriage to the great warrior of his age, but she must surely have been somewhat bemused on hearing that shortly before her arrival Richard, stripped to the waist, had gone to a church where he had confessed to 'sins against nature and the foulness of his past life', and after a ceremonial flagellation and an undertaking to sin no more had received absolution.

The nature of these sins is not revealed. Later it came to be assumed that they were homosexual, but there was not even a hint of this at the time. Monkish chroniclers had an open ear for scandal, and such leanings could not have been concealed from Richard's many enemies who would have been only too ready to spread word of them abroad. That Richard had a voracious sexual appetite was well known, and his affairs with women, including the birth of a bastard son, acknowledged. These were deplored by the pious who might have considered adultery 'a sin against nature'.

One chronicler, welcoming Richard's marriage to Berengaria, wrote that it was 'a salubrious remedy against the great perils of fornication', but there was no mention of pederasty. The only basis of Richard's addiction to this comes from an incident later in his reign when he was upbraided by a holy hermit who told him to remember the destruction of Sodom and to abstain from illicit acts, 'for if you do not God will punish you in a fitting manner'. But this is not conclusive as it has never been certain what were the sins of Sodom; there is nothing in Holy Writ about them being homoerotic. The book of Genesis states only that 'the men of Sodom were wicked and sinners before the Lord exceedingly', and that the Lord 'rained upon them brimstone and fire'. But the nature of their sins is unspecified.

Whatever Richard's sexual inclinations it seems that they did not extend in any marked degree to Berengaria. His treatment of her was always offhand; they spent little time together and had no children. When Eleanor left Sicily she put Berengaria in the care of her daughter, Joanna, the recently widowed queen, with orders that both of them were to accompany Richard to Palestine, and that he and Berengaria were to marry as soon as Lent ended. These instructions were carried out despite women having been barred on the crusade; but it was necessary for them to travel in a separate ship which ran into a storm and was washed up on the shores of Cyprus where Berengaria received rough treatment from the island's ruler, Isaac Comnenus. Richard, following later, deposed Comnenus and, Lent being by then over, married Berengaria who was also crowned Queen of England. This was followed by three days of festivities but it seems that Richard attracted notice by the amount of time he spent alone with Comnenus's beautiful daughter who was to accompany the royal party to Palestine.

When Richard reached Palestine (8 June 1191) he found the crusaders already there in disheartened mood partly because of their lack of success and partly because of the ravages of malaria, but he put new life into them. The port of Acre had been under siege for over a year and was still holding out, but Richard stepped up operations so that it was captured within a month; but it was followed by the most ghastly horrors.

The capture of Acre was a notable success for Richard, but only ten days later the crusade suffered a serious blow when Philip Augustus announced his intention of returning to France; the reason he gave was his contraction of malaria, but jealousy of Richard and an urge to stir up trouble at home may have been the main cause.

At the beginning of September Richard had a further success with the capture of Jaffa (present day Tel Aviv) but then his fortunes declined: he had quarrelled with other leaders of the crusade and some of these deserted, and he himself was greatly weakened when he contracted malaria. For a time he struggled on and by July 1192 he came within sight of Jerusalem, but by then he had realised that he was not going to be able to capture the city and was compelled to come to an agreement with Saladin whereby the Turks remained in possession of Jerusalem but Christian pilgrims were to be allowed to visit the holy shrines in safety.

At the end of September Berengaria, accompanied by Joanna and the daughter of Comnenus, was put on a ship bound for Europe. It was fortunate that she sailed separately from Richard, otherwise she might have shared his imprisonment in Germany. She had been in Palestine for fifteen months and little had been heard of her during that time; as always she kept a low profile; but it must have been a gruelling experience in the midst of men and women being killed sometimes in battle, sometimes in cold blood and many more dying from disease. And her journey to Europe was not to be without danger and hardship and took much longer than expected. By the end of 1192 she had reached Rome where she heard of the capture of Richard by the Emperor of Germany and it was considered prudent that she should remain there for the time being lest she too should become a victim of capture and ransom. But Pope Celestine III came to her rescue and provided her with an escort (including several cardinals) which took her to Genoa from where she sailed to Marseilles and then on to her dower lands in Poitou where she was to spend most of the rest of her life.

Little is heard of Berengaria after 1193. She was reported to have been active in raising money for Richard's ransom, but she was not summoned to be in England when Richard returned there from captivity and she was not present at his coronation service in Winchester Cathedral. They remained apart when Richard came to France while he waged war on Philip Augustus and also resumed his licentious lifestyle. But in 1195 he was solemnly warned by the holy hermit of the fate in store for him if he did not mend his ways. At first he paid no attention but when soon afterwards he fell dangerously ill he made a full confession and according to the chronicler, Roger of Hoveden: 'After receiving absolution took back wife whom he had not known for a long time, and putting aside illicit intercourse, he remained faithful to her, and they became one flesh and the Lord gave them health of body and soul.' But he did not give them offspring. In 1195 they spent Christmas together for the first time and afterwards she accompanied Richard on some of his campaigns. But she was not present at Chaluz in 1199 when he received his mortal wound from an archer, nor did Richard send for her to his deathbed; it was left to Eleanor to break the news to her on which she was said to have been inconsolable.

Berengaria was to live for a further thirty years. She was thought at one time to have been the only queen of England never to have visited the country, but research has discovered from safe passes granted to her that she did make occasional fleeting visits. At times during the reign of John she became almost destitute when that monarch failed to provide her with the money to which she was entitled, and she had to write urgent begging letters for relief. Otherwise, as was her wont, she led a quiet, retiring life, devoting much of her time and resources to works of charity. These included the foundation of the monastery of l'Espan where in 1230, when she was sixty-five, she took the vows of a nun. The date of her death is not known for certain but it is believed to have been soon afterwards.

ISABELLA OF GLOUCESTER (1160–1217) and ISABELLA OF ANGOULÊME (1186–1246)

Wives of John

No more complex character has been on the throne of England than King John. A bewildering mixture of contradictory qualities, he has baffled historians who do not agree as to his true nature. Reckless and judicious, grasping and generous, capricious and consistent are some of the adjectives that have been applied to him. But it surely cannot be denied that he was not an easy husband. His varying moods – at times passionately uxurious, at others violently enraged – would have tried the sufferance of a saint, and neither of his wives was that.

At the age of five John was betrothed to his second cousin, Isabella of Gloucester (otherwise Hawise), daughter of one of England's greatest landowners; but marriage was forbidden by the Archbishop of Canterbury on the grounds of consanguinity. Normally in such cases a dispensation was required from the Pope, but John was not prepared to wait for this, and when he was twenty-one was able to find a bishop prepared to perform the ceremony. For this defiance his lands were placed under an interdict, but this was lifted a few years later when a papal dispensation was forthcoming with the surely unrealistic condition that John and Hawise should refrain from sexual intercourse. Soon afterwards, however, they became estranged when no children were born; and in 1199, soon after becoming king, John, whose religious beliefs were adopted and discarded at will, affirmed that because of consanguinity the marriage had been invalid, and compliant bishops were found to annul it. To this Hawise made no objection; she probably regarded it as a merciful release and withdrew to her extensive lands, remarried twice and disappeared from the pages of history.

In the same year John married Isabella of Angoulême, the twelve-year-old daughter of one of his Norman vassals who was already betrothed to another of his vassals, and a particularly powerful one, the Lord of Lusignan and count of La Marche. There are different versions of how this came about. Contemporary monkish chroniclers, who were not averse to gossip, wrote how John on a visit to the Count of Angoulême fell insanely in love at first sight with his young daughter Isabella and, headstrong as ever, determined to marry her at once, which he did in Bordeaux Cathedral and then took her off to England to be crowned queen. In this he had the connivance of Isabella's father but provoked the bitter and lasting enmity of Lusignan, the jilted bridegroom. Another version, put forward by later historians bent on white-washing John, avers that the affair was not just a wild amorous fling but a carefully conceived plan to build up support in an important strategic area. If this was so it was, like so many of John's gambits, to fail. For two years later Lusignan took his grievance to King Philip Augustus of France who ordered John to appear before him in Paris to answer the charge, which John refused to do. Philip then denounced him as 'a contumacious traitor and confiscate of all his continental territories', and began an invasion of Normandy with consequences ultimately fatal to John.

At first Isabella had been a reluctant bride and had protested loudly and tearfully at the prospect of marrying a man twenty years older than herself from a strange, remote country of which she had hardly heard. But her pleas were unavailing and married she was, although it seems she did not take long to adapt and gained a hold over John so great that it was attributed by some to witchcraft and sorcery. There were days when he was so besotted that he could not be drawn out of bed with her and at times of crisis he seemed torpid and apathetic with thoughts only of love-making. Urgent business was left unattended and the King of France made further progress into Normandy while more of John's vassals, sensing which way the wind was blowing, changed their allegiance. By 1204 Normandy had been lost and the great Angevin empire of Henry II and Eleanor of Aquitaine broken up, and in this Isabella had had a significant role. A chronicler of the time wrote bitterly that 'Normandy had been lost under the quilt of a marriage bed.'

Of course the ecstasy was not to last. In time love turned into hatred and John and Isabella were on fighting terms, although not before she had borne him five children. In the last years of John's reign the behaviour of both of them was reckless and scandalous. John gave free rein to his lubricity, fathering seven known bastards and treating some of his paramours abominably.[1] Isabella too had her liaisons and on some of these John was alleged to have taken fearful revenge.[2]

John's ignominious failure in war and egregious behaviour in love led to the signing of Magna Carta in 1215 and then in the following year to a group of barons inviting the heir to the French throne (later Louis VIII) to invade the country, promising him the throne if he would rid them of the tyrant. Soon afterwards, however, John was taken seriously ill while making a progress through East Anglia which led to his death.[3]

At the time Isabella, with whom he had recently had some sort of reconciliation, was with her children in Gloucester and, as the country at the time was in a state of tumult following the French invasion, she lost no time in having her nine-year-old eldest son, Henry, proclaimed king and crowned in Gloucester Cathedral – there being no crown immediately available a gold collar of hers was used for the occasion. But the accession of Henry III was not without opposition. Some barons adhered to their compact with Prince Louis, and it was some time before the French forces were driven out and a regency council set up. It might have been expected that Isabella would be a member of this but she was omitted which was a clear indication of the low esteem in which she was held. 'A splendid animal rather than a stateswoman' was how a contemporary described her. Certainly her subsequent behaviour did nothing to improve her reputation.

Within a year she withdrew to her native Angoulême where a bizarre situation had arisen. Before John died he had felt obliged to come to terms with Isabella's former lover, Hugh de Lusignan now Count de la Marche, but this had only been achieved by betrothing to him his daughter, Joanna, in 1217 no more than seven years old. At thirty-four Isabella still retained her celebrated beauty and it was not long before she and the count had rekindled their former love. And so the unfortunate Joanna was dismissed back

---

[1] Compared with the twenty or so of his great-grandfather, Henry I, seven was not actually so many.

[2] Hanging their strangled corpses over Isabella's bed.

[3] Possibly poisoned in a monastery where he was staying. The monk who gave him the draught was ready to drink it himself as a token of good faith if it would remove such an odious tyrant.

to England (where she was later married off to the King of Scotland) and in 1220 Isabella and Hugh were to marry and to have eight children. Misfortune, however, was in store for them: partly, it was believed, at Isabella's instigation, the Count became involved in some unsuccessful wars as a result of which he was dispossessed of his territories and had to take refuge with his family at the court of the King of France where they were hospitably received by Louis IX (St Louis). But Isabella was not long out of trouble and when an attempt was made on the life of King Louis she was accused of having had a part in it. Whether or not this was so, she gave credence to it by fleeing the country and seeking safety in a religious house in Aquitaine where she was hidden in a secret chamber from which she never emerged and died there two years later.

Isabella was an archetypal *femme fatale*. Beautiful and perfidious, she brought disaster to both her husbands and by the end of her life was universally abhorred. The pseudonym of Jezebel by which she became known was not undeserved.

ELEANOR OF PROVENCE (1223–1291)

Wife of Henry III

For thirty-six years from the age of thirteen Eleanor of Provence was fated to prop up a weak and wayward husband sixteen years older than herself. Henry III had good qualities – charity, piety, kindliness, artistic taste – but very small powers of kingship. His reign of fifty-six years was one of the longest in English history but not one of the more glorious, witnessing conflict and civil war at home and unnecessary and unsuccessful wars abroad. It was, however, also productive of lasting benefits, notably the building of great cathedrals and significant developments in the evolution of Parliament.

It is surprising that, although he came to the throne at the age of nine and must have been considered a great matrimonial prize, Henry did not marry until twenty years later. For various reasons his first essays into marriage came to nothing, but at last in 1236 he was wedded to Princess Eleanor, one of the four daughters of the Count of Provence – all great beauties and all destined in time to become queens. The marriage was to prove happy and long-lasting: Eleanor was to bear him nine children and, unusually for kings at that time, Henry was a loving and undeviating husband.

It was some time before Eleanor's political influence was felt but she soon made an impact on life at court. In the sunny climes of her native Provence life was colourful and hedonistic and she was to find, as Eleanor of Aquitaine had before her, that by comparison life in England was sombre and crude. Most Anglo-Norman barons had little taste for the artistic, their pleasures being more physical, extending not much further than the hunting field and tournament lists. Like her namesake Eleanor attempted to introduce softer delights – music and poetry with troubadours and minstrels – and sanctioned the appointment of the first Poet Laureate. She also attempted to introduce more comfort and beauty into home life. English interiors at that time tended to be bare castle walls and unpaved floors covered with rushes. To these Eleanor added such luxuries, as they were then thought, as curtains, carpets and cushions and encouraged the uncouth English to eat using knives and forks rather than their fingers.

But, a civilising influence though she might have been, Eleanor was not popular in England. She was too extravagant and grasping. Henry lavished gifts of dress and jewellery on her, and she herself spent money recklessly whether it was there or not. Consequently royal finances were always in a parlous state, and she was forever devising ways of raising money, some of which were dubiously legal and which caused strong resentment.

An even greater grievance among the English was the bringing into the country of numerous foreign friends and relations of Eleanor's and bestowing on them highly paid offices of state. Her uncles fared particularly well: Peter des Rivaux was given the powerful and lucrative post of treasurer and keeper of the privy seal; and another, Boniface, with no relevant qualifications was appointed Archbishop of Canterbury where his behaviour was so provocative that he found it necessary to wear chain armour under his episcopal robes. 'Little by little,' wrote a monkish chronicler, 'the King invited such legions of Poitevins that they almost filled the whole of England and wherever he went he was surrounded by hosts of them.'

It was not at once that Eleanor's influence in the political field became apparent, but when it did, it was found to be harsh and reactionary. It was an age when reform was in the air. The barons had achieved significant limitations to royal powers by Magna Carta, and these were further curtailed when in 1258 Henry was compelled to agree to the Provisions of Oxford. To all concessions of royal authority Eleanor was strongly opposed and was always urging Henry to resist them and then to ignore them; and this did not go unnoticed and made her many enemies.

For a long time Henry held back from foreign wars as he was essentially a man of peace, his patron saint and model for kingship being the blessed Edward the Confessor. But pressure was always on him to regain the French territories lost by his father and when he succumbed he was always unsuccessful and became more heavily in debt than ever. In 1253 while he was abroad Eleanor was left as regent, but her rule was so despotic that it stirred up strong opposition particularly from a group of barons headed by a powerful nobleman of French origins, Simon de Montfort, who was also Earl of Leicester and married to one of the King's sisters.

In the following years the grievances of the barons became more intense; heavy and unlawful taxation, appointment of foreigners to top positions, breaches of Magna Carta and other contracts – all of these roused them to fury which was aggravated by Pope Clement lV, nominally Henry's overlord, who sent a legate to England to collect all the money he could from the clergy and to give full support to the King, freeing him from his oath to abide by the Provisions of Oxford. Ill-feeling came to a head in 1263. In that year Eleanor was involved in an ugly and dangerous incident when in attempting to escape from angry Londoners by river to Windsor her boat was bombarded from London Bridge with rocks, rotting carcasses and any missile handy amid shouts of 'Drown the witch!' From then the country was plunged into civil war for which Eleanor was in no small part responsible. In 1264 the forces of Simon de Montfort defeated those of the King at Lewes, and both Henry and his eldest son, Edward were made prisoners.

For one year then de Montfort became ruler of the country. He did not depose Henry but forced him into an agreement whereby his powers were greatly restricted. During this time Eleanor had found refuge at the court of the sainted Louis IX of France who was married to her sister and who treated her with every consideration. Adversity brought out the best in her and she immediately set about organising an army and fleet for the invasion of England. But these were not to be needed. For Simon de Montfort's position became untenable. He had managed to contain the powers of the King but was to find it much harder to contain those of the barons, many of whom were realising that the exchange of a weak and faltering king for a strong despotic ruler was not in their interests. Many of them, therefore, switched their allegiance.

King Henry was kept in honourable but secure custody by his brother-in-law but Prince Edward managed to escape and then to rally all forces hostile to de Montfort. In 1265 the two confronted each other in the battle of Evesham in which de Montfort was defeated and killed. Henry, present at the battle in captivity and narrowly avoiding death at the hands of royalists, was then restored to the throne and Eleanor returned from France along with a papal legate who, at her instigation, proceeded to excommunicate the leading rebels; but otherwise there was to be no great vengeance. Henry had his faults but was of a forgiving nature.

In the last years of her husband's reign Eleanor seems to have mellowed, becoming less oppressive and grasping and more given to piety and good works. When Henry died in 1272 his heir, Prince Edward, was away on a crusade and it was nearly two years before he returned to England during which time Eleanor was queen regent and, unlike on previous occasions, stirred up no trouble. In her nineteen years of widowhood she had to endure many family tragedies: of her nine children only two survived her. But she was well cared for by her son, Edward I, who was devoted to her. In 1280, when she was fifty-seven, she retired to the Abbey of Amesbury. As recorded in a chronicle: 'She laid down the diadem from her head and the precious purple from her shoulders and with them all worldly ambition.' However, she did not lay down her worldly goods, and before she took her vows she obtained a dispensation from the Pope enabling her to keep her dower lands as queen dowager of England and the income from them. She died in 1291 at the age of sixty-eight.

Eleanor, although often misguided, had been a courageous and capable queen consort. That a weakling like Henry had been able in a turbulent age to survive on the throne for fifty-six years was to a large extent due to her. Avaricious she certainly was but she was also charitable and encouraged Henry in his many good works and stimulated his interest in architecture and cathedrals. It is likely that she had a part in the rebuilding of Westminster Abbey and for this surely much can be forgiven her.

ELEANOR OF CASTILE (1241–1290)
and MARGARET OF FRANCE (1279–1318)

Wives of Edward I

Edward I is considered by many to have been the greatest English king of the Middle Ages, combining the administrative abilities of Henry II with the military prowess of Coeur de Lion. For thirty-six years he was married to Eleanor of Castile and no king has had a more loyal and supportive consort. She stood by him during a civil war in England, accompanied him on a gruelling crusade in which she may have saved his life and followed behind him in rigorous conditions during his campaigns in Wales. She also bore him at least fourteen children.

Eleanor was the only child of Ferdinand III of Castile and his French wife, Joanna Countess of Ponthieu. Her engagement to Edward occurred when his father, Henry III, was negotiating a peace treaty with her half-brother, Alphonso X, following an inconclusive war concerning his claims to Gascony, England's last remaining territory in France. At the time Edward was fifteen and Eleanor was twelve, but their marriage took place at once amid great rejoicing. Edward was already a popular figure, being of a different character to his father: Henry – meek, pacific and ineffective; Edward strong-willed, practical and belligerent. There were reports that in his youth he was wild and riotous like Prince Hal, later Henry V, and that like him he put these ways aside when he became king and assumed a more sober persona.

Edward's first test as a military commander came when at the age of twenty-five he defeated the rebel forces of Simon de Montfort at the battle of Evesham and restored his father to the throne. Four years later he announced his intention of going on a crusade which was ill-advised partly because of inadequate resources and partly because England was still in an unsettled state and he was needed there to support his father. However, he was not to be put off and Eleanor decided she would go too. There were even stronger reasons for her to stay behind – not only the rigours and dangers that would be encountered but she was also by then the mother of four young children. But she too was adamant. 'Nothing,' she declared stoutly, 'ought to part those whom God has joined, and the way to heaven is as near, if not nearer, from Syria as from England or my native Spain.'

Edward's plan was that he would sail to Sicily where he would join forces with the sainted French king, Louis IX, and they would then go on together to the Holy Land. But Louis became embroiled in a war with the Moors in North Africa where he died from a fever. It was then urged on Edward that he stood little chance of success on his own and the crusade should be abandoned. But Edward refused to give up, and on 9 May 1271 he landed at the port of Acre. He was to stay in Palestine for sixteen months during which time he was to discover, like his great-uncle, Richard I, before him, that the forces at his command were inadequate, that his allies were not to be depended on and there was no possibility of capturing Jerusalem. And so, again like his great-uncle, he made a truce with the Saracens and in September 1272 set sail for Europe, having achieved nothing except the kudos always accorded at that time to a crusader.

For Eleanor the months in the Holy Land must have been a fearful ordeal. Crusades always give rise to gruesome brutality – men killed in battle or (more often) dying from heat or disease or on occasions slaughtered in cold blood in acts of revenge. And Eleanor was in no condition to bear with these horrors. Shortly after arriving in Acre it seems (although details are scarce) that she gave birth to a daughter who died immediately, but she then became pregnant again and a year later another daughter was born (her fifth) who was later to become known as Joan of Acre. And then came the famous assassination attempt on her husband. It seems that an emissary of a Turkish emir managed to obtain an interview with Edward alone on the pretext of being converted to Christianity, but he was bent on murder and tried to stab Edward with a poisoned dagger. Edward was not, however, entirely taken by surprise and in the ensuing scuffle the would-be assassin was battered to death, but not before he had inflicted a wound on Edward's arm which turned septic so that his life was in danger. A story was to emerge years later that Eleanor sucked the poison out, but it is more likely that it was cut out by a surgeon in an agonising operation. For a time Edward was seriously ill and Eleanor, although just out of childbirth, nursed him devotedly so that he recovered and was able to leave Palestine three months later in reasonable health.

On the way home Edward and Eleanor stopped off in Sicily where tragic news reached them – the death of their two young sons; and soon afterwards came word of the death of Henry III. The death of his children Edward, and apparently Eleanor too, bore with composure but that of his father caused an outburst of grief. Stoically, if somewhat heartlessly, he declared: 'The loss of infants may be repaired by the same God that gave them, but when a man has lost a good father it is not in the course of nature for God to send him another.' Although he was now King of England Edward made no haste to return there, lingering for over a year in Gascony and other parts of France. When he and Eleanor did eventually arrive they were given a tremendous welcome and their coronation was one of the most splendid ever. The brave crusader king and his beautiful devoted wife went straight to the hearts of the people of England.

Once crowned Edward lost no time in exerting his authority. There was much to be done. The weak government of his father had allowed the great landed magnates to encroach on royal authority and take the law into their own hands, and Edward saw to it at once that these infringements were withstood and royal sovereignty reasserted. He also had enacted a number of statutes laying down the law on such matters as land tenure and the administration of justice which were of great importance as they tended to reduce the powers of the local feudal lords and increase those of royal officials who in time came to be known as the civil service. Edward is rightly acknowledged as one of England's great lawgivers.

Eleanor was Queen of England for eighteen years. Not very much is known of her during that time; what emerges is a somewhat mixed reputation: on the one hand as a loyal, devoted wife and mother of fourteen children, patron of poetry and the arts and benefactor of many charities: on the other as a hard and grasping landowner, extracting all she could from her tenants and none too scrupulous as to her methods of building up an ever-increasing land holding: in particular she secured debts owed by landowners to Jews and took over the lands pledged for them. This aroused the disapproval of the Church, and the Archbishop of Canterbury warned her that for Christians lending money on usury was a sin punishable by excommunication. In Eleanor's family life there was much tragedy: of her fourteen children only six survived into adulthood, but it is not apparent how greatly she was upset by this. She may have been a loving mother but certainly care of her husband always had priority over her children.

Unusually for that time there was at the beginning of Edward's reign a period of peace with France and rather than end this and try to regain the lands lost by his grandfather, John, Edward looked to extending his sovereignty in Britain.

The situation on the Welsh border had recently been turbulent. None of Britain's invaders – Roman, Saxon or Norman – had ever ventured on an invasion of Wales. The country was too mountainous and its inhabitants too ferocious. Instead the Normans had planted on the Welsh border 'Marcher Earls' with special powers and privileges to keep the Welsh tribesmen in check and ward off any raids into England. In time these Marcher Earls became over-powerful and a law unto themselves and almost as great a menace to the English as to the Welsh. The situation when Edward came to the throne was that the Marcher Earls had taken over most of Southern Wales but in the mountainous country in the north, known as Gwynedd, the native Welsh held out under a charismatic leader called Llewellyn with the title of Lord of Snowdon. He had been a troublesome neighbour, on occasions giving support to rebellious barons in England, notably to Simon de Montfort whose daughter he married. When Edward demanded that he should pay homage to him he refused and in 1277 Edward invaded Gwynedd and forced him to submit and recognise the King of England as his overlord. On this condition he was allowed to keep his position, but six years later he rebelled and once again Edward marched against him with the result that he was killed and Wales was conquered and incorporated into England by the Statute of Wales.

During Edward's Welsh campaigns Eleanor would usually accompany him, pregnant though she generally was. This involved spending long periods in bleak, comfortless castles which she tried to make more habitable by taking with her wall hangings, carpets and curtains. In 1284 Edward brought her to the half-finished castle of Caernarvon for the birth of her last child, the future Edward II, so that he could be presented to the people of Wales as a prince who had been born in Wales and could speak not a word of English.

Seventeen years later he invested him at Caernarvon as the first Prince of Wales.

In 1286 Edward became involved in Scottish affairs. In that year Alexander III rode his horse over a cliff on a dark night and was killed. His only direct heir was a young granddaughter, Margaret, daughter of the king of Norway, who was proclaimed queen, and a boat was sent to bring her back to Scotland. Much bloodshed and bitterness would have been avoided if she had arrived safely, for it had been agreed that she should marry the future Edward II of England and so unite the crowns of the two countries peacefully. But she died on the journey and there was then a disputed succession in Scotland in which Edward was involved and which was to lead in 1290 to him invading the country. As always Eleanor felt it her duty to go with him and followed behind. But on the way she fell mortally ill and at Grantham in Lincolnshire she died. When news of this reached Edward he was overwhelmed with grief and immediately called off the Scottish invasion and turned back to Grantham from where he escorted Eleanor's body to London. This was a slow progress and at each place where the cortege stopped he raised a monument to his wife, some thirteen in all of which the most famous was the last in Westminster named after his dear queen – in French *chère reine* – subsequently known as Charing Cross.

Eleanor did not live long enough to see the failure of Edward's attempts to impose his will on Scotland. He won every battle that he fought but thanks to the leadership of such patriots as William Wallace and Robert Bruce, Scotland was unconquered. After her death, Edward's character changed: once vital and ebullient he now became morose and withdrawn; his temper was unpredictable and relations with what was left of his family (of his fourteen children ten predeceased him) became ever more strained. In 1299 at the age of sixty he married for diplomatic reasons a French princess some forty years younger than himself. Margaret, daughter of the French king, Philip III, who was to bear him three children, but could do little to relieve the gloom that enveloped him. Only Eleanor might have done this. Edward's achievements for England deserved a less despondent old age.

ISABELLA OF FRANCE (1295–1358)

Wife of Edward II

Since the Norman conquest most of England's queens had been a blessing to the country – pious and charitable and a benign influence on their husbands. Such, however, cannot be said of Isabella of France who stands accused of adultery, treason and murder and has been dubbed 'the she-wolf of France'. That such a reputation is not fully justified has been contended by some modern historians. She was certainly guilty of adultery, and strictly, of treason, but of murder doubtfully, anyway not of her husband. And it could be argued that she was as much sinned against as sinning. Certainly she endured cruel and humiliating treatment. If she was one of the wickedest of English queens she was also one of the most long suffering.

Isabella was the only daughter of Philip IV of France, an ambitious and power-hungry monarch who had used her as a pawn in his designs since she was the age of four when, as part of a treaty with the English king, Edward I, she had been betrothed to his eldest surviving son, the future Edward II, eleven years her senior. Because of her age the marriage was not to take place until eight years later soon after Edward became King. Their wedding in Boulogne Cathedral was one of great grandeur attended by many crowned heads, and all seemed to be set fair: Isabella, by then twelve, had already become a famous beauty while Edward, although with no reputation as a warrior, was handsome and charming and gifted in the arts.

But there was trouble in store. For Edward was homoerotic and at the time in thrall to a talented and good looking courtier, one Piers Gaveston. Gaveston had first been appointed by Edward I to his son's court but had been banished when the old king became suspicious of their relationship. On becoming king, Edward II lost no time in recalling him and loading him with riches and honours including the royal dukedom of Cornwall and arranging a marriage for him to his niece, Margaret de Clare (daughter of Joan of Acre). This was madness and caused outrage. Isabella had been amazed when on her arrival in England after their wedding Edward had thrown himself into the arms of Gaveston, 'giving him kisses and repeated embraces' according to a chronicler, and showing much more attention to him than to her. Later she had been appalled when he had lavished on Gaveston extravagant gifts including jewellery that had been presented to him by his father-in-law as part of her dower. The treatment of Isabella at first was intolerable: for the most part neglected and, when noticed, looked on with indifference even contempt; and at the same time kept short of money. She complained bitterly to her father that she was almost penniless and that 'her husband was an entire stranger to my bed'. Philip IV was able to obtain more money for her but not more attention and it was several years before her marriage was consummated.

Edward was not the first homoerotic king of England. His great-great uncle, Richard I, had had similar proclivities, but he had managed to keep them under some sort of control so that people could turn a blind eye to them; but Edward made no attempt at concealing his relationship with Gaveston; on the contrary he flaunted it so that it was often mentioned in contemporary chronicles, one writing that 'like that of David for Jonathan his love for Gaveston surpassed that of women'. And another: 'I do not remember to have heard that one man so loved another.'

Richard I had been forgiven much because he was a mighty warrior but this Edward was not. He might have been as he was of great physical strength and not unskilled in the arts of war, but he was uninterested: like his grandfather, Henry III, he was essentially a man of peace (although not entirely so), preferring to occupy himself with gentle rural pursuits like hedging, thatching and ditching and keeping company with humble folk like grooms and carters rather than with great landed magnates. There were those who thought that he was little interested in being king and was all too ready to delegate his duties, but when these were imparted on an upstart like Gaveston, the fury of the barons would inevitably boil over. In 1310 a group of the most powerful of these banded together to form a body which came to be known as the Lords Ordainers. They decided that Edward was unfit to govern the country on his own and drew up a number of ordinances restricting his powers and laying down conditions including the dismissal and exile of Gaveston. To this, such was the weakness of his position, Edward felt compelled to agree. His father had left him with an empty exchequer and an unfinished war against Scotland and he needed all the support he could get. But he had no intention that Gaveston's exile should be permanent and after two years he was allowed back, as flamboyant and headstrong as ever.

Predictably this led to a baronial uprising which was headed by the King's cousin, Thomas Earl of Lancaster. Edward and Gaveston went north to confront the rebels but they had no success. Gaveston became stranded in the castle of Scarborough and was compelled to come to terms with his besiegers whereby he would surrender on condition that he was taken safely to the King before being put on trial by parliament. But this agreement was not honoured. On the way south he was waylaid by another group of barons in the Oxfordshire village of Deddington and taken off to Warwick where he was given a mockery of a trial in which he was not allowed to plead, and was summarily and brutally executed.

Meanwhile Isabella had been hustled around in the wake of her husband who had taken so little care of her that she had fallen into the hands of the rebels, but being held in some respect by them she was allowed to go free. During Gaveston's exile relations between Edward and Isabella had improved. Isabella was provided with a proper establishment and Edward treated her with consideration even generosity. Moreover their marriage had been consummated so that in 1312 Isabella gave birth to a healthy son, the future Edward III. She can hardly have been pleased by the return of Gaveston but she seems to have come to terms with him and certainly had no part in his death. For the time being she gave her husband full support in his contention with the Lords Ordainers, although she may have felt some division of loyalty as Thomas of Lancaster was her uncle.

The killing of Gaveston had caused a rift in the baronial party so that for a time pressure was off the King, but it came back strongly after his heavy defeat by the Scots at the Battle of Bannockburn. Thomas of Lancaster had kept away from this battle and may not have been unduly displeased at the outcome as afterwards the humiliated and nearly bankrupt Edward was to a large extent at his mercy. These were hard times for the King, but his relations with Isabella remained constant. Between 1316 and

1321 she bore him three children and her income became substantially greater on the death in 1318 of the dowager queen Margaret, widow of Edward I.

In 1321 Edward's fortunes were temporarily boosted following a bizarre incident in which Isabella was involved. While making a pilgrimage to the tomb of Thomas Becket at Canterbury she sought a night's lodging for herself and her entourage at the castle of Leeds in Kent, a royal demesne under the governorship of Lord Badlesmere. He was away at the time but his wife took it upon herself to refuse the Queen's request without her husband's permission so that Isabella was compelled to go elsewhere. Understandably she was infuriated by this and complained bitterly to the King who shared her anger and then proceeded to lay siege to the castle. For a time the intrepid Lady Badlesmere held out but was eventually forced to yield. If she had been male she could have expected the death penalty but the Plantagenets had scruples about putting women to death and she was sentenced to imprisonment.

This action of Lady Badlesmere, however, was to cause a division among the Lords Ordainers of which Edward was quick to take advantage and in the following year Thomas of Lancaster was brought to battle at Boroughbridge and defeated and captured and was shown no mercy. It was ten years since the death of Gaveston but Edward had always harboured a secret determination one day to have his revenge for it. Now the time had arrived and, usually mild and conciliatory, he proved vicious and vindictive. Altogether some 118 of Lancaster's adherents were put to death and their women folk too did not go free, many of them being herded into imprisonment in the Tower of London. This brutality cost Edward dear for it caused widespread anger and marked the beginning of his estrangement from Isabella who was shocked by the treatment of her uncle.

1322 saw the apex of Edward's fortunes: his most powerful rival had been overcome, Gaveston had been avenged, the Lords Ordainers were in disarray and parliament was induced to repeal those ordinances most restrictive of the King's powers. With wisdom Edward should have been able to consolidate his position, but he failed to do so. The main reason for this was that a new favourite had appeared on the scene.

For some time Edward had been relying increasingly on the services of two barons, father and son, both called Hugh Despenser.

The father was a faithful old servant who had stood by Edward loyally in his worst times and was described by a contemporary as 'an honourable, prudent, industrious and energetic old man'. But although he may have been all these things he also believed in feathering his own nest, and his acquisitiveness aroused great resentment, although nowhere near so much as that aroused by his son who was a much more ruthless and sinister character. There was some similarity between him and Gaveston: he was not so showy and exuberant but just as ambitious and avaricious and considerably more able; and his relationship with Edward was just as intimate. As with Gaveston, Edward entrusted him with great powers, married him off to one of his nieces and allowed him to enrich himself plentifully. Inevitably this caused furious anger and, as was his custom, Edward bowed before the storm and agreed to the exile of the Despensers; but they were soon back and after the downfall of Lancaster he let them become ever more extortionate and despotic. In the next years the younger Despenser became the most powerful man in the country. According to a chronicler: 'The King of England's right eye ... but an eyesore to the rest of the kingdom... His every wish became a royal command.'

Of course such a man exercising such powers made many enemies, and foremost among these was Queen Isabella. She was appalled at the prospect of another Gaveston and was determined to bring him down. For his part Despenser saw in her his main opponent and did all he could to humiliate her – overriding her orders, dismissing her French servants, sequestering her lands and separating her from her children. Miserably she wrote to the King of France: 'I am held in no higher consideration than a maidservant in the palace of the King my husband.' She had suffered in much the same way during Gaveston's ascendancy, but then she was a naïve, unsophisticated teenager; now she was approaching thirty, the mother of four children and considerably more versed in the ways of the world. In the battle she had to fight she showed a cunning and ruthlessness few would have suspected. At first she laid low, dissimulating, awaiting an opportunity, and this was soon to come.

In 1325 England and France became engaged in another war about Gascony, England's last remaining territory on the Continent. Both sides wanted peace but an impasse had been reached and desultory fighting continued. To Isabella it seemed that, as the sister of the new French king, Charles IV, she might be able to forge

59

an agreement, and so she proposed going on a peace mission to Paris, and to this Edward II agreed – a mistake that was to prove fatal. On arrival Isabella did manage to patch up some sort of a treaty but then insisted that to give it validity Edward should come to Paris to pay homage to Charles as his overlord in Gascony, and this she knew he would never do and so she then urged that their son, Edward, then aged thirteen, should come and perform the ceremony on his behalf. And to this, surprisingly, Edward agreed. Once the young prince was in Paris Isabella saw the strength of her hand: she was in a position to dictate to Edward terms on which she and their son would return to England: and prominent among these was the dismissal of the Despensers; and to this, as expected, Edward would not agree.

Isabella was then confronted with a momentous decision. If she were to obey Edward's urgent order to return home she would have to submit again to her deadly enemy and be reliant for her safety on a husband not notable for keeping his word. If, on the other hand, she were to defy Edward and refuse to come back except on her own terms she would be guilty of treason, her lands would be sequestered and she would become dependent for finance on her brother the King of France. It cannot be known for certain by what stages Isabella came to decide on the latter course of action. It seems probable that when she first came to Paris she was not thinking seriously of staying there after agreeing a treaty; but then events made her think differently. In the first place there was the arrival of her son and the realisation that she held a trump card. But there was perhaps a more compelling reason. For at the same time she was being strongly influenced by English *emigrés* in Paris who had fled there to escape the vengeance of the Despensers, and with one of these she fell deeply in love. Roger Mortimer was everything Edward II was not – dominant, virile, belligerent – and Isabella found him irresistible and made no secret of her passion, and it was common knowledge that they were lovers. Mortimer was a leading English landowner with vast estates on the Welsh borders and in Ireland where he had once been a strong and ruthless governor. But there was a blood feud between him and Hugh Despenser who held him responsible for the death of his grandfather, and this had resulted in his coming into conflict with forces of Edward II and being captured and sent to the Tower of London under sentence of death. This, however, was remitted and soon afterwards he made a daring escape for which there were signs of outside help.[1] When Isabella arrived in Paris he had been engaged for some time in gathering forces for an invasion of England and in this Isabella gave him her support. It was then that a character change became noticeable in her: gone was the dutiful, compliant wife to be replaced by a virago with mounting bitterness not only towards the Despensers but also towards her husband. It seemed as if the pent up fury of years was being unloosed.

Before an invasion of England could be launched there were setbacks to be overcome; although many had come forward to give their support there were those who held back. Pope John XXII was deeply shocked by the adulterous relationship between the Queen of England and a convicted traitor and told Charles IV of France that he must not tolerate their presence in his country – a direction with which Charles felt bound to comply so that Isabella and Mortimer and Prince Edward had to make a hurried departure from France and take refuge in the independent German state of Hainault (which included part of Holland) where she was given a heroine's welcome by Count William II. She must have told a pitiful tale of woe about being wronged by a cruel and perverted husband for the Count gave her every assistance for an invasion of England which was to be under the joint command of his brother John and Mortimer. Word of the venture soon spread around Europe and knights errant, some motivated by chivalry, some with an eye on the main chance, came flocking to offer their services.

In September 1326 Isabella's invasion force, some 2,000 strong, set sail and landed safely on the coast of Suffolk. There had been no opposition as the fleet which should have intercepted her was landlocked owing to a mutiny among the sailors. It was the first invasion of England from abroad since that of William the Conqueror in 1066 and was to be just as successful. From the first Isabella showed great talent in winning the hearts and minds of the English people, presenting herself as a beautiful, dishonoured wife with a fine upstanding young son, seeking redress and aiming at no more than rescuing her husband from evil counsellors. And such was

---

[1] Including drugged warders, a rope in place to lower him down the castle walls and a ship in readiness on the south coast to take him to France. At the time Isabella was in residence in the Tower and it was surmised later that it was she who organised the escape, but there is no positive evidence for this.

the popular detestation of the Despensers that people came rushing to her support. Meanwhile those loyal to the King faded away. Ten days later the citizens of London turned out to welcome her and in less than a month her forces were in Bristol where Edward had fled in the hope of rallying an army. There the elder Despenser was captured and summarily put to a ghastly death on the charge of treason which he surely had not committed. A few weeks later the younger Despenser was hunted down and he could expect no mercy. Isabella watched impassively as he was slowly dismembered and eviscerated.

It has been maintained by some that Isabella does not deserve the pseudonym 'She-Wolf of France'. Certainly some of her enemies were put to death with the maximum brutality, and squeamish she was not, countenancing horrible executions and viewing coolly the mangled remains of opponents when brought to her. But after her victory there was no widespread bloodbath. She was ready for reconciliation.

On 16 November Edward II was captured in Wales after an unsuccessful attempt to escape to Ireland and was imprisoned for the time being in Kenilworth castle in Warwickshire while his fate was decided. On this there was not full agreement. There were those, including the Pope, who would like to have seen Isabella reconciled to Edward who would remain king on certain conditions; but Isabella would have none of this. She was determined that he should be deposed and replaced by their son, then aged fourteen, with herself as regent until he reached his majority at eighteen. On this there was general agreement but there were difficulties as to how it could be achieved legally. There was no precedent, no king having been deposed since the Norman conquest. In 1327 a Parliament was assembled which voted unanimously in favour of deposition, but as it had not been convened by royal command it could be not be said to have force of law, and young Prince Edward was definite that he was not prepared to accede to the throne unless his father abdicated of his own free will and named him as his successor. One of Isabella's strongest supporters, the aggressive and devious Bishop Orleton of Hereford, was then sent to put pressure on Edward to conform, which by none too godly methods he succeeded in doing, and Prince Edward was proclaimed Edward III amid tumultuous rejoicing.

But this was not the end of the matter. What was to become of the ex-king? Was he to be exiled abroad? Kept in prison? Or done to death? The ultimate fate of Edward II is enshrouded in mystery. After a rescue attempt he had been moved from Kenilworth to Berkeley Castle in Gloucestershire where he was said to have been treated with great brutality – mocked and tormented, fed with foul unwholesome food and kept in a filthy chamber reeking of the carcasses of animals in the hope that he would sicken and die. According to the official version he died on 21 September 1327 'by an accident destined by fate', which, to say the least, is ambiguous. Whether he died a natural death or, as reported in some chronicles, he was killed in an horrifically brutal way which left no outward mark on his body cannot be known.[2] It is also not entirely certain that he did not escape from Berkeley Castle and live the rest of his life in obscurity abroad. Quite a plausible case can be made for this. But whatever Edward's fate the evidence is that he was not killed at the instigation of Isabella, much more likely at that of Mortimer. No accusing finger was pointed at her at the time and she put on a convincing show of grief at Edward's funeral.

The disappearance of Edward from the scene was, nevertheless, convenient for Isabella: it removed the main threat to the authority of herself and Mortimer. For the next three years they were the country's rulers. And they were to find this no mean task: they inherited wars with France and Scotland, the country's finances were parlous and there was much lawlessness and disorder particularly in the city of London where miscreants took advantage of uncertain conditions for their own ends. It is not clear whether Isabella or Mortimer exercised the greater power. At first Mortimer kept a low profile as it was felt necessary to keep their illicit relationship out of public view, but behind the scenes he was a dominant influence. Isabella had a mind of her own and was no puppet on a string but she did depend on him.

It was always likely that the delight with which she was greeted when she first arrived would not be sustained. It was soon to be seen that she and Mortimer were just as rapacious and despotic as the Despensers. The main blow to their popularity came when in 1328 they made what many considered an ignominious treaty with Scotland, conceding everything for which the English had been

---

[2] A red hot iron inserted in the anus.

63

fighting for the last fifty years – complete independence of Scotland free from English overlordship and the acknowledgement of Robert Bruce as the lawful king. In the situation in which England then was, with a war against France impending, this may have been a prudent move, but it was regarded by most people as a craven submission, and the reputation of Isabella and Mortimer never recovered from it. At the same time it was becoming more and more evident to what extent they were both feathering their own nests and abusing their powers.

Great anger was caused in 1330 when Mortimer engineered the death of Edward II's younger brother, the Duke of Kent, who had become convinced that Edward was still alive and was set on tracking him down and gathering support for him. This may have been injudicious and possibly treasonous to his nephew Edward III, but he should have been brought to trial before his peers and executed according to the law. Instead he was hauled before an improvised court, forced into a confession and rushed off to a summary (and botched) execution. Such high-handed treatment of a prince of royal blood was deeply shocking to the country's magnates who felt it might be their turn next. Already Henry of Lancaster, the King's cousin and Isabella's uncle, was in open revolt. At first, eager to avenge his brother Thomas's death after the battle of Boroughbridge, he had been one of Isabella's strongest supporters, but he had soon become discontented by Mortimer's rapacity and arrogance, and by the end of 1328 he had been joined by other magnates and the country was confronted with civil war. But then suddenly his rebellion collapsed and he was forced to go meekly and seek pardon from Isabella and Mortimer which was granted but on humiliating terms.

Of greater significance was the changed attitude of the young King Edward III, then approaching his majority and the end of Isabella's regency. Until then he had been a loyal son, submitting to his mother's authority and for her sake tolerating Mortimer. But recently he had become more independent and aware of Mortimer's mounting ambitions which, it seemed to him, might not stop short of kingship. So to forestall this he determined to strike first. On the 19 October 1330 Isabella and Mortimer were staying in Nottingham Castle which was heavily guarded with every entrance locked and barred with the keys under Isabella's pillow; but Edward discovered a secret passage leading inside, and during the night he and a party of well trusted armed men made their way through and took Mortimer by surprise. The next day he was taken in chains to London where he was arraigned before parliament on a charge of high treason, accusing him among other crimes of the murder of Edward II. His trial was hardly more fair than that of the Duke of Kent; for fear of incriminating Isabella he was not allowed to plead in his defence and was found guilty and condemned to be hanged. His body was left on the common gallows (later known as Tyburn) for two days and two nights for all to see.

If Mortimer was guilty of treason so, it might be thought, was Isabella. But Edward did not proceed against her; he loved her dearly and owed much to her and did not want her exposed to scandal especially, as will be seen later, as he was about to claim through her the throne of France. Mortimer's arrest and execution had been a traumatic experience for her especially as at the time she was reported to be pregnant. It was said that her mind became temporarily unbalanced and she had to be put in confinement out of harm's way. The result of her pregnancy is not known. Later she was provided for generously and spent the twenty-eight years remaining to her in comfort and some state. There were restrictions on her, particularly as regards her movements, and at first she was excluded from all political affairs. Most of her time she spent in Castle Rising in Norfolk, although she was able to acquire additional residences later on, and there her son visited her regularly as also did her grandson, the future Black Prince, vital and ruthless like her with whom she had a special affinity and whose triumphs at the battles of Crecy and Poitiers she lived to witness. In 1348 she managed to survive the ravages of the Black Death, which decimated the population of England, although one of her granddaughters died as a result of it. During these years she was said to have behaved 'with meekness' although she did not entirely lie low. She attended a number of state occasions including the one which inaugurated the famous new order of knighthood known as the Garter.[3] During the four years in which her cousin, the French King John, was held captive in England after the battle of Poitiers she saw much of him and is likely to have had a part in negotiating the final

---

[3] So called, according to tradition, because a lady's garter came adrift which caused some mirth until King Edward retrieved it with the famous words, 'Honi soit qui mal y pense' (Shame to anyone who thinks ill of it).

treaty for his release. She also saw something of her son-in-law, King David of Scotland and his wife Joan. After eleven years' captivity they were released, although, in view of her husband's infidelities, Joan was to return to England and became Isabella's close companion.

In her last years Isabella became much preoccupied with mortality. She was closely associated with the Franciscan friars and became a member of one of their lay orders. She also became involved in many charitable works. She died in 1358 at the age of sixty-three and Edward provided a magnificent funeral. She was interred in the Grey Friars' church at Newgate and, at her request, a casket containing the heart of her husband was laid on her bosom. What feelings inspired this wish can only be conjectured.

Isabella will always be a contentious figure. During the four years in which she exercised great power, greater than any other English queen apart from Margaret of Anjou, she achieved a temporary peace with Scotland but by promoting her son's claim to the throne of France she was instrumental in instigating what came to be known as the Hundred Years' War. Few will deny that deposing Edward II and replacing him with Edward III was beneficial to the country and she did it brilliantly, but she could not have done it without the support of Mortimer and this ultimately proved fatal.

PHILIPPA OF HAINAULT (c.1314–1369)

Wife of Edward III

'Never since the days of Queen Guinevere had so good a queen come to England nor any who had so much honour. And as long as she lived the realm enjoyed grace, prosperity, honour and all good fortune.' So wrote the Flemish chronicler, Jean Froissart, of Philippa of Hainault. Strongly prejudiced he may have been, as he had once been in her employment, but many would agree with him. Amid the barbarities of the fourteenth century her gentleness and compassion shone brightly. Her husband was a great warrior king, perpetually at war, usually victorious, a man in some moods charming and generous, in others brutally ferocious; and a loving if not a faithful husband. For her part Philippa was a loyal and devoted wife, always putting her husband's interests first and bearing him twelve children.

Philippa first met Edward when, with his mother Isabella and her paramour Mortimer, he took refuge at the court of her father, Count William of Hainault, after being expelled from France. Philippa, one of four daughters, at once attracted the attention of Edward, then aged thirteen and, although she had no authority either from Edward II or Parliament, Isabella took it upon herself to arrange a betrothal between them, and made use of the dowry which became payable to finance an army for the invasion of England. Edward was to take part in this and had a sad parting from Philippa, but he did not forget her and when the invasion had been successfully concluded his betrothal to her was confirmed by Act of Parliament.

Philippa arrived in England in December 1327 by which time Edward II had been put to death and his son crowned as Edward III, but, being only thirteen, effective power rested with his mother and Mortimer. Philippa's good nature and patience were to be tested to the utmost as she was treated with scant consideration or even courtesy. Edward was waging war against the Scots and it was necessary for her in midwinter to make the long, rigorous journey to the north of England where they were married in York Minster in January 1328. Philippa was then Queen of England but she was not treated as such as her mother-in-law was determined that she should not upstage her or impinge on the hold she had on the young king. So she was allowed no separate establishment of her own, the dower lands normally granted to the queen consort were withheld from her and for the time being she was to have no coronation. At the age of thirteen she was no match for the formidable Isabella and bore these slights meekly.

For three years Edward and Philippa were to remain under the thumb of Isabella and Mortimer, but 1330 was to see their liberation. Philippa had become pregnant and it was felt she should be officially crowned queen so there were no doubts about the succession. On 15 June she gave birth to a son, Edward, the future Black Prince, and four months later Edward III staged his coup against Mortimer, and Isabella was compelled to make over her dower lands to Philippa and go into retirement.

Just before her new found freedom, Philippa had a narrow escape from death. A magnificent tournament was being held in Cheapside to celebrate the birth of Prince Edward and the tower from which she was to watch it collapsed when she was in it. She was not badly hurt but when the matter was reported to Edward III he flew into a rage and ordered all the carpenters engaged on the job to be put to death. But Philippa pleaded with him, as she was to do later on a more famous occasion, and on her knees implored the King to spare them, which he could not forbear to do.

During Edward's reign of fifty years there were not to be many years of peace. There were intermittent wars with Scotland but there was a much more serious one with France which came to be known as The Hundred Years' War. There was no good reason for this. It derived from Edward III's claim on the death of his uncle, Charles IV without an heir, to the throne of France through his mother Isabella. But this had been barred by the Salic Law, and the French had accepted as King Charles's nearest male relative Philip VI, and had no wish for him to be replaced by the King of England.[1] Similarly many English people dreaded their king assuming the throne of France, a richer and more powerful country, and there would be a danger of England becoming a satellite. But perhaps the underlying reason was the love of Edward III and English barons for warfare. To them it was a form of sport in which great glory and riches could be won. The prosperous provinces of France were a tempting bait for plunder: bribes could be extorted and ransoms demanded. And for the King there was another vital consideration that foreign wars kept rebellious English barons occupied and distracted them from making trouble at home. These devouring passions the gentle and peace loving Philippa could not restrain; all she could do was to allay some of the horrors and miseries the war engendered, and these were indeed horrific – apart from the carnage of the battlefields, the burning of defenceless villages, the expropriation of peasants from their hovel homes, the killing in cold blood of innocent hostages. No doubt she felt pride in the historic victories of her husband and eldest son, but at Crecy she had to bear the loss of several relations fighting for France. At the time of the battle she was acting as regent in England and it fell to her to assemble an army to confront an invasion by King David of Scotland which she did effectively, and at the battle of Neville's Cross the Scots were heavily defeated and King David captured and brought to London for a captivity of twelve years. It is not clear whether Philippa was present on the battlefield, but it appears that she was there beforehand and exhorted her troops with stirring words.

Soon afterwards Philippa joined her husband in France where he was laying siege to the port of Calais – a long drawn out operation that was to last for nearly a year. For some reason Edward was insisting on staying there himself until the end. It was during this siege that there occurred the incident for which Philippa has become best known. The resistance of the people of Calais in gruesome conditions was heroic, but it drove Edward into a frenzy and he was intent on taking vicious revenge, and when the city finally surrendered he ordered that the six richest citizens should come out clad only in a shirt with a halter round their necks prior to being hanged. Those around him urged that such a callous deed would bring him great dishonour but he was not to be dissuaded. But then Queen Philippa added her voice and on her knees implored him to relent. 'Ah, gentle sir,' she begged, 'since I passed the sea in great peril I have desired nothing of you. Therefore now I

---

[1] The Salic Law barred women from ascending the throne of France. There was doubt as to whether it also barred a woman's offspring.

humbly require you in honour of the son of the Virgin Mary and for the love of me that we will take mercy on these six burgesses.' Such a plea the King could not resist, albeit reluctantly, and the burgesses were spared and even treated with kindness. And Calais was to be English for two centuries.

In 1348 Edward's reputation was at its height. The kings of France and Scotland were his captives, and his stature in Europe was such that the Electors of Germany offered him the title of Holy Roman Emperor which, on the strong insistence of Philippa, he declined; as well as claiming the throne of France it would be too much. In normal circumstances English arms might have gone on to further triumphs, but in 1348 England, like all other European countries, was struck by the fearful plague known as the Black Death in which one third of the population of London was believed to have perished. During the year that the plague was rampant Philippa and her family were able to keep their distance from London and the worst affected areas and escaped infection, the only casualty in the royal family being her daughter Joan who was struck down in Bordeaux on her way to marry a Spanish prince later known as Pedro the Bad (perhaps a merciful release).

Because of the Black Death there was a respite in the Hundred Years' War and it was not until 1356 that the English undertook another major invasion of France. This resulted in the battle of Poitiers where the Black Prince with an army of some four thousand found himself confronted by a French army of twenty thousand, but owing mainly to the deadliness of the English long bowmen he was victorious. Fearsome slaughter was inflicted on the French and King John and many noblemen of high rank were captured and taken back to England to be ransomed.

The battle of Poitiers established the Black Prince as the greatest military commander in Europe. At the time he was twenty-six and unmarried. Several brides had been proposed for him but he had not been interested, preferring a free-ranging life in which he had not been abstemious. But then he fell deeply in love with his cousin Joan, known as The Fair Maid of Kent; reputed to be the most beautiful as well as the richest woman in England. But as a marriage partner she was not ideal. Her past was shady: although only thirty-two she had had two husbands (one dead, one divorced) as well as a number of lovers; she had also given birth to five children. Unsurprisingly Edward and Philippa did not find her suitable as a daughter-in-law, but in 1360 the Black Prince went ahead and married her and because of his great reputation they felt obliged to accept her.

By then the war against France had taken a turn for the worse. An English invasion in 1359 had been a disastrous failure and in 1360 a treaty had been patched up whereby France regained possession of a number of English provinces including Normandy, Anjou and Brittany. But the largest, Aquitaine (comprising about one third of France) was retained and in 1363 the Black Prince was invested by his father with the sovereignty of it. But he was not to be a popular ruler. He and Joan lived in magnificent state, but this involved heavy taxation, and he showed great insensitivity in appointing English rather than Gascon noblemen to high office.

In England too all was not well. Failures in the war against France had caused discontent, and there were soon to be distressing signs of a deterioration in the condition and character of Edward III. He was no longer the heroic figure he had once been. He had long since been an unfaithful husband and a chronicler had noted early on that he was prone to 'the dissolute lusts of the flesh'. In his thirties he had been implicated in an ugly scandal in which he was alleged to have raped the beautiful and virtuous Countess of Salisbury; but the facts of the case were confused and it was hushed up. However, he did not mend his ways and in 1364 (when he was fifty-two) a woman called Alice Perrers, not beautiful but wilful and wily was to have an increasing hold on him. As a result the tone of his court became sordid and brash, and people at the time were shocked by 'the scurrilous wantonness of the ladies who adorned it'. Philippa, then, had much to put up with, and this she did with a good grace, even agreeing in 1366 to take Alice Perrers as a maid of her bedchamber. But by then the shadow of death was on her. She was suffering from a dropsical illness which in 1369 was to kill her at the age of fifty-five.

It was perhaps as well that Philippa did not live to see the degeneration of her husband and eldest son. After his disastrous rule of Aquitaine the Black Prince lost the prestige and glamour that had once been his. He became haughty and ungracious and fought wars in France and Spain where his ruthlessness and cruelty became a byword. Mercifully Philippa did not witness the last seven years of his life, and even more mercifully, was spared the last years of her husband who was laid low by a series of strokes and became ever more enfeebled. Gone was the great ruler – mighty in battle, wise and gracious in peace. In his place had come a pathetic old man, bereft of authority and respect and dominated by an avaricious mistress. A harsh fate indeed and one that surely would have been allayed if Philippa had not predeceased him.

ANNE OF BOHEMIA (1366–1394) and
ISABELLA OF FRANCE (1389–1411)

Wives of Richard II

Richard II became king at the age of ten. As the son of the Black Prince and grandson of Edward III it was expected that he would be another great warrior who would win victories and bring the war against France to a triumphant conclusion. But Richard was cast in a different mould. He had little love of warfare and did what he could to come to terms with the French. His tastes were primarily aesthetic and he was a patron of all forms of art. In this he was encouraged and assisted by his first wife, Anne, daughter of the King of Bohemia and granddaughter of a famous heroic figure, the blind King John who had fought so valiantly at the battle of Crecy on the side of the French and whose motto *Ich dien* (I serve) had been adopted by the Black Prince and has ever since been the motto of the Prince of Wales.

Bohemia was a central European state with no close ties with England. In promoting the betrothal the council which ruled the country during Richard's minority was looking for aid in the war against France. Otherwise there were no particular advantages: Anne was not a great beauty and she brought with her no dowry which Richard sorely needed at that time; but the marriage, albeit childless, was to be a happy one.

Anne arrived in England in 1382 when the country was in an unsettled state. The previous year had seen the great Peasants' Revolt when the country's rulers had been caught off guard and had been threatened with a holocaust. A rampaging mob had broken into London and, among other atrocities, had murdered the Archbishop of Canterbury and burned down the Savoy Palace of the King's uncle, John of Gaunt. The situation might have got out of hand completely but for the courage of Richard, then aged fourteen. At Smithfield he confronted the rebel horde and was in imminent danger of death when their leader, Wat Tyler, was struck down

73

and killed. But at the moment of crisis he did not lose his nerve: he rode intrepidly towards the raging peasants, telling them that he would now be their leader and promising them that if they dispersed he would grant all their demands. This was Richard's finest hour, but his promises were not to be honoured, and when later the men of property gained the upper hand a fearful vengeance was taken on all who had joined in the revolt. This was still being wreaked when Anne arrived in England and one of her first actions as queen was to plead for mercy for those who had been so basely betrayed.

The aftermath of the Peasants' Revolt was not the only trouble afflicting England at that time. It was a divided and unruly country, still at war with France, nearly bankrupt and with the large landed magnates taking every opportunity to encroach on royal authority. In his last years the once mighty Edward III had become incapacitated, and the war with France, which had once brought such glory, was failing, and the heavy taxation needed to keep it going was causing angry discontent. Such was the inheritance of Richard II, aged ten. For the first ten years of his reign Richard was in subjection to a clique of barons known as the Lords Appellant. As he grew older he found this dominion intolerable and was determined to be free of it, but this was not easily achieved.

The character of Richard II has always been ambiguous, containing as it does so many contrary facets – sharp astuteness with baffling folly, patience with impetuosity, tenderness and kindness with cruelty and bad temper. Like his great grandfather, Edward II, he had an effeminate vein which showed itself in his aesthetic tastes and his soft and sybaritic lifestyle. He loved to array himself and his court in magnificent clothes and jewellery, and saw to it that his palaces were luxuriously and exotically furnished.[1] He may too have had homoerotic tendencies. There were men with whom he had close relationships, notably Robert de Vere Earl of Oxford, handsome and engaging and similar in some ways to Piers Gaveston; on him he lavished great honours and riches, creating for him a new rank, that of marquis (of Dublin) and later imparting an even more extravagant title, that of Duke of Ireland. But he was not just a self-indulgent epicure. He was capable of exerting himself and was

---

[1] Particularly as regards the baths and latrines which for that age were exceptionally salubrious.

ruthless in pursuing his main objective, that of humbling the Lords Appellant. In this eventually he was to be successful, but then, consumed by *folie de grandeur*, he overplayed his hand and came to grief.

Anne did not live long enough to see all this happen. She died in 1394 at the age of twenty-eight. She had been a devoted and supportive wife and her influence on Richard was always beneficial. Had she lived longer it is possible she might have kept him on course and prevented some of the follies which ruined him. In the country she was much beloved although she was accused by some of being grasping both on her own account and that of her attendants from Bohemia. But the people of England have always been ready to resent what they see as foreigners profiting at their expense. They might have appreciated more the way Anne enriched the country's cultural life, notably in her patronage of the first great English poet, Geoffrey Chaucer.

Richard always loved her dearly and was devastated by her loss, so much so that he ordered the palace in which she died to be razed to the ground as he could not bear to be reminded of her death. He was not, however, to remain a widower for long. Two years later he astounded everyone by taking as his second wife the eight-year-old daughter of Charles VI of France, a strange union at any time but especially so with England and France still intermittently at war. But Richard had always wanted peace with France, and the agreement he made with Charles concerning the marriage provided for a thirty-year truce as well as containing a secret clause by which the French king would send help if Richard should be in danger again from rebellious barons.

If there were those who were alarmed at the prospect of a second Isabella of France as queen, they need have had no fears. The young princess was no she-wolf. She was found to be lively and somewhat precocious and at her splendid wedding in Calais showed poise and aplomb. But she was to be queen for only three years for all of which time she was in the care of suitably high-born governesses.

The sands were running out for Richard. His extravagant lifestyle dependent on heavy and sometimes unlawful taxation had made him many enemies particularly in the turbulent and rebellious City of London, and his friendship with France was not popular. The story of his overthrow is well known – how he banished his cousin,

Henry Bolingbroke, son of John of Gaunt, for ten years and then on the death of the latter sequestrated his estates which he had promised not to do. This was a fatal error but Richard, having just brought down the leaders of the Lords Appellant, thought he was strong enough to strike at Henry who he may have believed would be too powerful a rival when he had returned from his exile and taken possession of the vast estates of his father. But his high-handed action caused general alarm. The large property owners thought that if this could happen to Bolingbroke it could happen to them and rebellion began to spread. Richard's fundamental mistake was to overestimate the strength of his position; after such a provocative act and with disaffection growing he should have been on his guard. To go off, as he did, on an expedition to Ireland was the height of folly as it left England open to an invasion by his cousin who gained widespread support in the same way as Isabella and Mortimer had done sixty years before. And Richard was to suffer the same fate as his great-grandfather – imprisoned and then done to death in mysterious and probably brutal circumstances.

And so at the age of twelve Isabella became a widow. She was treated with consideration by the new king, Henry IV, who had hopes that she would marry his eldest son, Henry of Monmouth, later Henry V, but this she refused to do. She would have no truck with her husband's murderers. A suitable arrangement should have been made for her return to France, but this had to be delayed when her father suffered a bout of insanity. When she did eventually go in 1402 it was on ungenerous terms – without her jewellery which had been given away and without most of her dowry which should have gone with her. Four years later she was wedded to her cousin, the heir to the Duke of Orléans, five years her junior. Four years after that she died in childbirth. A brief and tragic life.

MARY DE BOHUN (1370–1394) and
JOANNA OF NAVARRE (c.1370–1437)

Wives of Henry IV

Henry IV is one of the more controversial kings of England. Was he a heroic character who rescued England from a despotic and irresponsible monarch and then ruled the country wisely and beneficently? Or was he a duplicitous manipulator who contrived to depose and put to death the rightful king and then seize the throne to which he was not the lawful heir?

Throughout a reign beset by plots, rebellions and civil disorder he was faithfully supported by two wives, one English and one Spanish, the former bearing him six children, the latter nursing him devotedly in his last days when he was tormented by disease including epilesy and (probably) leprosy.

Henry's father was the third (surviving) son of Edward III, John Duke of Lancaster, known to history as John of Gaunt, a man of immense wealth and limitless ambition. At the age of thirteen Henry had been married to a rich heiress, Mary de Bohun (aged eleven), daughter of Humphrey de Bohun Earl of Hereford and Essex and hereditary Constable of England. Owing to the bride's tender years the marriage could not be consummated for the time being, but when it was children came in profusion – six in eight years including Henry of Monmouth, the future king Henry V.

It seems that Henry was a faithful but absentee husband. His was a roving and restless disposition. He was constantly touring the Lancaster estates and accompanied his father in wars against France and Scotland; and in 1390, when there was a period of comparative peace at home, he went off to East Prussia to join the Teutonic Knights in a crusade against the infidel Lithuanians. Two years later he set off with a large retinue across Europe on a pilgrimage to the Holy Land where he was filled with a deep desire, which remained with him for the rest of his life, to liberate the country from the Mohammedan Turks.

In 1394 soon after his return to England Mary de Bohun died in giving birth to their sixth child. Left with six children under eight it might have been expected that Henry would have looked rather urgently for another wife, but it was to be eight years before he married again. And during that time his life was to change dramatically.

There had always been rivalry and some hostility between Henry and his first cousin Richard II. They were of a different ilk – Richard aesthetic and peaceable, Henry belligerent and hyperactive. They had, however, lived in reasonable amity until the civil war of 1387 when Henry took the side of the Lords Appellant and led their army to victory at the battle of Radcot Bridge, and for this Richard never forgave him.

The story of Henry's banishment and his return to England to depose Richard and have him put to death has been told in the previous chapter. The speed with which he overran the country was extraordinary and was perhaps mainly due to his declaration when he first landed that he came only to retrieve his father's estates, not to replace Richard as king. Whether he changed his mind, or it was always his intention, cannot be known, but he might well have shied away if he could have known the turmoil that was in store for him as king. At the core of this was the fact that he was not Richard's lawful heir; he was descended from Edward III's third son, but there were those alive who were descended from his second son, Lionel, Duke of Clarence. Edmund Mortimer, Earl of March, was only eight in 1399, but he was by birth the lawful king of England, and when troubles arose for Henry his name was always to the fore.

In 1402 Henry remarried. His second wife was Joanna, dowager Duchess of Brittany, a widow of thirty-two with six children.[1] During his exile he had visited the court of John Duke of Brittany, and his wife Joanna, who gave him help for his projected invasion of England. He must have made a deep impression on the Duchess as three years later after the death of her husband and without ever seeing Henry again she accepted him in marriage. Joanna was the daughter of Charles III, King of Navarre, whose evil ways, particularly his practice of necromancy, had brought to him the soubriquet of 'the bad'. Her upbringing, like many

---

[1] The first widow to be Queen of England since the Norman conquest.

78

princesses of that time, had been unstable. At the age of ten a betrothal was arranged for her with the King of Castile, but this was soon broken off. In the following year she and her brother were taken as hostages by the King of France for the good behaviour of their father. Then at sixteen she was wedded to John IV, Duke of Brittany, who was known as 'the valiant' but who had a reputation for bad temper and treachery. It was hardly a romantic affair: the Duke had been married twice before and was old enough to be her grandfather. But contrary to expectations he proved a kindly and considerate husband and during their thirteen years of marriage she was to bear him nine children (three died in infancy).

Henry and Joanna's marriage was regarded with suspicion at the court of the King of France. The King, Charles VI, was only intermittently sane, but the regent, the Duke of Burgundy, insisted as a safeguard that Joanna should leave her three sons under his protection. There was also a difficulty because Henry and Joanna were cousins (through her mother) and a dispensation was therefore needed from the Pope, which was more complicated than it might have been as there were then two popes, but the matter was satisfactorily arranged and the marriage was solemnised in the first place by proxy, rather strangely with one of Joanna's knights standing in for her in a low-key ceremony in Eltham Palace. When Joanna arrived in England in the following year there was another wedding in Winchester but, unexpectedly, not in the cathedral but in the small church of St Swithun.

The first four years of Henry's reign had been deeply troubled. In trying to establish some sort of law and order in the country he had resorted to despotic measures which had alienated many of his one-time supporters and there had been a number of plots and rebellions, some in the belief that Richard was still alive and was waiting his opportunity to return and drive out the usurper. Henry was also confronted with religious dissidents. For some time an Oxford don, John Wycliffe, had been attacking the doctrines and customs of the Church, teaching that people should take their religion straight from the Bible, not from bishops and priests who taught versions too favourable to themselves and their own well-being. The wealth of the Church, the special status of priests, soft-living monks and rapacious friars came under his attack as well as pardons, indulgences, confessions, pilgrimages and the doctrine of transubstantiation.[2]

The greatest moment of danger to Henry came in 1403 soon after Joanna's arrival in England when there was a rebellion led by the Earl of Northumberland and his fiery son known as Harry Hotspur who were aggrieved that Henry had withheld money due to them after their defeat of a Scottish invasion in the previous year. However, they were decisively defeated at the battle of Shrewsbury which put Henry's throne out of danger for the time being. But dangers persisted particularly in Wales where a vicious guerrilla war was being fought.

For a woman of thirty-two and a mother of nine Joanna was still a beauty; she was also of sterling character, but like other foreign queens she encountered hostility in England. The Hundred Years' War was in abeyance at the time but anti-French feeling was prevalent, and although Brittany was not part of the kingdom of France it was under the overlordship of the French king and thought to be subservient to him; and besides Breton pirates were preying on English ships in the Channel and were even raiding south coast towns. And so Joanna was regarded with suspicion and people were inclined to find fault with her, accusing her of extravagance and being surrounded by an excessive number of Breton attendants. Parliament was always prying into her private affairs, something which previous kings would not have tolerated, but owing to the insecurity of his position Henry felt he had to submit to its demands. For it was not by right of birth but by proclamation of a Parliament (albeit not a legal one) that he was king, and what Parliament had given it could take away. And so Joanna was obliged not only to make economies in her household but also to send away most of her personal staff, even including cooks and chambermaids.

In spite of the dangers that beset him Henry was to remain on the throne until he died from natural causes at the age of forty-seven. His last years were miserably unhappy. The deposition and killing of Richard II weighed heavily on his conscience as did the putting to death of numerous rebels including an Archbishop of York, which some thought almost as great a sin as the murder of

---

[2] This laid down that the bread and wine when consecrated in the Eucharist was changed physically into the body and blood of Christ.

Becket. He longed to atone for his misdeeds by leading a crusade to the Holy Land, but he was never able to do this. There were always pressing matters for him to attend to in England. And his health broke down completely: he suffered from epilepsy and was afflicted with a terrible skin disease similar to leprosy when his body was covered with painful and ugly pustules so that he dreaded appearing in public. He became so weakened that the proper governance of the country became beyond him and he was aware of this but resisted all attempts by his heir to take over kingly duties. For Joanna the care of such a tormented husband as his life ebbed gradually away was a gruelling task but one from which she did not shrink.

She was to outlive Henry by twenty-four years. It might have been expected that she would have a prosperous and untroubled widowhood. She had been endowed amply by Henry with property of all sorts – castles, towns, manors, fee farms – and she received too a dower from Brittany. Her relations with the new king, Henry V, her stepson, had always been good, and he was grateful for her help in keeping Brittany neutral in the war he was waging against France. She must, however, have had mixed feelings about this, for she had many relatives whose first allegiance was to the French king. At the battle of Agincourt she lost a brother and son-in-law fighting for France; and her second son, Arthur, was horribly wounded and taken prisoner and in the victory celebrations in London paraded through the streets with other eminent captives.

Whatever her feelings might have been Joanna always gave her stepson full support and there seemed to be complete trust between them. But then suddenly came a bombshell. On the orders of the King, who was in France at the time, Joanna was charged with witchcraft and conspiring with others to bring about his downfall by practice of the black arts. Apparently this had been reported by a Minorite friar who had once been her confessor. It seems incredible that Henry V could have believed such a story but he proceeded to take drastic action: the Queen Dowager was confined in one of her castles, stripped of all her possessions (including furniture and clothing) and her staff was dismissed. She was to be kept in reasonable comfort but was to be allowed no freedom of movement nor any contact with the outside world. The full truth of this extraordinary incident will never be known as Joanna was never brought to trial and the friar who accused her was killed in a quarrel with an enraged priest. The most likely explanation is that the King, who was in dire financial straits at the time, coveted her wealth which she had perhaps been too assiduous in amassing since coming to England. Whatever the reason she was to remain in confinement for three years, but as the King became aware of approaching death in 1422, his conscience troubled him and he ordered that full restitution be made to her which was tantamount to an admission that the charges against her had been trumped up.

In spite of tribulations Joanna was to live to the ripe old age (for that time) of sixty-seven, fifteen years into the reign of her step-grandson, Henry VI, by whom she was treated kindly.

CATHERINE OF VALOIS (1401–1437)

Wife of Henry V

No queen of England has had a more bizarre life story than Catherine of Valois. After a miserable childhood when her mother treated her abominably and her father was intermittently insane, she was married to the great conquering hero of the age and became the mother of the only King of England who was also for a time King of France. Then for the rest of her life came obscurity, married (or perhaps not married) to a lowly courtier of Welsh origin by whom she had three sons, one of whom was to be the founder of the Tudor dynasty.

Catherine was the younger sister of Queen Isabella, second wife of Richard II. Her father, Charles VI, was amiable, ineffective and schizophrenic; her mother, Isabella of Bavaria, was evil and licentious, spending such money as she had on herself and her lovers so that her children were neglected and often went hungry and ill-clothed. In time, however, Catherine was to grow into a renowned beauty and was much sought after in marriage, particularly by Henry V, the young King of England. But marriage negotiations with him were difficult as he was obsessed by a dominating ambition: he saw himself not only as King of England but also of France and then as the leader of a great Western crusade to free the Holy Land from the Mohammedans. To this vision all else was subordinate, and great as was his love for Catherine, he would only marry her on the most rigorous terms which included a massive dowry and the restoration of Normandy and Aquitaine as well as the recognition of himself as heir to Charles VI.

Such terms could not be accepted and in rejecting them the Dauphin, Catherine's brother, added a stinging insult – a box of tennis balls as being 'fitter playthings than the provinces'. To which Henry responded by saying that the balls 'should be struck back with such a racket as should force open the gates of Paris'.

And so Henry set out to conquer France with all the suffering that that entailed – slaughter on the battlefields, cities besieged and burned and fertile farmlands laid waste. At the battle of Agincourt in 1415 the French suffered their heaviest defeat and were compelled to sue for peace and agree to Henry's terms including his marriage to Catherine which occurred soon after the signing of the Treaty of Troyes in 1420. But this did not put an end to all fighting and Catherine, during what might have been her honeymoon, had to accompany her husband while he besieged cities and fought battles in which hundreds of her fellow citizens were killed. Strangely there are no recorded instances of Catherine, like previous queens pleading for mercy and moderation. She seems to have looked on the barbarous treatment of some of her compatriots with detachment.

There was a break from warfare at the end of 1420 when Henry and Catherine went to England where they were received rapturously. The English people had paid dearly for Henry's victories but they did not begrudge them; there was no one they loved more than a victorious monarch. But Henry could not linger in England. He was soon called back to France to deal with a dangerous situation, leaving Catherine behind to give birth to a son, the future Henry VI. She had been instructed that he should not be born in Windsor owing to the prophecy of a soothsayer that the conquests of Henry of Monmouth would be lost by Henry of Windsor. But this behest she failed to obey – fatefully, as will be seen.

Henry and Catherine's marriage was to last no more than two years. In August 1422 Henry died of a mortal disease, probably dysentery, at Vincennes, three miles from Paris. He took some time a-dying and it might have been expected that Catherine would have been at his deathbed. She was in Paris at the time and could easily have been summoned but no call came, which seems to suggest that their love affair was not as ardent as that portrayed by Shakespeare. Dutifully she accompanied his cortège back to England and saw him interred in a splendid tomb in Westminster Abbey. But she did not appear to be weighed down with grief and did not remain a widow for long.

What happened to Catherine in the next thirteen years is cloaked in mystery. Queen Dowager though she might have been, she disappeared from the scene. She did not attend her son's coronation in Westminster Abbey in his eighth year nor was she present when he was crowned King of France in Paris in the following year. It later transpired that at some point she may have married an undistinguished courtier of Welsh origin by the name of Owen Tudor. Little is known of him except that he was descended from a Welsh chieftain called Theodore, later transmuted to Tudor, and that he had fought with Owen Glendower who may have been his godfather. Later he had been at the battle of Agincourt and then taken into the court of Henry V where he occupied the modest position of clerk of the Queen's wardrobe. No record has been found of his marriage to Catherine but it is certain that she bore him three sons, the eldest of whom married Margaret Beaufort, a great-granddaughter of John of Gaunt, and was created Earl of Richmond by Henry VI, and had a son, Henry, who was to become Henry VII. Owen was thus the progenitor of the Tudor dynasty. It seems extraordinary that Catherine was able to live for so long in obscurity with her low-born Welsh husband and three sons without attracting the attention of the government, but in 1435 there was trouble. The regent, Henry VI's uncle, Humphrey Duke of Gloucester, had Catherine confined in a convent, her sons were put into another one and Owen Tudor was imprisoned in Newgate.

Catherine was to die two years later at the age of thirty-six, weighed down by grief and, perhaps, a troubled conscience. She did not live long enough to see the expulsion of England from all of France (except Calais) but she did witness a succession of English defeats, following the appearance on the scene of Joan of Arc, and may have felt that these were due to her disobedience in giving birth to her son in Windsor. It might be expected that she would also have been troubled by the fate of Owen Tudor and their sons, but there is no evidence of this. In the will she drew up shortly before her death they are not mentioned. It almost seems as if she was complicit in the covering up of her relationship with Owen Tudor. In this, as on other occasions, there is something strangely heartless about Catherine. Although Queen of England for two years and Queen Dowager for fifteen she made little impact on the country. During her son's long minority she might have been a powerful and influential figure, instead of which she was tucked away out of sight with a minor courtier. The inference is that she was a beautiful face and not much more.

On her death she was accorded a funeral worthy of her rank and laid to rest in Westminster Abbey, but the original epitaph on her tomb described her only as the widow of Henry V with no mention of her as being the wife of Owen Tudor. It may be that it was because of this that the epitaph was subsequently removed by her grandson, Henry VII. And her mortal remains were not to remain in peace. On the accession of her great-grandson, Henry VIII, her body was exhumed and found to be in such a state of preservation that with the consent of the King her bones were put on public display. For three centuries they could be viewed and even handled by morbid sightseers (including Samuel Pepys). It was not until the nineteenth century that her relics were finally moved into a suitable resting place.

MARGARET OF ANJOU (1430–1482)

Wife of Henry VI

Margaret of Anjou was the most ill-fated of English queens. The quarter of a century in which her husband was king must have been the unhappiest and most humiliating in the country's history, seeing, as it did, the loss of the English lands in France, a bloody and brutal civil war in England and the virtual extinction of the Plantagenet dynasty. And in these disasters Margaret had a leading role. Her life was tempestuous and heroic and mostly wrong-headed, and its failure was all the more tragic because she was one of the most beautiful and gifted of women.

Considering the turbulence of the times and in contrast to the rest of her life, Margaret's childhood was calm and contented, although not without its dramas. When she was two years old her father, René, the younger son of the Duke of Anjou, was captured in battle and held captive for six years pending the payment of an impossibly high ransom.[1] During that time he accumulated more kingdoms and titles. On the death of his elder brother he became titular Duke of Anjou and Count of Provence, and then a year later on the death of a female relative, King of Naples and the two Sicilies and, for good measure, King of Jerusalem. But these honours were illusory. Most of Anjou was then occupied by the English; there was another strong claimant to the throne of Naples; Sicily was beyond his reach, and Jerusalem was in the hands of the Turks. Left to himself René might have been inclined to let most of these titles lapse; his was not a war-like disposition, his main interests being music and art in which he had some ability. But his wife, Isabella of Lorraine, was made of sterner stuff. She was one of the great female warriors of that time, and while he was a prisoner she took up the cudgels on his behalf, both in her

---

[1] His captor, Philip, Duke of Burgundy, was well known as 'The Good' in spite of having fathered thirty-seven bastards.

native Lorraine and in Naples where she had some success; and René, though still in prison, was acclaimed king.

Meanwhile Margaret had been left in Anjou in the care of her grandmother, another female warrior who had once led a French army to a rare victory over the English. Her upbringing of her granddaughter had been strict but enlightened, seeing to it that she was given an education befitting her intelligence. When Margaret was seven her father was released from captivity, but he was always to be something of a lame duck; he did not for long remain King of Naples and, forsaking his other far-flung kingdoms, settled in Anjou where enough problems awaited him.

In the 1440s France was still suffering from the ravages of the Hundred Years' War. The country was teeming with homeless and hungry peasants, as well as brigands and robber barons. Law and order was rarely prevalent. The writ of the French king Charles VII extended over only a small part of France, most of which was still occupied by the English; but since the mission of Joan of Arc and the death of Henry V their power was on the decline, and this was soon to gather pace. Charles was proving a more capable ruler than might have been expected. He had developed much from the timid Dauphin into whom Joan of Arc had put some mettle and had had crowned king. Since then he had been successful in uniting French factions and was laying intelligent plans for the eventual expulsion of England from France, and in these Margaret of Anjou, his niece by marriage, was to have a part to play.

By the age of fifteen Margaret had grown into a notable beauty and was much sought in marriage. It is not known how she first came to the attention of Henry VI, but it was probably through his great-uncle, Henry Cardinal Beaufort, who had been deeply impressed both by her beauty and her forceful character. It seemed to him that she was just the wife for the weak willed and faltering Henry. And so he painted her in glowing colours and Henry, hitherto a reluctant lover, had responded enthusiastically and set about in earnest acquiring Margaret as his wife.

In the prolonged negotiations which ensued it might be expected that Margaret's father, Duke René, would have the leading role but this was taken over by the King of France who saw in his beautiful niece a useful pawn in his dealings with England. She could be of critical importance in the influence she brought to bear on her irresolute husband. And he must be made to pay dearly for her by making concessions about English lands in France, in particular renouncing English rule of the strategically important province of Maine. To come to terms on these matters a conference was convened in the Angevin city of Tours, attended by representatives of the French king, René and an English delegation headed by one of the King's chief ministers, the Duke of Suffolk. The bargaining between the two sides was keen: Henry VI wanted Margaret almost at any price, Charles VII insisted on the surrender of Maine to which Suffolk was reluctant to agree as he knew that his many enemies at home would be at his throat for such an abject surrender. In the end an agreement was reached by which Margaret was to marry Henry, and Maine was to be ceded, but this was to remain secret for the time being. There was also to be a truce of two years in the Hundred Years' War. The English would have liked a permanent settlement but so long as they occupied lands in France this was not possible.

Of course Margaret had no part in these dealings. Whether or not she liked the prospect of becoming Queen of England was not considered relevant. She might well have had qualms about being parted from her home and family at such a young age and being sent to the land of France's traditional enemy and being married to a king whose reputation was hardly heroic. But it did not occur to her to make objection. The throne of England was still one of the most potent in Europe.

After matters had been settled there was a delay of a year before the marriage was solemnised and Margaret set out for England. The main reason for this seems to have been the penury of Henry VI. Such was his plight that he was unable to find enough money at once to give his future wife an appropriate royal reception; also the Queen's apartments from long disuse had fallen into decay and needed extensive renovation. Finance was eventually found, however, and early in 1445 the Duke of Suffolk returned to Anjou to bring Margaret to England. But first there was a magnificent marriage service in Nancy Cathedral attended by many of Europe's royalty, although not by the bridegroom who stayed at home, the Duke of Suffolk acting for him by proxy. This was followed by eight days of festivities – pageants, tournaments, feasts – before Margaret set out on a stately journey to England. At all stages she was received rapturously by local inhabitants but she was gravely embarrassed by shortage of ready money. Her father had been unable to provide her with any and her uncle had been unwilling to, and so in order to pay bills for incidental expenses she had to resort to borrowing from her attendants or even pawning some of her wedding presents. The last part of her journey proved traumatic. In crossing the Channel her ship was badly battered in a gale and she arrived in England in a state of collapse, suffering not only from *mal de mer* but also from a disease which might have been chicken pox so that she had to lie low for several days before meeting her husband and going through another marriage service at Tichfield in Hampshire. Before proceeding to London, however, Henry felt it necessary to send for new clothes for his wife as the ones she had brought with her were barely presentable.

In spite of the rigours of her journey Margaret made an immediately favourable impression on the people of England. If they could have known the fateful role she was to have in their history they might have been inclined otherwise, but for the time being they were charmed by her grace and beauty and were not put off because she was French – one of the enemy – and came dowerless and so liable to be a charge on the taxpayer.[2]

It cannot have taken Margaret long to realise how parlous was the state of England at the time of her arrival. Since the battle of Agincourt the positions of England and France had been reversed. In 1415 France had a weak king of unsound mind, unable to cope with feuding nobles and helpless in face of a powerful invading army. In 1450 it was the English who had a timid king presiding over a divided country with an inadequate army. The brilliant victories of Henry V had brought the country great glory but had also brought it to the verge of bankruptcy. Henry VI was laden with debts he could not pay; everywhere there were signs of poverty and discontent and at times pestilence; law and order was precarious and in places anarchical. And the great victories had not succeeded in conquering France: despite heavy defeats in battle and the devastation of large areas of the country French national pride was unbroken and had been fanned into life by Joan of Arc. Since her appearance the war had been going increasingly in France's favour and by the time Margaret became Queen of England there were those who were convinced that the English should make peace as

---

[2] Her father, René, was unable to provide any money for a dowry but, feeling that he ought to produce something, bequeathed to Henry his hereditary claim to Majorca and Minorca – entirely valueless as his authority over these islands was nil.

soon as possible on the best terms available, otherwise eventually they would be driven out of France altogether. But this 'peace party' was strongly opposed by a 'war party' who wanted to revive the triumphs of Crecy and Agincourt and carry on fighting until ultimate victory. In view of these deep divisions England was in great need of a strong, decisive ruler, but this Henry VI could never be. Tender hearted, weak minded and deeply pious, he had no gifts of leadership and was quite incapable of controlling the warring factions by which he was surrounded.

When Margaret first arrived in England at the age of fifteen she did not immediately become involved in politics. Although by then Henry had officially been of age for seven years he had been content to leave most of the government to others – principally to his uncle, Humphrey Duke of Gloucester ('Protector of the Realm') and his great-uncle, Cardinal Beaufort, then approaching eighty. With the death of both of these in 1447 chief power rested with the Duke of Suffolk, to whom Margaret was devoted. But he was to become intensely unpopular in the country partly because of misgovernment and partly because of his insatiable rapacity – he was forever amassing riches and positions; and because of his closeness to Margaret his unpopularity spread to her. Increasingly it was suspected that her first loyalties were to her father Duke of Anjou and her uncle, the King of France, rather than to her husband King of England. There was outrage when in 1448 it became public that Maine had been ceded to Anjou, and for this Margaret was blamed (bitterly but wrongly). In the next year the truce with France came to an end and this was followed by a string of English defeats so that by 1450 all of Normandy had been lost. And with every French success Margaret became more reviled. In 1450 too she lost her main prop and support, the Duke of Suffolk. He had been sent into exile by Parliament but had been seized off the ship in which he was travelling and hacked to death by a barbarous mob who blamed him for all their wrongs.

1450 was a fateful year for England, for besides the setbacks and losses in France there was a serious rebellion at home, led by one Jack Cade, an ex-soldier and said to be an outlaw. It followed a similar course to the Peasants' Revolt of 1381. A rabble army took the government by surprise and broke into the City of London where it robbed and murdered freely before it was persuaded to withdraw by promises given and subsequently not honoured. Margaret, later to show herself the most bellicose of queens, came out of this incident without distinction. Henry VI, stirring himself out of his usual stupor, wanted to lead his forces into battle, but Margaret prevented him and led him off to the safety of Kenilworth in the Midlands, a notable contrast to the behaviour of Richard II seventy years before.

The English defeats in France cannot, of course, be attributed to Margaret. It was not her fault that owing to chronic shortage of money English forces had been run down, nor was it due to her that the French had gained a marked superiority in one particular arm, that of artillery. Gunpowder was to play an ever more significant role in warfare and was to mark the end of the predominance of the English longbow. The responsibility for the English disasters must rest to some extent with Henry VI who hated all warfare, never took part in a battle and did nothing to boost either the weaponry or the morale of his armies. But the main responsibility should lie with the governor-general of Normandy, Edmund Duke of Somerset, a grandson of John of Gaunt and cousin of Henry. It may be that the English situation in Normandy was so weak that no one could have saved it, but certainly Somerset did not cover himself with glory, and it came as a surprise to many that on his return to England, Henry, influenced by Margaret, showed him great favour and made him his chief minister.

It was this that brought into the political arena one who was to have a crucial role in the following years. Arguably Richard Duke of York had a better claim to the throne than Henry VI, being descended through the female line from Edward III's second son, Lionel Duke of Clarence whereas Henry was descended from Edward III's third son, John of Gaunt. In his youth he had won great honours in the war against France and more recently had shown himself a capable ruler of Ireland. The signs were that he would be a much stronger and more effective king than Henry, but for the present he protested that he was not seeking the throne, only that as heir-presumptive he should have a more prominent role in government; in particular he demanded the dismissal and disgrace of Somerset whom he blamed bitterly for the losses in France and whom he regarded as his deadly rival; because he was a fellow great-grandson of Edward III who might seek to replace him as heir-presumptive to Henry. It was this rivalry between the House of Lancaster and the House of York which was to be the basic cause of the Wars of the Roses.

In 1450 on his own initiative Richard left Ireland and landed in Wales with a small force and advanced on London. On the way he was joined by a number of supporters who looked on him as a deliverer from a weak and corrupt government; but he found that most of the nobility kept their distance, suspecting him of being self-seeking and over-ambitious. And so when he reached London Richard was at pains to emphasise his loyalty to Henry VI and stress that he only came to bring about the dismissal and disgrace of the Duke of Somerset. But in this he was unsuccessful; for Somerset was firmly supported by Margaret and therefore by Henry. Recently Margaret's authority had been increasing. She had been taking a more active role in politics and had usually been getting her way; but she realised that her influence had to be concealed as the people of England had no love for 'petticoat government'. And so the pretence had to be maintained that all her decisions came from either the King or Somerset. Henry was totally devoted to her and almost always ready to be guided by her; Somerset too tended to be submissive and so in his confrontation with Richard he had her full support, which was unfortunate for the country. It should be the role of the monarch to mediate between factions and seek reconciliation, but this was not in Margaret's nature. She was always violently partisan. If she had been less so the Wars of the Roses might have been avoided.

At first Richard of York was stalled. Somerset remained in office and most of the baronage was unwilling to break its allegiance to Henry VI who had been king for twenty-nine years, was the Lord's Anointed and who, in spite of evident weaknesses, was held in some reverence for his piety and beneficence. And so for the time being Richard withdrew to his stronghold in the Welsh Marches to await a change of fortune, and this was soon to come.

In 1453 following a heavy defeat at the battle of Castillon England lost all of Gascony which had been hers for three centuries since the time of Eleanor of Aquitaine. This left only Calais in France under English rule. In the same year there were two other events of momentous importance. After eight years of marriage Margaret at last gave birth to a child,[3] a son who immediately

---

[3] The child's legitimacy was questioned, Henry not being thought capable of fathering him. On being presented with the baby Henry, then on the verge of dementia, looked at him blankly and said that it must have been born of the Holy Ghost.

replaced the Duke of York as heir-presumptive, and the latter had to realise that his chances of becoming king by peaceful means had receded. At almost the same time Henry became insane. Whether it was the schizophrenia which had afflicted his grandfather, Charles VI of France, is not clear, but it had the effect that his mind went completely blank and all form of communication with him became impossible. For as long as she could Margaret kept his condition secret, but this could not last and it became necessary to set up a regency for which Margaret immediately put forward her claim, but this found no favour in Parliament, and a Great Council proceeded to appoint the Duke of York as 'Protector and Defender of the Realm'. This was a bitter time for Margaret: her arch enemy had taken over the government; Somerset, her friend and main supporter, was in the Tower; and her husband was insane. But her courage was undimmed. She became fanatically determined to uphold the cause of her demented husband and infant son. And in time events took a turn for the better: after sixteen months Henry recovered and was able to announce in Parliament that the Duke of York was relieved of his position and the Yorkists he had appointed to high office were similarly dismissed. At the same time Somerset was set free and became once again the King's chief minister.

But Richard of York was far from finished. For the time being he withdrew to his estates in the north of England where he found support from powerful nobles, notably the Earl of Salisbury and his son Richard Neville, Earl of Warwick.[4] Between them they were able to raise a formidable army and moved south, while at the same time Somerset raised an army for the King. It was while the two armies were in transit that they clashed, almost it seemed by accident, at St Albans where the first battle of the civil war was fought. It was hardly more than a skirmish – lasting one hour, with only 5000 troops engaged and no more than 120 casualties. But it was a Yorkist victory: Somerset was killed and Henry VI, who had been no more than a spectator at the battle, was captured and taken off to London by the Duke of York who resumed, temporarily as it proved, the title of Protector of the Realm.

Although the battle of St Albans was on a small scale it was not without significance. For it set the pattern of the thirty years'

---

[4] To become in time the most powerful man in the country, known as 'The Kingmaker'.

civil war which was to be brutal and treacherous and almost entirely without honour. Most of the barons taking part did so from no high-minded motives but out of greed and self-interest and changed sides whenever it suited them. Of chivalry there were few signs. Most odious of all was the cold-blooded killing of prisoners after each battle, resulting in blood feuds and vengeance being wreaked whenever possible. And it was at St Albans that the pattern for this was set when a number of Lancastrian captives were horribly put to death.

The battle was followed by four years of uneasy truce during which the fortunes of the two sides fluctuated. At first the Duke of York was dominant but then his rule became as unpopular as that of the Duke of Somerset and there was a Lancastrian resurgence. Left to themselves it is likely that Henry and Richard could have come to terms. Henry, whose sanity was still intermittent, wanted peace at almost any price and would have been thankful to leave affairs of government to Richard while he devoted himself to his main interests of theology and education.[5] He even agreed at one stage that he should be succeeded as king by Richard rather than by his own son Edward. But any such idea was totally abhorrent to Margaret. Compromise and conciliation were not in her nature. For her it was a battle to the death, and although she sometimes put on a peaceful face, she always knew that the succession of her son to the throne depended on the elimination of all Yorkist claimants. And so with her rare beauty and dauntless personality she became the standard bearer of the Lancastrians, forever stirring up trouble for the Yorkists, courting popularity and negotiating secretly for aid from foreign rulers. For the continuation of the civil war for nearly twenty years she was as responsible as anyone.

Open warfare broke out again in 1459, and as always fortunes varied. At the battle of Northampton in 1460 the Yorkists were victorious, which prompted Richard to claim the throne, but this was not a popular move and he did not pursue it. At the battle of Wakefield soon afterwards he was defeated and killed, and on Margaret's orders his severed head, crowned with a paper crown, was placed above the gates of the city of York. Wakefield also saw the elimination of other leading Yorkists especially of the older

---

[5] Among his educational foundations were the College of the Blessed Mary of Eton and King's College Cambridge.

generation so that younger men came to the fore, notably Richard's son, Edward the new Duke of York and future Edward IV, and Richard Neville Earl of Warwick, on his way to becoming 'the Kingmaker'. Only a month after Wakefield Edward at the age of nineteen led his forces to victory at the battle of Mortimers Cross. Meanwhile Margaret, who had been rallying allies in Scotland, led a mainly Scottish army in an advance southwards. This was an error as it took no account of the deep-rooted hostility between English and Scots, and many Lancastrian sympathisers became alienated. She gained a minor victory at the second battle of St Albans and was poised to move on London, but it became clear that Londoners would resist to the death being overrun by a horde of barbaric Scots, and they were forced to retreat northwards, robbing and raping as they went. They were brought to battle at Towton close to York and heavily defeated. Margaret and Henry with their young son, Prince Edward, managed to escape to Scotland, but for the Lancastrians who were captured no mercy was shown. Never has there been such a bloodbath in England – some 36,000 killed either in battle or slaughtered afterwards.

After Towton England lay at the feet of Edward Duke of York, Henry VI was deposed and on 26 June 1461 Edward was crowned king in Westminster Abbey as Edward IV. The Wars of the Roses might then have come to an end, but not as long as Margaret was alive. Her zeal and determination were undimmed. Never would she be deflected from fighting for the rights of her husband and the son she adored. Based in Scotland she stirred up all the trouble she could for the new English king, but she had to realise that, such was the strength of his position, he could only be dislodged by forces from abroad.

And so in April 1462, with her son in tow but leaving her husband behind, she left for France to see what support she could find there. But she was to be disappointed. Her father, René of Anjou, was too stretched by his own problems to give aid, and her cousin Louis XI, the new King of France, pressed on all sides by rebellious nobles, was wary of becoming involved in a war with England. However, eventually, in return for a pledge of the return of Calais as a surety, he did make her a loan, along with 2000 men-at-arms under the command of a capable and charismatic commander, Pierre de Brézé, who was to prove Margaret's most loyal, and possibly loving, adherent.

With this small force Margaret set out to invade England in October 1462; but the expedition was to be dogged by misfortune. Margaret had insisted on landing in the north of England where help from the Scots might have been forthcoming; but her little fleet was scattered in a storm and one vital ship with most of the equipment and money on board was lost as also were many of the soldiers. However, she and de Brézé managed to struggle ashore and at first had some minor successes. A few important fortresses were captured, Henry VI was brought from Harlech Castle in Wales where he had been sent for safety, and their forces were joined by a number of Lancastrian loyalists. But in 1463 Edward IV and Warwick came up from the south and inflicted a decisive defeat on them at the battle of Hexham.

It was (probably) after this battle that the most famous of legends concerning Margaret originated. The story goes that she and her son, Edward (aged ten), fled into the recesses of Hexham Forest where they became irretrievably lost and fell among thieves who stripped them of all valuables but then proceeded to quarrel among themselves about the distribution of them; and while this was going on Margaret and her son made their escape. But then as darkness closed in they became ever more hopelessly lost and were in total despair when they suddenly found themselves confronted by a gigantic man of fearsome aspect who was clearly a bandit-in-chief. But Margaret was equal to the occasion and made an impassioned plea, throwing herself and her son on his mercy and imploring him that if he had a heart which could be touched by pity and that if he had once had a mother who had stooped over his cradle he would take care of this child who was the son of the rightful king and heir to the crown of England. In saving him he would save his soul and his country. Few could resist Margaret in such a supplication. Certainly not the giant robber who took them back to his hovel home where they were cared for by his wife and were eventually reunited with a search party of de Brézé. The validity of this story may be doubted, but as Sir Winston Churchill in his famous *History of the English Peoples* used to say of similar stories: 'If it is not true it ought to be.'

Somehow after the battle of Hexham Margaret and her son and the faithful de Brézé managed to escape from England to the Continent where they landed in the domains of Charles Duke of Burgundy (now in his seventies) who received them courteously but would not be drawn into any of their political schemes. The situation in France at that time was unstable. The new French king, Louis XI, a devious and unscrupulous character, was bent on a united France under his dominion. With the English expelled from the country (except for Calais) this involved subduing the principal barons of whom the most powerful was the Duke of Burgundy who was resisting all attempts to bring him into line. In this conflict both the King and the Duke were anxious not to antagonise the King of England, and so for the time being they kept their distance from Margaret who then had to take refuge with her father René in Anjou. Here bad news soon reached her: Henry VI, left in hiding in the north of England, had been tracked down and brought to London where he had been paraded through the streets like a common criminal, pinioned to his horse and pelted with filth by the populace on his way to the Tower where he was lodged in squalid and humiliating conditions.

The outlook for a Lancaster restoration, therefore, looked bleak indeed. But Margaret still did not give up hope and, unknown to her, events in her favour were unfolding in England. Recently Edward IV had become ever more reliant on his chief supporter, the Earl of Warwick. In battle and times of crisis Edward was superb – competent, decisive and fearless; but when danger was removed he lapsed all too readily into a life of ease and self-indulgence where his pleasures took precedence over everything, and affairs of state were unloaded on to others.[6] This state of affairs well suited Warwick who took on more and more responsibilities, enriching himself lavishly in the process. For a time the partnership worked well but then it came under strain. In 1467 Edward made a secret and most imprudent marriage to Elizabeth Woodville. From then on the differences between Edward and Warwick intensified. In the conflict between the King of France and the Duke of Burgundy Warwick wanted an alliance with the former while Edward increasingly favoured the latter, and this came to a head in 1468 when Edward arranged a marriage between his sister, Elizabeth of York, and the new Duke of Burgundy, Charles the Bold. From then on a rupture between Edward and Warwick became inevitable and it was expedited

---

[6] As a foreign ambassador (Philippe de Commines) wrote at the time: 'He gave himself up wholly to pleasure and took no delight in anything but ladies, dancing, entertainment and the chase.'

by the favours being showered on Elizabeth Woodville's numerous relations. To Warwick it became clear that the Woodville family was constituting a threat to his authority which he could not tolerate. And therein lay an opportunity for Margaret.

At first Warwick bided his time, concealing his intentions, but in 1469 in spite of strong opposition from Edward he brought about a marriage between his daughter, Isabella, and Edward's younger brother, George Duke of Clarence who, he thought, might be of use when it came to a showdown. But in the event this proved a vain hope as George was found to be weak and unreliable, and held in little respect by anyone.[7] Before making a move Warwick also made sure of general support from the King of France who was becoming alarmed at Edward's developing alliance with the Duke of Burgundy.

Warwick's coup came in September 1460 when a delegation of Yorkists, headed improbably by the Archbishop of Canterbury, roused Edward from his sleep and took him into custody in one of Warwick's castles. After that for the next two years events in England were so volatile that few could comprehend them. Following the abduction of Edward the situation was unique – two kings both in prison and the fate of the country apparently in the hands of the 'Kingmaker'. What would he do? Restore Henry VI and the Lancastrians? Come to terms with Edward IV and the Yorkists? Or even put his son-in-law Clarence on the throne? The last of these options was soon ruled out owing to Clarence's obvious inadequacy, and Warwick was not yet ready to come to terms with Margaret. So it was necessary for him to release Edward and try to come to an agreement with him. But the mistrust between them had become too great, cooperation was impossible and by March 1470 Edward had gained the upper hand and Warwick had to leave the country hurriedly and seek refuge with the King of France. Louis XI received him hospitably but considered, as was his wont, how he could best serve his own purposes. Threatened by a closer alliance between Burgundy and Edward IV, it seemed to him that the latter had to be diverted by stirring up the English civil war and this, he thought, could best be achieved by an alliance between Margaret and Warwick. This might seem impossible as they had been the deadliest of enemies. To Warwick, cynical and heartless,

---

[7] 'False, fleeting, perjured Clarence' (Shakespeare, *Richard III*).

it would be no problem; he could easily feign friendship and change his allegiance. But to Margaret, passionate and sensitive, it was unthinkable. When she hated it was with a blazing intensity which could not be subdued, and there was no one she hated more than Warwick. He, more than anyone, had been the cause of her troubles. It was he who had deposed her husband and had him dragged through the streets of London to be imprisoned in the Tower. And it was he who had accused her of betraying England to France and had proclaimed her an adulteress and her beloved son a bastard. How could she possibly come to terms with such a man? But the wily King of France thought it could be managed. He saw that for the sake of her son Margaret would make any sacrifice and if she could be persuaded that it was in his interests for her to treat with Warwick she would succumb – as eventually she did. But not before at a ceremony of reconciliation she had let loose a torrent of fury and cursed Warwick as a coward and a traitor. But Warwick was thick skinned enough to stand up to this and on bended knee he begged her forgiveness which at length was forthcoming. He then took a solemn oath on a relic of the True Cross, which had somehow made its way to Angers Cathedral, that he would be a faithful subject to Henry VI, Queen Margaret and Prince Edward. And Margaret similarly promised to treat him as a faithful subject. And this was not all that was required of her: as a guarantee of their compact a marriage was proposed between Prince Edward and Warwick's daughter, Anne Neville. This was a particularly bitter pill for Margaret to swallow. A deal, perhaps temporary, with Warwick was one thing but to have him for ever as the father-in-law of her only son was another matter, and she resisted the idea fiercely, but in the end her hand was forced not least by the Prince himself who, at the age of seventeen with Plantagenet blood stirring in his veins, was greatly attracted by the young lady and was eager to marry her.

After the sealing of the pact between the arch enemies, events moved swiftly. Seven weeks later with a small fleet and men-at-arms provided by the King of France, Warwick landed in south-west England. Edward at the time was in the north and seems to have paid scant attention to this incursion, thinking it a minor matter which he could deal with at his leisure, but he was mistaken and for once was caught napping so that Warwick, gaining allies as he went, reached London three weeks later and Edward, finding himself deserted by some close supporters, was obliged to flee the country and take refuge with his brother-in-law, the Duke of Burgundy.

In London Warwick, having stabilised his position, released from the Tower, Henry VI, a pathetic bedraggled figure who had been a prisoner for the last five years and treated none too kindly; but he was washed, tidied up and adorned with a blue cloak belonging to Edward, and once again paraded through the streets of London, but this time not as an outcast, hooted and derided, but hailed delightedly as the rightful king.

To Margaret, waiting anxiously in France with her son, the news of Warwick's success and Edward's flight was a wonder. She had hopes that at long last her luck was turning and her bitter and relentless struggle was to be rewarded. But, fatally, fearful for the safety of her son, she delayed coming to England where she was urgently needed as a focal point for loyal Lancastrians. The fates never favoured her for long, and when she finally set out she was held up by contrary winds, and in the meanwhile Edward IV had made a comeback. Urged on by the Duke of Burgundy and provided by him with a small fleet and a token force, he landed in March 1471 in Ravenspur in Yorkshire. There support for him was not readily forthcoming so that he felt it necessary to announce that he came only to claim his dukedom not the throne. But then backing for him began to grow, and his brother, George Duke of Clarence, the great defector, deserted Warwick and came over to his side. Then, acting with customary speed and boldness, he outmanoeuvred Warwick and was in London a month later where he once again proclaimed himself king; and once again too the wretched Henry VI, 'a sack of wool' as a contemporary described him, was returned to his cell in the Tower. Edward then lost no time in bringing Warwick to battle, which he did at Barnet in Hertfordshire where he gained a decisive victory in which 'the Kingmaker' was killed, his body stripped naked and brought to London and put on show in St Paul's.

On the very next day Margaret landed in south-west England and was so dismayed by the news of Barnet that she had thoughts of returning at once to France; but, partly on the insistence of her son, she was persuaded to persevere and to make contact with a strong Lancastrian force in Wales under Jasper Earl of Pembroke. However, she was intercepted on her way at Tewkesbury by Edward

IV who won another overwhelming victory after which the young Prince Edward was put to death. This was a mortal blow for Margaret, one from which she never recovered. If she had been male she too would have been killed but, like all Plantagenets, Edward recoiled from killing women and he must have realised that with the death of her son she was no longer a threat; all fight had left her; her cause was dead. But to make doubly sure, he saw to it that Henry VI too was done to death – how and by whom is not known but it must surely have been with Edward's connivance. A brutal and horrible murder certainly it was but it must also have been a deliverance. No English king has had a more wretched existence. Longing to be left alone to his books and his devotions he had been hauled on and off the throne, dragged around from place to place and forced to do things he loathed. In the midst of the horrors of the civil war he alone had pleaded for peace, mercy and conciliation, but no notice was taken of him. On his death, however, there seems to have been some awareness of his saintliness and his tomb at Chertsey was visited by pilgrims in search of healing.

After the battle of Tewkesbury Margaret was treated with studied cruelty. She was brought to London and lodged in the Tower but not allowed to see her husband before he was killed. Later she was given a minimal allowance and permitted to live with one of her oldest friends, the Countess of Suffolk (widow of the man who had negotiated her marriage twenty-five years before). Here she might have been allowed to die in peace but in 1475 (when she was forty-six) Edward IV suddenly ordered her into close captivity. The reason for this is not clear but soon afterwards Edward forsook his alliance with the Duke of Burgundy and made a peace treaty with the French king, one clause of which stipulated that Louis would pay a ransom of 50,000 crowns for Margaret. It soon became clear, however, that this was not done out of altruistic feelings for his cousin; he had ulterior motives. For although Margaret had been expropriated from nearly all her rights and possession in England, in France, following the deaths of her mother, brother and nephew, she had become the legal heiress of her father, René, whose domains included Anjou, Provence, Lorraine and Bar, and on these Louis was casting a covetous eye. If he could acquire them for the price of Margaret's ransom it would be money well spent. And so in 1476 Margaret had to sign a document making over all her worldly rights and possessions to the King of France, which she did meekly and obediently. There was a time when she would have been roused to fury by such demands, but no longer. Now that she had no heir to inherit from her she had become indifferent. All she wanted was an untroubled life away from a cruel and scheming world; but even this was not easy to find. Her father, René, now seventy-five, as always in financial straits and in thrall to a second wife less than half his age, was not welcoming, but eventually a modest dwelling was found for her in Anjou where she lived humbly and penuriously until her death at the age of fifty-two in 1482.

And so it came about that the woman who had once been the most admired princess in Europe and the most powerful queen consort of England ended her days in poverty and neglect. Her place in history was assured, but not as a heroine who had fought so desperately and sacrificed so much but rather as the dominating fury of England's bloodiest civil war.

ELIZABETH WOODVILLE (c.1437–1492)

Wife of Edward IV

Elizabeth Woodville was the first English-born queen and the first commoner since the Normans, and her marriage to Edward IV was a rare case of a love match rather than one formally agreed for reasons of state. No queen at the time of the Wars of the Roses could expect an easy life, and Elizabeth had her full share of turmoil and tragedy: she saw the execution of her father, two brothers and a son by her first marriage, and then her two sons by Edward IV, known to history as the Princes in the Tower, disappeared mysteriously. Her own life saw many vicissitudes: at one time leading a quiet inconspicuous life in the country, then living in state as Queen of England, then on two occasions seeking sanctuary in Westminster Abbey and finally enclosed in a religious house in Bermondsey.

Elizabeth was the daughter of Richard Woodville, a knight of no high degree who had served as steward to Henry V's younger brother, the Duke of Bedford, when he commanded the English armies in France. There he attracted the attention of the Duchess of Bedford, a high-born lady, daughter of the Count of Luxemburg and said to be descended from Charlemagne, and at one time the second lady in England after the Queen. On the death of the Duke they married, to the dismay of her family who considered the marriage beneath her. However, it proved stable and in due course they had twelve children of whom Elizabeth was the eldest. At the age of thirteen she was married to John Grey, by whom she had two sons before he was killed fighting for the Lancastrians in the second battle of St Albans in 1461. Following the Yorkist victory at Towton in the following year and the accession to the throne of Edward IV the lands of the Greys, like those of other prominent Lancastrians, were sequestrated and at the age of twenty-five Elizabeth was left a penniless widow with two young children.

In her despair she embarked on a bold course of action: she

heard that Edward IV sometimes came hunting in the forest of Whittlebury near her home in Grafton, Northamptonshire, and she planned to waylay him and beseech him to restore the lands of the Greys for the sake of her two young sons. This ploy proved all too successful. It was to have momentous consequences. It is not too much to say that it changed the course of English history. For Edward – handsome, vital and intensely physical – was entranced by her beauty and was to give her much more than her family lands. He expected that she would join the ranks of the many women with whom he had his way. But to his amazement Elizabeth was not to be won like that; she played for higher stakes and stipulated that favours would only be granted within marriage. 'I may be unworthy to be Queen,' she said demurely, 'but I value my honour more than to be a concubine.' This was a reaction to which Edward was not accustomed and it might have caused him fury and frustration, but instead it made him all the more frantic to achieve his purpose. Such beauty combined with such virtue he found irresistible. As a contemporary chronicler put it succinctly: 'the less she gave the more she allured'. If a marriage there had to be, a marriage there would be, and one took place in darkest secrecy in a small parish church attended only by Elizabeth's mother, a lady in attendance, the priest and a boy to sing. Never had a king been married so unceremoniously.

A more unsuitable and inopportune marriage can hardly be imagined. Edward at the time was newly and insecurely enthroned and his great need was for a prestigious union with a member of a ruling dynasty which would bring him greater status and badly needed finance. Instead he married an impecunious English widow, of no high birth, from a Lancastrian family and five years older than himself. At first secrecy was maintained with Edward making surreptitious visits to his wife after dark or slipping away unobtrusively during a hunting expedition, but there came a time when the affair had to come to light, for the Earl of Warwick, who had done more than any man to make Edward king, was in the process of arranging a marriage for him with a relation of the King of France. When this was approaching consummation Edward had to admit that he was no longer free to marry. Understandably Warwick took this hard; he had been grossly deceived. It marked the end of his alliance with the Yorkists and his switch to the Lancastrians. This would almost certainly have happened in time, but it was accelerated by the bestowal of great favours on the Woodville family. Elizabeth's siblings all expected to be provided for and Edward, generous to a fault, saw to it that they were. Most of them were found marriage partners among the higher ranks of the nobility (including a bizarre match between a young man in his twenties and the wealthy dowager Duchess of Norfolk, thrice widowed and old enough to be his grandmother).[1] In addition, Elizabeth's father was appointed Constable of England with no particular qualifications for the post. All of this was bitter gall to Warwick. It was clear that his hold over the King was slipping and he was being edged out by the Woodvilles, and this he resented and was powerful enough to resist. In the next two years it was sometimes Edward and sometimes Warwick who was ruling the country. During the period of Warwick's ascendancy Elizabeth with three of her daughters found it necessary to rush into sanctuary in Westminster following the release from gaol of all prisoners who were running riot. There she was to remain for nearly a year during which time she was to give birth to the future Edward V. While there Warwick could have made life difficult for her, but he showed little inclination to do so, and Elizabeth and her family were left in discomfort but in peace.

Following his victory at Tewkesbury and the elimination of his main rivals Edward IV was able to devote himself to the life he loved best – what a contemporary described as 'pastimes, pleasures and dalliance'. Hunting was his favourite sport but there was as well a profusion of pageants, games, tournaments and banquets with as many as fifty dishes. These were to kill him by the age of forty. But he was still no weakling. For the last twelve years of his reign he was active and enlightened in the country's government: predatory barons were subdued and lawlessness suppressed. And he was always a popular figure, partly because of his charm and bravura and partly because he kept taxation low. This he was able to do because he had other sources of income: the confiscation of Lancastrian estates and the payment of ransom money brought him large sums as also did England's wool trade with Flanders which he encouraged and in which he participated profitably himself. He even made warfare pay. In 1476 he mounted a massive invasion of France for which Parliament paid, but soon after landing he proceeded to make peace with the French king on

---

[1] Nevertheless, she was to outlive him.

advantageous financial terms. A nine-year truce was also agreed as also was a bethrothal, never to be formalised, between Edward's eldest daughter Elizabeth and the Dauphin. The two kings met in bizarre circumstances. For greater security their negotiations took place on a bridge over the river Somme and each enclosed in a mesh cage. After embracing (with difficulty) they thrashed out terms for peace.

With the conclusion of this lucrative treaty came nine years of peace and prosperity, something England had not known for many years. The only event to cause a stir on the domestic front was the attainder and death of Edward's brother, George Duke of Clarence. Contumacious as ever, he finally overstepped the mark, taking powers he did not have to put people to death and then, insanely, to question the legitimacy of his two brothers, Edward IV and Richard Duke of York, leaving himself the rightful king. This was too much and he was sent to the Tower under sentence of death where he was said to have perished by drowning in a butt of Malmsey wine.

Richard, later Richard III, is one of history's enigmas. Was he the hunchbacked monster created by Sir Thomas More and Shakespeare, capable of one heinous crime after another? Or was he, as some strongly maintain, a courageous soldier and enlightened ruler who was woefully wronged and misunderstood? During the early part of his life he seemed to be the latter. He had served his elder brother faithfully and capably and was generally held in high regard and there was no mention of any physical deformity. And his private life seems to have been beyond reproach. Whatever else he was he was no voluptuary.

The people of England owed much to Edward IV for his firm and, by the standards of the time, just government. But certainly he set no high moral tone. His court was shamelessly profligate. No English king has indulged himself more lavishly, eating and drinking to excess and making no attempt to curb his inordinate sexual appetites. There was never any likelihood of his being a faithful husband and Elizabeth seems to have accepted this. During his last years he was openly in thrall to one Jane Shore, wife of a City goldsmith and to this too Elizabeth made no objection. Not that Edward's treatment of her otherwise was cruel and heartless. She continued to bear him a steady stream of children – ten in all – and she was well provided with money for her various extravagances, mainly in the field of art and literature where she showed some discernment; among those she patronised was William Caxton who set up the first printing press in England at that time. But although her influence was in some ways beneficial Elizabeth was never well liked. It was not forgotten that on her father's side she was low born and there were those who always regarded her as an upstart. And, as is often the case with those suddenly raised to a much higher station in life, she tended to be haughty, standing on her dignity and keeping even the elderly and exalted on their knees in her presence. And she was always demanding and out for what she could get for herself and her family. The fears some people had of an ever-growing Woodville faction were not without foundation. In the end they were to be her undoing.

The period of peace Edward brought to the country came to an abrupt end when he died unexpectedly in 1483. This left a power vacuum as his heir was a boy of twelve and there was strong contention among various factions to gain control of him. At first advantage lay with the Woodville family, headed by Queen Elizabeth, who was in London where a son by her first marriage, the Marquis of Dorset, had taken control of the Tower of London with the royal treasury while one of her brothers was in command of a powerful fleet in the Channel. At the time of his father's death the new King, Edward V, was in Ludlow on the Welsh border under the tutelage of his uncle, Lord Rivers. Word was sent to him there that he should repair to London as soon as possible for an early coronation in order to forestall any other contenders to the throne. Chief among these was his uncle, Richard, Duke of Gloucester, who was then in the north of England where he had been fighting against the Scots. He was the one Elizabeth feared most – with good reason as it proved – but at first he behaved with great rectitude, acknowledging Edward V as the lawful king and taking an oath of fealty to him. But he lost little time in coming south to London and, whether by accident or by design, his route coincided with that of his nephew. The two parties met at Stony Stratford in Buckinghamshire and at first all was geniality and loyalty, but then Richard changed his tune and brought about the arrest of Lord Rivers and other attendants on trumped up charges and took his young nephew into care under the pretext that he was in danger from evil and ambitious people. They then proceeded to London where he did not arrive until after the day (4 May) appointed for Edward's coronation.

On arrival in London Richard continued for a time to proclaim his loyalty to his nephew and that he was doing no more than protecting him; but he was feeling his way, seeing how far he could go. His next objective was to gain possession of Edward's younger brother, Richard Duke of York,[2] who was with his mother in sanctuary. Great pressure was brought to bear on her to let him go and at length, much against her will, she yielded, fearing perhaps that eventually he might be abducted. And so he joined his brother in the Tower, never to be heard of again.

Soon afterwards a large army loyal to Richard arrived in London from the north and with this behind him and promises of support from some noblemen he was ready to take the final step – of deposing his nephew and declaring himself king. On 22 June Doctor Shaw, a Cambridge divine and brother of the Lord Mayor of London, was put up to giving an inflammatory sermon at Temple Bar in which he made wild accusations about Edward IV, saying that he was not the legitimate son of his father, Richard Duke of York, but of some foreign archer. This was not the first time this had been alleged as Edward was very different in build and appearance from his father and two brothers, but few had taken it seriously and it caused great shock and resentment particularly to Richard's mother, the Dowager Duchess of York who was naturally outraged at being branded an adulteress. Richard was quick to see that this fabrication was backfiring and something more was needed. And so a few days later his principal supporter, the Duke of Buckingham, was induced to make a speech to Parliament averring that Edward's marriage to Elizabeth had been brought about by the witchcraft of her mother and that it was null and void because Edward had previously been betrothed to another. This made him a bigamist and therefore all Elizabeth's ten children were illegitimate and so barred from the throne which left Richard the rightful monarch. Buckingham must have spoken with great eloquence because the reaction of Parliament to this balderdash was at first muted, but on the following day it voted that Edward V be deposed and Richard be petitioned to take the throne, which with a suitable show of reluctance he agreed to do. Extraordinarily all this seems to have met with general acclaim and twelve days later Richard

---

[2] Then aged nine but already a widower, having been married at the age of six to the daughter of the Duke of Norfolk who died soon afterwards.

was crowned king, and at his coronation were most of the greatest in the land.

Soon afterwards, however, an increasing number of people had serious doubts about Richard III as he had now become. As well as the ruthless way he had made himself king there were other high-handed and illegal actions which had caused anger. Rumours were beginning to circulate about the two young princes. Nothing had been heard of them for some time and people were wondering what had become of them. It would have been easy for Richard to scotch those whisperings by displaying them in public, but this he did not do. The fate of the Princes remains a mystery. That they disappeared is certain but how, when and where they died cannot be known. The account given by Sir Thomas More thirty years later based on the confessions under torture of Sir James Tyrrel does not hold water, and the bones of two children discovered under a staircase in the Tower in the reign of Charles II proves nothing conclusively nor did the examination of these bones by experts in 1933. In 1483 many believed that they had been done to death on the orders of Richard III, and this was one of the reasons why so many turned against him. In that age people were not squeamish, but the killing of children could not be condoned.

When Elizabeth Woodville heard of the deaths of her sons she was still in sanctuary and according to a contemporary chronicler 'she fell into a swoon and lay lifeless a good while; after coming to herself she weepeth, she cried out aloud and with lamentable shrieks made all the house ring, she struck her breast, tore and cut her hair, and overcome in fine with dolour, prayeth also her own death, calling by name now and then among her most dear children, and condemning herself for a mad woman for that, being deceived by false promises, she had delivered her younger son out of Sanctuary, to be murdered of his enemy.'

To the great inconvenience of the monks of Westminster Elizabeth and her three daughters remained in sanctuary for nearly a year, but this could not continue indefinitely. In March 1484 Richard solemnly affirmed to Parliament that if they came out they would be treated kindly and protected from harm and suitable husbands would be found for the daughters. Trusting in these promises Elizabeth emerged soon afterwards. Perhaps she felt she had no alternative. It seemed that Richard was firmly enthroned and for the sake of her daughters she had to come to terms with him. Still her subsequent friendly relations with him are hard to explain. He had almost certainly been responsible for the killing of her two sons and was certainly responsible for the judicial murder of her brother, Lord Rivers; besides he had bastardised her husband and declared her marriage to him invalid. And yet she was to be found adhering to him rather than to his rival, Henry Tudor (later Henry VII) and writing to her son by her first marriage, the Marquis of Dorset in France, that he should abandon him and return to England. She even appears to have countenanced a possible marriage between her daughter, Elizabeth of York, and Richard on the death of his wife, Anne Neville in March 1485.

She did, however, give some support to the first uprising against Richard in October 1483. This was led by the Duke of Buckingham, once Richard's closest ally; but it came to nothing. Buckingham's forces were held up by floods on the river Severn and were then easily dispersed and he himself captured and put to death, while the fleet of Henry Tudor, coming from France, was scattered in a storm. Elizabeth was still in sanctuary at the time, but she let it be known that if the rebellion were to be successful she would give her blessing to a marriage between her daughter, Elizabeth and Henry Tudor.

Nearly two years later in August 1485 Henry attempted another invasion. This time he landed successfully at Milford Haven in his native Wales. It seemed a desperate venture. He had with him only a small force, mostly of mercenaries who could not be relied on, while Richard was ready for him with an army twice as large. The battle of Bosworth should have been an overwhelming victory for him, but the defection of Lords Stanley and Northumberland turned the tables so that it was Henry who triumphed and Richard who was killed.

One of the first actions of Henry VII, as Henry Tudor now became, was to keep his promise to marry Elizabeth of York, eldest daughter of Edward IV, thus uniting the two houses of York and Lancaster. It might have been expected that relations between Henry and his mother-in-law would have been reasonably harmonious, and at first they were. The title of Queen Dowager was restored to her, the Act of Parliament invalidating her marriage to Edward IV was repealed, and she was invested with extensive lands. But for some reason she was not content and seems to have been implicated in the rebellion of 1487 centred round Lambert Simnel, who claimed to be the Earl of Warwick, son of the ill-fated George Duke of Clarence. For her part in the rebellion (not, it would seem, a very active one) Elizabeth was stripped of all her lands and sent to live in a religious house in Bermondsey. Why she should have sought to undermine the position of her daughter's husband is hard to understand. It may be that she thought that Warwick, a weak and ineffective character believed to be mentally retarded, would be a more pliant king than Henry.

Elizabeth was to live for five more years. Relations with her son-in-law were clearly strained but she was not publicly disgraced, and she might have embarked on a new life if an extraordinary idea of Henry VII had come to fruition – that at the age of fifty-eight she should be wedded to James III of Scotland, some twenty years younger; but from this she was saved by James's sudden death. When she died in 1492 she might, as mother of the Queen, have been accorded a state funeral, but this was denied her and she was buried with the minimum of ceremony, unattended by the King and Queen, in St George's, Windsor beside Edward IV.

By then she had seen the deaths of nearly all her large family – five brothers, six sisters, four out of five sons (by two marriages) and two out of seven daughters. Her life had been tragic and tumultuous, but her place in English history must be assured as the grandmother of Henry VIII and great-grandmother of Mary Tudor, Elizabeth I, Edward VI, Mary Queen of Scots, and the progenitor of all succeeding monarchs.

ANNE NEVILLE (1456–1485)

Wife of Richard III

Anne Neville was the daughter of the legendary 'Warwick the Kingmaker' and wife of Richard III, England's most reviled king. Not surprisingly she had a sadly troubled life. At the time of her father's ascendancy she lived in splendour in one of his castles attended by numerous servants and surrounded by his private army bearing the distinctive badge of a bear and ragged staff. But this changed abruptly when Warwick quarrelled with Edward IV and had to take refuge in France. While there he made an alliance with Margaret of Anjou which was sealed by the marriage of her son, Edward, to Anne. It seems that, unlike most arranged marriages, this was a love affair, each devoted to the other; but it lasted a pitifully short time, Edward being killed a few weeks later on the field of Tewkesbury. Anne was with her mother-in-law at the scene of the battle, and after the defeat of their forces both had a struggle for survival.

Anne was first taken into the household of her elder sister, Isabella, who was married to the reckless George Duke of Clarence. They were Warwick's only offspring and following his death the previous year at the battle of Barnet they were in line for an enormous inheritance which should have been shared between them, but Clarence coveted the whole of it for his wife. So he contrived that Anne should be hidden away out of sight disguised as a domestic servant. He hoped that thus she would be safe from all suitors. But she had attracted the attention of Clarence's brother, Richard Duke of Gloucester, who was wanting to make her his wife (along with her rich inheritance), and eventually after two years he managed to find her, put her into sanctuary and then marry her (1473). There then followed a bitter and sordid dispute between the two brothers about the distribution of the Warwick estate, eventually settled by Edward IV.

Soon afterwards both Isabella and Clarence died, and Anne was left with great estates but by then in the throes of an unhappy marriage and in rapidly deteriorating health. Her years of privation had weakened her and she was suffering from consumption. During the twelve years of her marriage she had had a number of pregnancies all of which had miscarried except one, a son, Edward, whom she loved dearly. Although never in love with the cold and impassive Richard she was a dutiful wife, accompanied him on his campaigns and presided over his hospitality. What she thought of the events of 1483 when he made himself king and of the disappearance of the Princes in the Tower is not recorded; but she was at his side during his splendid and long drawn out coronation and later when he made a royal progress through the Midlands and the North. But by then her health had broken down and in March 1484 she was devastated by the death of her son. Afterwards she had nothing to live for and a year later at the age of twenty-nine she died.

Such then was the brief unhappy life of Anne Neville – almost unrelieved tragedy. On the day of her death there was a total eclipse of the sun, thought by some to be not without significance. After her death rumours were abroad that she had been poisoned – that Richard, desperate for an heir, wanted her out of the way so that he could marry someone able to bear children. Many believed that he had contrived the death of his nephews and was capable of any crime. Richard was aware of this mounting hostility and tried to curry favour with acts of clemency and popular appeal, but these had little effect. He lacked his elder brother's compulsive charm and always there was suspicion. It was believed that he was wanting to marry his niece, Elizabeth of York, but finding this impossible, he made a statement to Parliament denying any such intention and at the same time angrily rebutting rumours about the poisoning of Anne. That he should have felt this necessary was thought by some to reflect an uneasy conscience.

ELIZABETH OF YORK (1466–1503)

Wife of Henry VII

Elizabeth of York was to have a crucial role in English history. As the oldest daughter of Edward IV and the wife of Henry VII she was to unite the houses of York and Lancaster, so bringing an end to the Wars of the Roses and the founding of the Tudor dynasty. She was also the mother of Henry VIII and the grandmother of Elizabeth I and Mary Queen of Scots.

Elizabeth was born in 1466 and was considered by some to be heir-presumptive to the throne until the birth of her brother (future Edward V) five years later. Like nearly all princesses at that time her life was soon bedevilled by confusion and danger. When she was four years old her father was forced into temporary exile by 'Warwick the Kingmaker', and her mother, Elizabeth Woodville with her four daughters, had to take sanctuary in Westminster – not the last time that this happened. With the return of Edward IV six months later the family was released, and following his victories at Barnet and Tewkesbury, they were to lead relatively stable and affluent lives for the next twelve years.

This period of peace came to an end in 1483 with the death of Edward IV and the seizure of the throne by Richard III. At the first sign of this happening Elizabeth Woodville with her daughters and youngest son, Richard Duke of York, lost no time in hurrying into sanctuary again where they were to remain for the next ten months. For Elizabeth of York, then seventeen, this was to be the bleakest and most harrowing time of her life. Enclosed in claustrophobic quarters and surrounded by troops posted by Richard to prevent escape or unauthorised communication with the outside world, the family had to endure not only privations but a series of terrible events. Against her better judgement the Queen was persuaded to release her younger son to join his elder brother in the Tower. Then came the appalling news that the Queen's brother, Lord Rivers and her son by her first marriage, Richard Grey, had

117

been summarily put to death without trial. And then came the dreadful act of Parliament invalidating Elizabeth Woodville's marriage to Edward IV and bastardising all of their children, followed by the proclamation of Richard as king. Out of the narrow windows of the monastery cells Elizabeth and her sisters were probably able to glimpse Richard's magnificent coronation procession. The situation seemed as gloomy as possible, but when affairs were at their worst hopeful news percolated through: Henry Tudor Earl of Richmond, one of the last Lancastrians to have a claim to the throne, had escaped to Brittany where he was gathering support and had undertaken, if he became king, to marry Elizabeth of York.

Henry's claim to the throne was a weak one. It came through his mother, Margaret Beaufort, a great-granddaughter of John of Gaunt Duke of Lancaster (fourth son of Edward III), but even this was not clear-cut as her grandfather, John Beaufort, had been born out of wedlock when his mother, Catherine Swynford, had been John of Gaunt's mistress, and although he subsequently married her and her children were legitimatised by Act of Parliament, there were those who still regarded them as of bastard strain.

Henry Tudor was born in 1456 when his mother was no more than thirteen but already a widow as her husband, Edmund Tudor, had been killed in the Wars of the Roses six months before. Soon afterwards she married Sir John Stafford and became separated from her young son who was brought up mainly by his uncle, Jasper Earl of Pembroke. After the battle of Tewkesbury they both escaped to Brittany where Henry was to remain for the next fourteen years. He was later to say that during this time he was either a fugitive or a captive; both his movements and his finances were under the control of the Duke of Brittany who was basically supportive of his designs on the English throne but who was under constant pressure from Edward IV to extradite him to England. Although often in danger Henry was able to stay put in Brittany and became the leading Lancastrian claimant, despite there being others who had superior rights by birth. His standing was due mainly to his mother, a lady of wide renown and influence who strongly promoted his cause.

Although they had been leading Yorkists, Elizabeth Woodville and her family, while they were in sanctuary, had been sustained by thoughts of this Lancastrian in exile, but at the beginning of 1484 the position of Richard III still seemed secure and in March of that year the ex-Queen at last yielded to his exhortations to come out of sanctuary.

In a public statement he had promised that if she did, no action would be taken against her and she and her daughters would be well provided for. She did not trust him, but was finding life in sanctuary intolerable and so, in spite of the killing of Rivers and Grey and the disappearance of the two young princes, assumed to have been murdered, she came to terms with him, and for the time being renounced her support of Henry Tudor.

Two months afterwards Richard's only son died as also a year later did his wife, Anne Neville. He then became intent on marrying again in order to have an heir, and it seemed that he entertained the idea of wedding his niece, Elizabeth of York, but this caused outrage and had to be abandoned. In any case such a marriage could hardly be advantageous to him as Elizabeth was still officially illegitimate. But he was concerned that she might escape to Brittany and marry Henry Tudor, so she was banished to a remote castle in Yorkshire.

During his two years as king Richard tried hard to endear himself to his people. He made gracious royal progresses through the country and tried to project the image of a wise and just ruler, but he still inspired mistrust, especially regarding the fate of the two young princes. Even in that brutal age the murder of children was considered unforgivable. And so support for Henry Tudor continued to grow so that in the summer of 1485 he was able to mount an invasion and defeated Richard at the battle of Bosworth, and immediately afterwards he confirmed his betrothal to Elizabeth of York. But he did not marry her at once, waiting until after he had been crowned king. The reason for this was almost certainly that Elizabeth, once the Act of Parliament bastardising her had been repealed, had as the daughter of Edward IV a superior claim to the throne to his own, and he did not want it to appear that he was king by reason of his marriage to her. Similarly he did not want to seem to owe his crown to Parliament and so he did not call one until after his coronation.

Henry was twenty-eight when he became king. Until then nearly all his life had been spent either in Brittany or in Wales; he had not spent more than a few months in England. Partly because of this and partly because of the fragility of his right to the throne rebellions against him were soon to break out. He was beset by enemies. Such leading Yorkists as were still alive and some disaffected Lancastrians were ready to join forces against him. And abroad Margaret Dowager Duchess of Burgundy, sister of Richard III, was always stirring up trouble, and the kings of France and Scotland were ready to join in. It was Henry's great achievement that he overcame all opposition and sustained the Tudor dynasty in power.

The rebellion centred round Lambert Simnel broke out within a year of Henry's coronation. It is incredible how many people were conned into believing that this son of an Oxford tradesman was the Earl of Warwick, despite the real earl being taken out of the Tower and paraded in public. But support for him, particularly in Ireland, grew apace, and when he landed in northern England it was with a larger force than Henry had had at Milford Haven two years before; and the danger from him was intensified when he was joined by a leading Lancastrian, John de la Pole Earl of Lincoln. But his army was defeated by Henry at the battle of Stoke and his leading supporters put to death. For Simnel himself there was a different fate: he was treated as a bad joke and sent to work as a scullion in the king's kitchens.

A more serious rebellion was to break out five years later, and once again a pretender was at the centre of it. Perkin Warbeck, a good looking youth from Flanders, was being employed as a model to show off the fine apparel of his master, and he so impressed some Yorkists in Ireland that they thought he must be of royal descent, and if he was not he could be made out to be. To find a royal prince whom he could impersonate was not easy, but he was finally presented as Richard Duke of York, the younger of the two Princes in the Tower who was said to have escaped from the clutches of his uncle and been brought up in secrecy abroad. There were many people who believed his story or said they did, and the revolt soon assumed serious proportions. Perkin was crowned Richard IV in Dublin Cathedral, and the King of France gave him support, as did the King of Scotland, who also gave him an unfortunate royal relation in marriage. Perkin must have acted the part with great skill as some of Henry's most trusted advisers, including the Lord Chamberlain, joined forces with him. It was five years before the revolt was finally suppressed and Warbeck captured and made to confess. His fate was harder than that of Lambert Simnel: he was imprisoned in the Tower

Isabella of France, wife of Edward II.
© National Portrait Gallery, London.

Philippa of Hainault, wife of Edward III.
After Edward Blore (1787-1879).
© National Portrait Gallery, London.

Anne of Bohemia, wife of Richard II.
Godfrey Prest.
© National Portrait Gallery, London.

Margaret of Anjou, wife of Henry VI.
Benjamin West.
Fulham Palace Collection.
© Courtauld Institute of Art.

Elizabeth Woodville, wife of
Edward IV, in sanctuary with
son, Richard Duke of York.
Richard Westall (1765-1836).
© National Portrait Gallery, London.

Elizabeth of York, wife of Henry VII.
British School.
Formerly Stanford Hall Collection.
© Courtauld Institute of Art.

Catherine of Aragon, first wife of
Henry VIII.
© National Portrait Gallery, London.

Anne Boleyn, second wife of
Henry VIII.
Edward Scriven, after William
Hilton (1786-1839).
© National Portrait Gallery, London.

Jane Seymour, third wife of Henry VIII.
Hans Holbein the Younger (1497-1543).
© National Portrait Gallery, London.

Anne of Cleves, fourth wife
of Henry VIII.
Hans Holbein the Younger
(1497-1543).
© National Portrait Gallery, London.

Catherine Parr, sixth wife of
Henry VIII.
William Henry Mote; John William
Wright.
© National Portrait Gallery, London.

Anne of Denmark, wife of
James I.
Attributed to Marcus
Gheeraerts the Younger.
© National Portrait Gallery, London.

Henrietta Maria, wife of Charles I.
After Sir Anthony Van Dyck.

The five eldest children of Charles I, 1637. Sir Anthony Van Dyck (1599-1641).

Anne Duchess of York, first
wife of James II.
Sir Peter Lely.
© Scottish National Portrait Gallery.

Mary Beatrice of Modena,
second wife of James II.
Kneller.
Weston Park Collection.
© Courtauld Institute of Art.

and later put to death after an alleged escape attempt (along with the unfortunate Earl of Warwick).

It was not until after the suppression of the Simnel revolt that Henry allowed the coronation of his wife, Elizabeth, to go forward. By then he felt he had established himself sufficiently as king not to need any back-up from his wife. The coronation was a splendid one, attended by the greatest in the land in full regalia, for although Henry was by nature parsimonious, he was aware of the importance to a king's prestige of a fine display.

At the time of her marriage Elizabeth was only nineteen, but her passage to the altar had been long and eventful. At the age of four she had been betrothed to a nephew of Warwick the Kingmaker, but on his downfall it had been cancelled. Her father, Edward IV had then had thoughts of marrying her to Edward Plantagenet, son of Henry VI and Margaret of Anjou, but this too came to nothing. More important was her betrothal in 1476 (at the age of ten) to the Dauphin as part of her father's peace treaty with Louis XII of France. This was treated seriously and for a time she was known in England as the Dauphine and prepared for life in the French court; but then, abruptly, to the fury of Edward IV, the French king reneged on his agreement, and Elizabeth was left to look elsewhere. For a time various plans were aired but these had to be put aside when in the reign of Richard III she was declared illegitimate. Her only prospect then was for a private marriage. But this changed with the triumph of Henry VII, and Elizabeth soon settled into the role of not only a dutiful wife but also a fruitful one: a son, Prince Arthur being born eight months after marriage and seven more children in due course.

The name of Arthur had been specially chosen by Henry. In Wales and Brittany he had been imbued with the history and legends of the Celts, and had convinced himself that through his grandfather, Owen Tudor, he was descended from the great Welsh chieftain and mystic, Cadwallader, who had fought against the Anglo-Saxon invaders in the seventh century. Cadwallader had prophesied that one day the ancient line of British kings would be restored through a Welsh king, and Henry harboured ideas that this could be himself, hence the name of Arthur for his eldest son and the insistence that he be born in Winchester, the capital of King Arthur. Of Elizabeth's eight children three were to die in infancy and Arthur at the age of sixteen. Until her death her family was always her main concern.

121

She was not politically minded and had never aspired to be queen regnant which by birth she had a right to be. She and Henry were devoted to each other and she had a beneficent influence on him, softening the edges of a character apt to be hard and avaricious.

One of the crosses Elizabeth had to bear was her mother-in-law. Margaret Beaufort was one of the great ladies of the age. Of learning and piety she had the qualities of a saint but was not easy to live with; she tended to take all management on herself so that Elizabeth could not feel that she was mistress in her own household. She had been married three times and Henry was her only child. Like nearly everyone both Henry and Elizabeth treated her with awe. It must be doubtful if Henry would have become king without her. She was to outlive Elizabeth by six years.

Elizabeth died in 1503 at the age of thirty-seven, soon after giving birth to her eighth child who died a few days later. She lived long enough to see her son Arthur married to Catherine of Aragon but she died four months later. Henry was desolated by his wife's death. He loved her dearly and had become increasingly dependent on her for domestic happiness. He was to outlive her by six years and during that time the tone of his court deteriorated markedly: music and poetry were replaced by gambling games and low forms of entertainment such as freak shows; and Henry himself became gloomy and introverted and his least attractive traits – coldness and avidity – became more pronounced. At times his behaviour verged on derangement as when in looking for a second wife he considered marrying his widowed daughter-in-law Catherine of Aragon and then her half-mad sister Joanna. In his last years the cares of kingship weighed on him ever more heavily, and he died an unhappy and embittered man, regretted by few.

Elizabeth's place in English history, though vital, was inconspicuous. She was destined always to be in supporting roles, but these she fulfilled with courage and selflessness. It should perhaps be remembered of her that she was the only English queen to be the daughter of a king (Edward IV), the sister of a king (Edward V), the wife of a king (Henry VII), the mother of a king (Henry VIII) and the grandmother of a king (Edward VI).

CATHERINE OF ARAGON (1485–1536)

First Wife of Henry VIII

No queen has had a more profound effect on English history than Catherine of Aragon. Although it was the last thing she herself would have wished, the Reformation, when it came, was to a large extent due to her. By her intractable refusal to agree to the annulment of her marriage to Henry VIII she drove him to extreme measures which set the country on a different course.

Catherine was the daughter of Isabella Queen of Castile and Ferdinand King of Aragon whose marriage had brought about the unification of Spain, later completed by the expulsion of the Moors from Granada. Isabella was one of the great women of her age, learned and a patron of the arts as well as being a formidable force on the battlefield. Of her ten children, Catherine was the fifth, born when the war with the Moors was at its height.[1] Later she was brought up in the Moorish palace of Alhambra where Isabella saw to it that she had a serious classical education. She was to be profoundly influenced by her mother from whom she inherited a deep piety and rigidly orthodox beliefs, fiercely intolerant of any signs of heresy. Isabella may have driven the Moors out of Spain but she also introduced the Inquisition.

The idea of a marriage between Catherine and Henry VII's son Arthur first arose when Catherine was two years old and Arthur one. Their parents were drawn together by a common hostility towards France, although the Spaniards could not but be apprehensive about a marriage to a future king of England in view of the treatment meted out recently to English kings – three deposed and put to death in fifteen years – and Henry's position as King of England was far from secure. In 1497, however, when both Catherine and Arthur were twelve, they were formally betrothed and in 1500 a marriage treaty was agreed whereby

---

[1] Isabella was back with her army one day after Catherine's birth.

Catherine would come to England in the following year for the wedding.

After first being driven back by a violent storm in the Bay of Biscay (which some regarded as a portent) Catherine finally reached England in October 1501 where she was given a rapturous welcome. The people of England took her to their hearts at once, admiring her simple piety and unpretentious dignity, and appreciative too that she had within her a strain of Plantagenet blood, her mother (like many others) being a great-granddaughter of John of Gaunt. She was not perhaps a great beauty, being short of stature and inclined to plumpness, but she had a fresh complexion with an English rather than a Spanish demeanour.

The wedding ceremony took place amid great splendour on 14 November in St Paul's Cathedral in which, ironically, Catherine was given away by Arthur's younger brother, Henry, then aged ten and later to become her second husband. In celebration the City of London put on a magnificent display of pageantry, and even Henry VII was prevailed on to dig deep in his pockets to mark the occasion. Amid such tumultuous rejoicing Catherine could not but be gratified but she must too have had some concerns. There was a problem of communication: although she had been designated as a future queen of England for fifteen years she had been taught no English and few at court spoke Spanish so it was necessary to resort to basic Latin which was restrictive. And Catherine must have had anxiety about her husband; for Arthur, unlike his sturdy younger brother, was a delicate youth; pallid and undersized (even shorter than Catherine), he seemed younger than his fifteen years and hardly ready for marriage. At the wedding festivities he did not even dance with his wife, she performing a stately Spanish measure with her attendant ladies, while he danced in English fashion with an English lady of the court.

It cannot be known how their marriage would have developed as it lasted only five months. After the wedding it was necessary for Arthur to return to the Welsh Marches where as Prince of Wales he presided over the administration. There he was later joined by Catherine in the middle of a particularly rigorous winter which was too much for Arthur's frail health so that he sickened and died.

On the death of Arthur both Henry VII and King Ferdinand sought ways of turning the new situation to their advantage. At heart they wanted the same – that Catherine should marry Arthur's younger brother Prince Henry, but terms for this were not easily agreed, and it was not until after the death of Henry VII seven years later that the marriage took place. It was not then considered a disadvantage that Catherine was five years older than Henry, although in time it was to become so. It was also thought not to be a major impediment that Henry would be marrying his deceased brother's widow which was contrary to canon law, it being confidently expected that the Pope would grant a dispensation allowing it. The main stumbling block which caused the matter to drag on for so long came from the payment of Catherine's dowry over which both her father and father-in-law were determined to do the other down. Among the questions to be settled were what should happen to the part of the dowry already paid by Ferdinand in consideration of Catherine's marriage to Arthur, also whether the remainder should take the form of cash or plate and jewellery. Henry VII, because of his inordinate love of it, wanted the former, while Ferdinand, forever short of ready money, wanted the latter. In the squalid and drawn-out wrangle between the two kings the person to suffer acutely was the unfortunate Catherine, as each king regarded it as the responsibility of the other to provide for her immediate needs with the result that neither paid her anything and she was often in dire straits, having to sell her jewellery to pay for food and clothing.

The plight of Catherine between the death of Arthur and that of Henry VII was woeful. Her father seemed indifferent to her suffering and treated her as little more than a bargaining counter while Henry VII behaved towards her with customary meanness. In 1504 Pope Julius II, after some hesitation, granted a dispensation allowing Henry and Catherine's marriage, but by then Henry VII was holding back as in that year Catherine's mother, Isabella, died with the result that Castile and Aragon became for the time being separate states again with Ferdinand king only of Aragon. This meant that he was a less powerful ally than he had been and consequently his daughter of less value in the marriage market. Henry VII of course realised this and wanted to delay his son's marriage to her in case something more profitable became available. And so he insisted that Henry and Catherine be kept apart, and just before his son reached the age of consent (fourteen) he was compelled to make a formal renunciation of his betrothal to Catherine so as to make public that he was open to other offers.

125

Following the death of her prospective mother-in-law, Elizabeth of York, in 1503 Catherine had other crosses to bear. The behaviour of Henry VII became ever more abnormal. He even entertained ideas of marrying Catherine himself, but this was firmly vetoed by her parents who said it was 'a thing not to be endured'. His idea of marrying Catherine's half insane sister, Joanna, also came to nothing after her father, Ferdinand, hard and unscrupulous as ever, had her put away in an asylum so that he could assume power in what was by rights her kingdom of Castile.

Elizabeth of York's death also resulted in life at the English court becoming drab and disreputable. Henry had little interest in music or the arts and his taste for entertainment was crude. And so Catherine had few opportunities for enjoyment or self-fulfilment. In her loneliness she sought consolation in austere religious practices – fasts, vigils, pilgrimages – in which she came under the domination of her father confessor, an unscrupulous and oppressive Franciscan friar, Fra Diego, who aimed to take over her life completely. By 1509 Catherine came close to breaking point and decided that she would return to Spain and devote herself to a religious life, but from this she was saved by the death of Henry VII and the accession of Henry VIII who straight away made her his wife so that at last she became Queen of England.

Quite suddenly then Catherine's life was transformed from one of penury and neglect dominated by a cold hearted father-in-law to one of excitement and activity led by a loving and exuberant husband. The latter was indeed a marvel among monarchs. Of great physical strength and boundless energy he excelled in all manly sports – wrestling, riding, jousting, tennis among others. On the hunting field he would wear out eight horses in one day and in the tiltyard few could stand up to him. And at the end of the day he would go dancing through the night, 'leaping', as a contemporary wrote, 'like a stag'. Nor were his attainments only physical. He was a scholar, well versed in the classics and scriptures, and a musician, able to compose, read at sight and play many instruments. And in addition he was blessed with good looks and possessed of the vast fortune hoarded by his father.

Marriage to the young Henry must have been exhilarating if sometimes exhausting. Each day was overflowing with activity – balls, banquets, hunts, pageants, tournaments – and the court was constantly on the move from one royal palace to another as food

126

and drink in one ran out and piles of debris and stinking ordure mounted up. Catherine would grace all these functions with her presence but usually as a spectator rather than a participator. She was held back partly because of her numerous pregnancies but especially because her main interests were elsewhere. Religious devotions and works of charity were always her prime concern; for these she was held in high esteem. She also had a reputation for scholarship: she read widely and liked to gather round her learned men of the time. The Dutch scholar, Erasmus, has recorded that in religious discussion with her husband she was shown to advantage.

Compared to the life she had lived before and what was to come later her first seven years as queen were to be for Catherine a period of peace and well being. Henry loved her dearly and treated her kindly and generously: she was allowed plenty of money and had a staff of some hundred and sixty in attendance on her. For her part she assumed gracefully and capably the role of queen consort. That her husband had complete trust in her was shown in 1513 when he left the country to lead an invasion of France and nominated her as regent with full powers which she exercised to great effect; for when a Scottish army, thinking to take advantage of the King's absence, invaded England, Catherine showed some of the martial talents of her mother, Isabella, and rallied forces which at the battle of Flodden inflicted one of the heaviest defeats ever on a Scottish army.

These honeymoon years, however, were not without storm clouds. Henry may have been a loving husband but not altogether a faithful one. It might have been expected that with his vibrant vitality and masculine charms he would have taken after his grandfather, Edward IV, of whom it was written that 'no woman was there anywhere but he would importunely pursue his appetite and have her'. But Henry was not so licentious. Sidelines he did have but not indiscriminately. It has been said of him that he was the only English king to have had more wives than mistresses. At first he tried, although not successfully, to conceal them from Catherine who could not but regret them but decided that she had to turn a blind eye. Her own behaviour was always above reproach and she never failed to abide by her motto of *Humble and Loyal*. In almost every way she was a perfect queen consort, but in one crucial matter she was unsuccessful: she had not been able to bear a surviving male heir to the throne. It had not been for want of trying: she was believed to have given birth to four sons in six years, but they had all been either stillborn or had died in infancy. The only child to survive was a daughter, Mary, born in 1516 when Catherine was thirty-one. It was becoming apparent that she was unable to have more children and this weighed on Henry heavily. He was convinced that if he died leaving only a daughter, her succession would be disputed and there would be civil war as there had been four hundred years ago when Henry I had tried to impose his daughter, Matilda, as queen, and Henry dreaded that this should happen again.

The decline in Henry's love for Catherine and the fading of her influence on him began in 1514 when she was twenty-nine (considered then to be middle aged). In that year Henry joined with the King of France in an alliance against Ferdinand, King of Spain so that Catherine was in the invidious position of her father and husband being at war. The same year saw the rise of Thomas Wolsey, son of an Ipswich butcher, to the post of Lord Chancellor and for the next fourteen years to be Henry's chief minister. From the first Catherine disliked and mistrusted him, as the King came to rely more on him for advice and less on her. In 1518 she had her eighth and last pregnancy, resulting in yet another stillborn baby and by then Henry had become convinced that she would never bear him a son. By then too Catherine had lost her looks. Continual pregnancies had taken their toll. When she was thirty a foreign diplomat had written that she was 'rather ugly than otherwise', and a few years later the King of France was to describe her brutally as 'a deformed old woman'.

In 1524, when Catherine was forty, relations with Henry had been severed. They lived apart for much of the time and did not sleep together. But at first Henry did not think of a divorce. He had other ideas. One was to promote as his successor an illegitimate son known as Henry Fitzroy, borne to him by a woman about the court, one Bessie Blount. At the age of eight, honours and appointments were heaped on this child, including the dukedoms of Richmond and Somerset, the earldom of Nottingham and the office of Lord High Admiral. But if it was Henry's intention that he should succeed him as king, it was not acceptable. Catherine was outraged that her daughter, Princess Mary, should be superseded by a bastard and for once expressed herself forcibly. Another idea was that Princess Mary should marry Catherine's nephew, Charles V, the Hapsburg Emperor of Austria and King of Spain; and their son should succeed to the throne of England. A betrothal between them was agreed but then suddenly the Emperor reneged on it and married a princess of Portugal instead. Other similar marriages might have been arranged, but the situation changed completely when, perhaps for the first time in his life, Henry fell desperately in love.

Catherine had been tolerant of Henry's digressions, and he had treated her with tact and respect and they had kept up appearances. As late as 1520 the Dutch scholar Erasmus could write of them: 'What family of citizens offer so clear an example of chaste and concordant wedlock.' But the wedlock was soon to be under severe strain when about 1526 Anne Boleyn arrived on the scene. She was one of Catherine's maids of honour, and Henry became totally infatuated by her, and when she refused to grant favours unless she was his wife, Henry's thoughts turned in the direction of having his marriage to Catherine annulled.

Henry had always been an orthodox Roman Catholic and when in 1517 Martin Luther had launched his historic attack on the Church over the sale of Indulgences, Henry had entered into vehement and at times abusive controversy with him, denouncing 'the corrupt teachings of this weed, this dilapidated, sick and evil-minded sheep'. And Luther had retorted by describing Henry as 'raving like a strumpet in a tantrum'. But Henry had also written a scholarly and cogent thesis rebutting Luther's argument for which the Pope at the time had granted him the title of *Fidei Defensor* (Defender of the Faith). When he became desperate to marry Anne Boleyn, Henry hoped that his marriage to Catherine could be annulled legally, and he thought he had found a means of achieving this in the Old Testament book of Leviticus where it is stated: 'If a man shall take his brother's wife it is an unclean thing; he hath uncovered his brother's nakedness. They shall be childless.' Henry was able to persuade himself that the reason Catherine had not borne a son was that their marriage was contrary to God's holy law and was therefore invalid. She had never been his lawful wife and so he was free to marry Anne. But plausible as this might seem in some eyes there were objections. The verse in Leviticus was ambiguous, referring not to sons but to children and Catherine had borne him a daughter, and it might not necessarily have applied

129

to a deceased brother. Also Leviticus was contradicted by a verse in the book of Deuteronomy which laid it down that it was the duty of a husband's brother 'to go unto his widow and take her to him to wife'. Of greater significance was the fact that in 1503 Pope Julius II had granted a dispensation allowing the betrothal of Henry to Catherine, and what Henry required in 1527 was that the current pope, Clement VII, should decree that his predecessor had been mistaken. This in normal circumstances he might have been prepared to do, but at the time he was at the mercy of the Austrian emperor, Charles V, whose troops had recently overrun Rome and who was not prepared to see his aunt Catherine put aside as having been no more than Henry's concubine and her daughter Mary (to whom he had once been betrothed) branded as a bastard.

Henry had hopes for a time that Catherine would agree to an arrangement whereby she would retire discreetly to a religious house and acquiesce tacitly to the invalidation of their marriage. But to this she was rigidly opposed. She believed fervently that her marriage to Henry had been lawful and that to set it aside would be a sin endangering the souls of both Henry and herself. By making this decision and sticking to it she probably did not realise that she was altering the course of English history.

For Henry became more determined than ever to have an annulment. And so he embarked on what came to be known as 'The King's Great Matter' which was not to be settled for six years.

His first step was to set up a tribunal to give judgement on the case. This was headed by two papal legates, Cardinal Wolsey who could be relied on to give a favourable verdict and a Cardinal Campeggio sent from Rome by the Pope with instructions to delay giving judgement as long as possible so as to avoid giving offence either to the Austrian Emperor in whose power he lay or to Henry VIII who was one of his strongest upholders. In carrying out this brief Campeggio was to be all too successful: taking more than twice as long as was necessary to travel from Rome to London, and on arrival he immediately took to his bed with an acute attack of gout. He then took every opportunity to make difficulties and delay proceedings.

Before the tribunal began to operate Henry became aware that his move to oust Catherine in favour of Anne was not at all popular, and he felt it necessary to assemble a group of notables – nobles, clergy, city aldermen among others – to put forward his case. This was unashamedly hypocritical. Although he had long been out of love with Catherine and was angry with her for thwarting him, he praised her fulsomely as 'a woman of sweet gentleness and humility … of all good qualities pertaining to nobility she is without comparison'. He asked his listeners to believe that it was at the dictates of his conscience that he was questioning the legality of their marriage, that it was only his tender love for Catherine that had prevented him bringing the matter up before, and that it was his dearest wish that their marriage would be declared lawful as he would willingly marry her again. Not many can have been deceived by these protestations but, as time was to show, very few were prepared to speak out on Catherine's behalf.

When after a delay of fifteen months the tribunal at last began its proceedings they were indeterminate and nothing was achieved. When Catherine appeared before it she ignored the cardinals and fell on her knees before Henry and implored him passionately that 'for all the love that has been between us and for the love of God not to distress her, and to let [her] have justice and right'. She then left and refused all demands for her to return, for which she was officially condemned as 'contumacious'. She also demanded that the enquiry be held in Rome rather than in London which Campeggio said should be considered, offering as it did another opportunity for delay. Otherwise the tribunal spent much time trying to ascertain if Catherine's marriage to Arthur had been consummated as it had been ordained that on this depended whether or not her marriage to Henry was legal. Catherine had taken a solemn oath on the blessed sacrament that although she had been to bed with Arthur seven times she had remained *virgo intacta* and incorrupt as when she emerged from her mother's womb. But this was disputed by Henry who instigated intrusive personal enquiries to prove his point. After sitting for a few months the tribunal was adjourned by Campeggio for the holiday season and it was not reconvened.

By then Henry was boiling with impatience. He was enraged that his 'Great Matter' should be stalled in this way and even more so when the Pope summoned him to appear before a tribunal in Rome. The idea of the King of England appearing before an Italian court to plead his case he considered an outrage. In his fury he looked around for a scapegoat and found one in Wolsey. For fourteen years the great cardinal had been the virtual ruler of the country and had served the King devotedly, but during that time he had made many enemies (including Anne Boleyn) and they had been poisoning Henry's mind against him. Although he had done his best to expedite the 'Great Matter' he was indicted for treason in 1530 and would almost certainly have ended up on the block had he not died on his way from the north to face trial.

Meanwhile Henry had been much taken with the idea of an obscure churchman, Thomas Cranmer, that the legality of his marriage should be referred to theological scholars at European universities so that their opinions could be given due weight by the Pope in coming to his decision. 'This man hath the sow by the right ear,' he is said to have exclaimed. And so emissaries were dispatched who were able by means partly theological and partly mercenary to obtain the judgments that were required. But unfortunately the Pope became aware of what was happening and, under pressure from the Emperor, issued a bull banning the subject of Henry's marriage from public discussion. So the opinions of the scholars were of little help and the King's 'Great Matter' was no further forward.

Henry's impatience could then no longer be contained and he began to entertain thoughts of making a break with Rome. In his youth he had once declared that he was 'so bounden to the See of Rome that he could not do enough to honour it. We will set forth the Pope's authority to the uttermost.' But as Pope Clement VII continued to prevaricate and Anne became ever more pressing he had other thoughts. In 1531 he declared himself head of the church in England and as king held 'plenary, whole and entire power ... without the intermeddling of exterior persons'. This was confirmed by the Act of Supremacy passed by Parliament in 1534.

In 1532 'The Great Matter' became more urgent when, six years after she had first attracted Henry's attention, Anne Boleyn became pregnant, and in 1533 Henry married her secretly, thus becoming in some eyes a bigamist. Soon afterwards Thomas Cranmer was appointed Archbishop of Canterbury and, as was required of him, set up a court of enquiry into the validity of Henry's marriage to Catherine – very different from the one presided over by Wolsey and Campeggio. To this Catherine was summoned to attend which she refused to do, saying that the matter rested with the Pope's court in Rome, for which she was once again condemned as 'contumacious'. As expected Cranmer gave judgement that her marriage to Henry was invalid whereas that to Anne was legal. This was confirmed in 1534 by the Act of Succession which laid down that Henry would be succeeded by Anne's offspring rather than Catherine's daughter, Mary, who was declared illegitimate. A further attempt was made to persuade Catherine to accept the situation. The Dukes of Norfolk and Suffolk visited her at Ampthill where she had been banished, and told her she could expect more generous treatment if she agreed, but she was not to be moved. At the same time she was informed that she had been downgraded from queen to princess dowager, a title she refused to accept.

Catherine's desolation was now complete. Her treatment had been brutal: branded as Henry's harlot and her daughter bastardised, deposed as queen and replaced by a woman who had once been her maid of honour. She had also lived to see her husband degenerate from a handsome, affable, generous youth into a gross, diseased, vindictive tyrant. But perhaps her greatest grief was the country's break with Rome – the overruling of the Pope and the demeaning of the church which to her was sacred. When she died in 1536 there was little to comfort her. Only this – that she had once declared that if she had to choose between two extremes, she would choose extreme sadness rather than extreme happiness. In the midst of the greatest unhappiness there was always some consolation, whereas it was always too easy to forget things of the spirit in the midst of great prosperity.

ANNE BOLEYN (c.1501–1536)

Second Wife of Henry VIII

Anne Boleyn (or Bullen as sometimes rendered), like Catherine of Aragon, was to have a major role in English history. She too, although in an entirely different way, was to hasten the coming of the Reformation. For seven eventful years Henry VIII was in thrall to her when few queens have exercised such power. Her influence was not always beneficial; she could be cruel and vindictive and was never popular; but she did not deserve the gruesome ending of her life. And one should surely be grateful to her for begetting the future Elizabeth I.

Anne's family was well connected. Her father was descended from a line of wealthy London merchants, and had come to hold positions at court where he was often employed in missions abroad owing to his fluency in foreign languages. Her mother, who died when Anne was aged eleven, was the sister of the Duke of Norfolk and a powerful figure in the court of Henry VIII. Anne was introduced into court life at an early age. When thirteen she became a maid of honour to Henry VIII's younger sister, Princess Mary, when she went to France to be married (much against her will) to the elderly and debauched Louis XII.[1] The French king, however, was not to live for long and on his death Mary returned to England to marry her great love, the Duke of Suffolk. But Anne remained in France and took service with the French Queen Claude, wife of Francis I. She was to spend seven years in the French court which made a deep impression on her. Between the strict propriety of Queen Claude and the exuberant licentiousness of Francis I she learned to steer an ambivalent course. She also learned much else – poised and beautiful manners, gracious and flirtatious talk and the finer points of love making.

These arts she was to deploy with consummate skill on her

---

[1] She was eighteen, he was fifty-two.

return to England in 1521 to become maid of honour to Queen Catherine. At the time her sister Mary was current mistress of Henry VIII, but soon afterwards she married and left the court, leaving the coast clear for Anne; but it was to be five years before her love affair with the King began. In the meanwhile she might have married a very desirable bachelor, Henry Lord Percy, son and heir of the fifth Earl of Northumberland, to whom she became engaged; but for some reason the King, although not yet smitten by her, disapproved and ordered Wolsey to put an end to the affair which he did with a heavy hand, thereby incurring Anne's bitter hostility which eight years later was to cost him dear.

It seems to have been in 1526, when Anne was twenty-five and Henry thirty-five that he first fell in love with her. Queen Catherine was then forty-one with faded looks, a melancholy disposition and apparently incapable of further child bearing. Henry was desperate for a change, and no one could have been more different from Catherine than Anne. Whereas the former was decorous, devout and strictly correct, the latter was mercurial, quick witted and sharp tempered. It seems she was not a great beauty. A foreign diplomat wrote at the time: 'Madam Anne is not one of the handsomest women in the world. She is of middling stature, swarthy complexion, long neck, wide mouth, bosom not much raised, and in fact nothing but the King's great appetite – and her eyes which are black and beautiful.' And another contemporary wrote: 'Beauty and sprightliness sat on her lips; in readiness of repartee, skill in the dance and in the playing of the lute she was unsurpassed.'

Whatever Anne's qualities Henry was totally captivated by them and became infatuated as he had never been before. 'So much in love was he,' wrote a foreign diplomat, 'that God alone can abate his madness.' People were amazed at the latitude he allowed her; she could speak to him in a way no others would have dared, and the more fiery and reckless she became the more he seemed to revel in it. Quarrels they had in plenty, but they always made them up and their love making afterwards was all the more passionate. But Anne was insistent that full favours would not be granted outside marriage; she was not prepared to be another of Henry's mistresses and this made Henry all the more frenzied and determined to marry her.

Henry had hoped for a quick and discreet annulment of his marriage to Catherine, but in this he had been thwarted partly by the firm stance taken by Catherine and partly by the prevarication of Pope Clement VII who was a virtual prisoner of Catherine's nephew, the Emperor Charles V. After four years of delays Henry had finally broken loose and, taking the law into his own hands, denied the authority of the Pope and declared himself 'supreme head of the Church of England as far as the law of Christ will allow'.[2] Catherine, who refused to acknowledge this, was banished from court and honours and riches were then heaped on Anne including the title of Marquess of Pembroke, unique for a woman. Soon afterwards she became pregnant and in January 1533 Henry married her in deepest secrecy – secrecy being necessary as his marriage to Catherine had not yet been annulled. Later in the year, however, the newly appointed Archbishop of Canterbury, the obsequious Thomas Cranmer, set up court and pronounced Henry's marriage to Catherine illegal and so his recent marriage to Anne was valid. This was followed by a magnificent coronation for Anne (when she was six months pregnant) for which large crowds turned out but which gave her a mixed reception: there was some cheering and waving of caps in the air, but there was also some booing and caps left on heads. For Anne was not generally popular, there being much resentment at the way Queen Catherine had been put aside for a younger woman of dubious reputation and regarded by some as 'the royal whore'.

Anne's coronation was the summit of her success – Queen of England, recognised by nearly all the leaders of church and state, still in the love of her husband and bearing a child everyone expected to be a boy. Anne realised that everything depended on this. If she bore Henry a male heir she would be safe in his love, but not otherwise. When the child she was carrying turned out to be a girl, the future Queen Elizabeth, it was a tremendous disappointment to Henry. From then on he became increasingly vexed by her tantrums which he no longer found erotic and was telling her that he could lower her as much as he had raised her. He came to realise too how self-seeking and vindictive she was, particularly in the treatment she urged for Queen Catherine and her daughter Princess Mary. As punishment for their obstinacy they were to be kept apart and confined in rigorous and unhealthy conditions. Anne demanded among other things Catherine's jewellery

---

[2] This last was added to ease the conscience of some churchmen.

and state barge, causing the Spanish ambassador to remark that 'God grant she may content herself with the said barge, the jewels and the husband of the Queen.' Treatment of Princess Mary was even more ruthless. After the birth of Elizabeth Mary was not only bastardised but compelled to become maid of honour to her younger half-sister and Anne was boasting that she would marry her off to 'some varlet'. She even urged that she and Catherine be put to death, but this Henry dared not do partly because of the outrage it would cause and partly because of the revenge that might be taken by Catherine's nephew, Emperor Charles V.

Renunciation of the Pope in 1531 had been formalised by the Act of Supremacy passed by Parliament in 1534, and already before that, with the help of a ruthless and capable secretary of state, Thomas Cromwell, Henry had induced Parliament to pass a number of laws curbing the powers and privileges of the Church and of the Pope in particular who for his part had declared Henry's marriage to Anne illegal and passed sentence of excommunication on him, to which Henry had retorted that he 'did not care a fig for all the Pope's excommunications'.

This open breach with Rome could not but cause concern in the country, and there were those then (as today) who put the main blame for it on Anne; but this is mistaken. It is true that she was sympathetic towards religious reform: there were abuses she thought ought to be suppressed, monasteries that should be investigated and in some cases closed down, and she was in favour of English translations of the Bible being made generally available. And there was a strong body of opinion in the country in favour of such reforms. The measures passed by Parliament were not in support of the annulment of Henry's marriage, and it was unfortunate that they were mixed up with it.

By 1534 it was becoming noticeable to many that Anne was out of favour. The French ambassador reported that 'the King was tired to satiety of her'. In 1535 she became pregnant again and the birth of a son might have saved her, but in the following year she miscarried and this sealed her fate. Already by then Henry had become attracted by one of Anne's maids of honour, Jane Seymour – gentle, submissive and of pale complexion in contrast to Anne's fiery temperament and angry outbursts. By April 1536 he and Thomas Cromwell were planning for Anne to be removed from the scene. Cromwell's spies reported to him that the Queen had at times behaved indiscreetly with certain men and charges of adultery might be brought. And so on 24 April a commission was appointed to look into certain 'treasonable conspiracies', as yet unspecified, in which Anne might be involved. As was expected the commission found that there was evidence that Anne had committed adultery with four men and had conspired to kill the King. Of the four men one, Mark Smeaton, a court musician, confessed under torture to his guilt; the other three, who were of noble birth, maintained their innocence, but they were all put on trial and sentenced to death. By then Anne too had been arrested and committed to the Tower.

Anne had earlier become aware of the danger she was in and had been at pains to present a new image of herself as a godly matron devoted to good works and pious practices, but this was not altogether convincing and she was still regarded by most people as spiteful and self-seeking, and she was to arouse little sympathy in the ordeal that awaited her. On 15 May, along with her brother, Lord Rochfort, with whom she was accused of incest, she was arraigned for high treason before a court of twenty-six noblemen headed by her uncle, the Duke of Norfolk. The trial, conducted in the Great Hall of the Tower of London in front of a large crowd (estimated by the Spanish ambassador to be as many as two thousand), bore all the hallmarks of a put-up job. Evidence was scanty and unconvincing. The Lord Mayor of London, one of those sitting in judgement who had had experience of trials, later stated that he 'could not observe anything in the proceedings against her but they were resolved to make an occasion to get rid of her.'

Before the trial Anne had shown signs of the great strain she was enduring – sometimes in tears, sometimes laughing hysterically at the absurdity of some of the charges brought against her – but during the trial, in which she was not allowed an advocate to speak for her, she was composed and dignified, giving 'wise and discreet answers' to the questions put to her. But the outcome of the trial was never in doubt: she was convicted of 'wronging her husband with four persons and with her brother,' and was condemned to death in a manner to be prescribed by the King. But Anne was not entirely innocent. She had been guilty of reckless behaviour but almost certainly not of adultery; and in any case this charge fell apart when two days before her execution Archbishop Cranmer, pliant as ever, on orders from the King pronounced her marriage to Henry invalid. The reason for this was to bastardise Princess Elizabeth and so clear the way for any children Henry might have by Jane Seymour to succeed to the throne. But if his marriage to Anne was invalid how could she have committed adultery?

As the day of her execution approached Anne, usually so fiery and volatile, became calm and resigned. The governor of the Tower, Sir William Kingston, in his last report wrote that he had seen 'men and also women executed and they had been in great sorrow, but to my knowledge, this lady hath much joy and pleasure in death.' To the end she protested her innocence. Just before her execution she sent to Henry a message, simple and dignified but tinged with irony: 'Commend me to His Majesty and tell him he hath been ever constant in his career of advancing me; from a private gentlewoman he made me a marquess, from a marquess to a queen and now he hath left no higher degree of honour, he gives my innocence the crown of martyrdom.' There was too some sarcasm in her last words on the scaffold: 'I come here only to die and thus to yield myself humbly unto the will of my Lord the King. I pray God to save the King and send him long to reign over you, for a gentler and more merciful prince was there never.' Certainly she could expect no mercy from Henry who wanted her dispatched as quickly as possible, but he did at least see to it that there should be some seemliness in the circumstances of her execution – in the comparative seclusion of Tower Green rather than the open site of Tower Hill, and the most expert headsman in Europe was brought over from France who with his special 'sword of Calais' could be relied on to sever her head with one blow.

The execution of Anne was a monstrous crime. Even the most sanguinary and merciless of medieval monarchs had foreborne to put a queen to death, and on a trumped up charge. Anne had lived dangerously and her fall was to be expected but not so brutally and gruesomely. Henry, however, showed no remorse. On the following day he became betrothed to Jane Seymour and within ten days was wedded to her, and the woman he had once loved so passionately had been expunged from his mind.

JANE SEYMOUR (1509–1537)

Third Wife of Henry VIII

Jane Seymour was Queen of England for rather less than eighteen months. During that time she said or did little that was memorable apart from bearing Henry VIII the son he had been wanting so desperately for so long. Because of this and because of her reputation for humility and a warm heart she was a popular queen and acclaimed by Henry as his favourite wife. It was beside her that he was buried.

In 1535 Henry VIII in the course of a west country progress was the guest of Sir John Seymour of Wulfhall in Wiltshire. Sir John was sheriff of the county and a man of some standing but not a member of the old nobility. His wife was of aristocratic lineage, being descended from Edward III and so a distant cousin of the King. Five years previously Sir John had been involved in a family scandal when he was found to have been consorting with the wife of his son, Edward, by whom he was believed to have fathered two sons. Tudor society, not easily shocked, was outraged by this and it might have caused a major disruption in the Seymour family but the matter had been settled: Edward put his wife into a nunnery, disinherited the sons and later married Lady Anne Stanhope, a lady of great respectability. By 1535 the scandal had subsided and the King's visit was an indication that the family was not in disgrace. But it was also to do more than that for it seems to have been the first time that Henry took serious notice of Sir John's daughter, Jane.

At the time Jane was twenty-seven years old, almost middle aged by Tudor standards, of no great beauty and no intellectual, but modest, mild and unassuming which to Henry, then becoming estranged from his termagant wife Anne, had great appeal. Henry might have noticed her before as she had held positions at court from an early age and in 1535 was a maid of honour to Queen Anne, but it was not until then that Henry's attention to her became marked. This caused keen interest at court where its members considered switching their allegiance from the old favourite to the new. Particularly interested were Jane's two brothers, Edward and Thomas, who saw advantage to themselves in the King's love for their sister, and they encouraged her and advised her as to how she should respond, and she was to be an apt pupil and to play her part with some adroitness. She saw clearly that what Henry wanted in a wife was loyalty, docility and chasteness. She must not be won too easily. She must have her principles and stick to them. An opportunity to show this occurred when she received from the king a purse full of gold with a letter in his own handwriting which she kissed but returned unopened along with a prim message beseeching the King 'to understand by my prudence that I am a gentlewoman of good and honourable family, without reproach, and have no greater treasure in the world than my honour, which I would not harm for a thousand deaths. If the King should wish to make me a present of money, I beg him to do so when God shall send me a husband to marry.' It might have been expected that Henry would have taken this amiss but to the contrary he was delighted and longed for her all the more.

There were those at the time and others since who suspected that Jane's gentle, demure demeanour was not entirely genuine and that underneath lay a hard core of steel. The Spanish ambassador reporting to his master, the Emperor Charles V, hoped that 'no scorpion lurks under the honey'. One who had no doubts on this score was Queen Anne who soon became aware of what was going on and would have liked to dismiss Jane from her court but dared not do so for fear of angering the King. And so to her rage and frustration she had to sit by and watch while her position was undermined by her handmaiden.

Jane's first triumph came in 1536. In that momentous year, which saw the death of Catherine of Aragon, the execution of Anne Boleyn, the closing of the first monasteries and a major rebellion known as the Pilgrimage of Grace, she was married to Henry VIII and became Queen of England. It had taken her hardly seven months. The same feat had taken Anne Boleyn seven years. Established as Queen, Jane had other objectives and in not all of these was she successful. Her religious views were conservative: she regretted the breach with Rome and was deeply grieved by the closing of the monasteries and she attempted to intervene with her husband on both these matters, but was sharply rebuked and told to mind her business and to remember that the last queen had died as a result of meddling in state affairs. And Jane was prudent enough to accept this and to conform more closely to her motto – 'Bound to serve and obey'.

In another matter, however, she had some success. She felt she had to do something to relieve the plight of the King's elder daughter, the Lady Mary as she was known. Mary was then twenty and her life had been one of almost unrelieved misery. She had seen her mother, to whom she was devoted, put aside and her marriage invalidated and so rated as no more than a harlot, and she herself had been declared illegitimate, forced to subject herself to her younger half-sister Elizabeth and treated with disdain and cruelty by her stepmother Queen Anne. After her mother's death she had remained banished from court and family life, her father refusing to have anything to do with her unless she signed a document acknowledging that he was the head of the Church of England and that her mother's marriage had been invalid. This for a long time she refused to do as she thought that such an untruth would endanger her immortal soul. Jane pleaded with her to do so and pleaded with Henry to take her back into favour, but unavailingly. Finally, however, Mary gave way, persuaded that for a statement made under great duress she would have absolution from the Pope. Then Henry relented and Jane was able to restore an affectionate relationship between them. She would have liked to do more and bring her back into the line of succession, but here she found she was venturing on dangerous ground and did not press the matter.

Jane's greatest triumph came in 1537 when she gave birth to a son, the future Edward VI. When it became known that she was pregnant there had been a wild outburst of excitement even greater than that following the pregnancy of Anne Boleyn two years before. Once again doctors and astrologists and other seers all predicted that the baby would be a boy, and this time they were right. The rejoicings when on 12 October 1537 his birth was announced were unprecedented. The King was beside himself with joy. For nearly thirty years he had been longing for such a consummation and had had only disappointments and false hopes. Various reasons had been put forward for these, notably the illegality of his first marriages; but there had also been rumours about his potency. Anne Boleyn, among many indiscretions, had let it be known that this was apt to be intermittent. And so he regarded the birth of a son as not only settling the question of the succession but also as a vindication of his masculinity. But his joy was soon marred. Jane had had a long and difficult labour and two weeks later she died of a fever. Grief at this was general and genuine. In the brief time she had been Queen Jane had become well loved; her warmth and humility and particularly her kindness to the Lady Mary had won many hearts. For a time Henry was desolate and withdrew into solitude but it was not long before he was looking out for a fourth wife.

What if Jane had survived? Might her soothing effect have calmed Henry enough to prevent the furious rages and monstrous brutalities of his old age? The country would not have witnessed the farce of his marriage to Anne of Cleves, and the wayward Catherine Howard would not have ended up on the executioner's block. In 1547, when Jane would have been thirty-nine, her son succeeded to the throne at the age of ten. During his minority would she still have been content to 'serve and obey'? The history of Britain might have been different.

ANNE OF CLEVES (1515–1557)

Fourth Wife of Henry VIII

Anne of Cleves was Queen of England for six months. No king's marriage has ever come to an end so quickly (or so peaceably). Anne has been treated lightly by history: depicted as graceless and unsightly and dubbed cruelly 'the great Flanders mare'. Failings she may have had but she was no mere figure of fun. She was amiable and kindly and always popular, kept her head on her shoulders and had an astute eye for her best interests. Of all Henry's wives she obtained from him the best treatment.

Desolated as Henry had been by the death of Jane Seymour he had, nevertheless, within a month started looking around for another wife. There might well have been a maid of honour waiting on the sidelines to engage his attention, but the political situation at the time required that he should make an advantageous alliance with a foreign power. Henry was insistent, however, that other matters besides political considerations should be taken into account. The comeliness and character of a possible bride were of essential importance, otherwise, as he had once asserted, marriage would be 'a displeasure and torment' rather than the 'pleasure and quiet' it should be. And so before committing himself Henry went to great pains to find out personal details of eligible princesses. He told the French ambassador that he would like to have them assembled in Calais for the purpose of comparison; but this was too much for the French king, Francis I, who said that princesses could not be lined up for inspection like a lot of ponies to which the ribald ambassador added that next he would be wanting to mount them for a trial run. And for once Henry had to back down. But he was not deterred from other investigations. He sent his court painter, Hans Holbein, round Europe to make likenesses of possible candidates, and his ambassadors were told to make close scrutinies.

In seeking a foreign wife Henry, perhaps predictably, was to encounter some hesitancy. At forty-six he was hardly a romantic figure – enormously obese, with a flaming temper and a festering and evil-smelling wound in his leg which would not heal. And the fates of his three previous wives must have been a grim warning to any successor. A prime candidate was a French princess, Mary of Guise, a widow of twenty-two with good figure and proven fertility, but when she heard that Henry was interested in her she lost no time in becoming betrothed to his nephew, James V of Scotland. Highly suitable too was Christina, Duchess of Milan and daughter of the King of Denmark, a widow of sixteen and a great beauty. But she too held back in spite of impassioned entreaties made to her by Henry's ambassador who could bring himself to say of his master that he was 'the most gentle gentleman that liveth, his nature so benign and pleasant that I think to this day no man hath heard many angry words pass his lips'. But Christina was not deceived and was reported to have said that Henry's first wife (her great aunt) was suspected of having been poisoned, that his second wife was innocently put to death and the third lost for lack of keeping in her childbed.

Anne of Cleves had not at first been among the forerunners. It was reported of her that 'she was praised for her virtue and modesty but nothing much else,' and furthermore that she was 'not highly educated, could not sing or play any instrument, exhibited little humour or cheerfulness and spent most of her time sewing.' When the English ambassador went to have a look at her and her sister he found them 'wrapped up in such monstrous habit and apparel that their figures and faces could hardly be seen.' And when he remarked on this he had no sympathy from their brother, the Duke of Cleves, who asked tartly if he expected to see them naked. But somehow these adverse reports came to be overlooked, and the portrait of Anne by Holbein, manifestly flattering, entranced Henry, and so under strong pressure from Thomas Cromwell who stressed the political advantages of such a match and Henry's increasing impatience for another wife after two years of widowhood a marriage was agreed.

Anne's journey to England was a triumphal progress. Accompanied by a huge entourage of some two hundred and sixty people and two hundred horses she travelled overland to Calais (still an English possession) where she was delayed for two weeks owing to bad weather, but the governor spared no expense in entertaining her. She finally arrived in England on 27 December 1539 where she was greeted exultantly. But then things went terribly wrong. Henry came down to meet her at Rochester and was aghast at what he found. She was nothing like what he had expected. Her features were angular and she was tall and thin and gauche. He told Cromwell that he was so struck with consternation and never so much dismayed in his life as to see a lady so far unlike what had been represented. 'I like her not,' he kept repeating. His immediate thought was to extricate himself from the marriage, but Cromwell told him this would bring him disgrace throughout Europe and might land him in a war with Cleves. Henry could not but see the force of this and resolved to go through with the wedding which was due to take place three days later. In the meanwhile he showed commendable restraint. Although seething with anger at having been deceived he showed no outward signs of it and his manners to Anne were impeccable so that she did not realise for several weeks that anything was amiss. Just before the wedding, however, he told those around him: 'My lords, if it were not to satisfy the world and my realm, I would not do what I must do this day for any earthly thing.'

Henry and Anne were married amid great splendour on 6 January 1540; but ahead of them lay the bridal bed. This was hardly one of roses: Anne reeked of body odour and Henry's suppurating leg stank abominably. Moreover Anne had no knowledge of the facts of life, and so had no idea of what to expect. It seems that Henry groped for a time but was in no way aroused by her and the marriage was not consummated. Next day he told Cromwell: 'Surely, my lord, I liked her before not well, but now I like her much worse. She is nothing fair and have very evil smells about her ... I have left her as good a maid as I found her.' He then became determined that his marriage to her had to be annulled, but this should be done legally and with as much propriety as possible: and so for the time being he continued to share his bed with her, and so unworldly and naive was Anne that she continued to think nothing was wrong. But this could not last: her ignorance of sexual matters became known to her ladies-in-waiting, one of whom enquired boldly if she was still a maid. 'How can I be?' she replied, 'when I sleep every night with the King? When he comes to bed he kisseth me and taketh me by the hand and biddeth me "Good night, sweetheart", and in the morning kisseth me and biddeth "Farewell, darling".' She seemed to think that this was enough for child bearing, but her ladies thought the time had come to tell her that more was needed, and when she realised that Henry had been holding back she became seriously alarmed and wondered what was going to happen to her.

Unknown to her Henry and his lawyers were investigating how an annulment might be achieved. It seemed for a time that it might be done relatively easily as earlier in Anne's life there had been talk of her marrying a prince of Lorraine, and if this had amounted to a pre-contract her marriage to Henry could be invalidated. But nothing positive on this score could be ascertained and it had to be abandoned. Grounds for annulment, then, had to be non-consummation and for this to be established Anne's cooperation was necessary. If, like Catherine of Aragon, she was obstinate and refused to have anything to do with the matter, it would have stalled. But Anne was found to be willing, even eager, to give assistance. Marriage to Henry was something of which she was not sorry to be quit.

And so a charade was enacted to give the business an appearance of legality. In March 1540 Henry solemnly informed Parliament that in view of the rumours prevalent of a pre-contract between Anne and the Prince of Lorraine, his conscience would not allow him to consummate their marriage, and that although he had shared a bed with Anne every night for four months he never took from her by true carnal copulation. Parliament then affirmed that non-consummation constituted enough grounds for annulment and petitioned the King to have the legality of his marriage investigated by a convocation of clergy, and to this the King graciously consented. And so in due course on 9 July the convocations of York and Canterbury found Henry's marriage 'null and void'.

In return for her compliance Anne was treated generously: she was granted a handsome financial settlement which included Richmond Palace and the manors of Hever and Penshurst, and was accorded the title of 'King's Sister' with precedence over all other ladies apart from the new Queen and the King's two daughters. For her part Anne had to agree to remain in England and become a naturalised British subject, thus ensuring her silence and subjection to the King. A further condition of imprecise meaning banned her from 'playing the woman' – presumably stirring up trouble and making difficulties. To these conditions she was happy to agree and so was able to lead a quiet, untroubled and affluent life. She also agreed to write to her brother, the Duke of Cleves, assuring him of her satisfaction at the turn of events and that the annulment was indeed genuine, her body having been 'preserved in the integrity which I brought into this realm'. Understandably the Duke was not happy at the way his sister had been treated, regarding it as an insult to his country, but as long as Anne took the attitude she did and remained in the jurisdiction of the English king there was little he could do.

Anne has been criticised for the ready way she accepted Henry's terms. She might, it was felt, have shown more of the spirit of Catherine of Aragon. But she surely took the prudent course. In England she could live comfortably, even luxuriously, on the edge of life at Court and enjoying the simple things which gave her pleasure including a glass or two of wine. A drawback was that she was committed to a life of celibacy, but after her experience with Henry this may have been no great deprivation. The alternative was to forfeit her allowance and return to Cleves, but this would be humiliating and would lead to impoverishment and constraint, under the thumb of a dictatorial mother and possibly married off by her brother to some minor princeling. In England she was to be content. She was on good terms with Henry, so much so that on the downfall of her successor, Catherine Howard, rumours were abroad that Henry might take her back into queenship but these were absurd. When Henry married the plain and mature Catherine Parr there were those who believed that Anne was jealous and was reported to have declared that the bride was nowhere so beautiful as she was, and this may have been true as since living a single life and eating and drinking plentifully Anne had filled out and, according to one contemporary, was 'half as beautiful again.' More likely is a remark attributed to her that 'a fine burden madam Catherine has taken upon herself'.

In her old age Anne became a meticulous housekeeper, worrying about the cost of everything, particularly servants of whom she never seemed to have enough. In the reign of her stepson Edward VI payments of her allowance fell into arrears and she made desperate requests not only for these to be made good but also to be increased, but it was considered by the Council of Regency that she was well provided for. Having converted to Roman Catholicism she was to survive the troubles of the reign of Mary Tudor but was not to survive into the reign of Elizabeth to whom she was specially attached.

Anne died in 1557 at the age of forty-one and was interred in a magnificent tomb of black and white marble in Westminster Abbey. She was widely lamented as she had always been popular. A contemporary chronicler recorded of her: 'A lady of right commendable regard, courteous, gentle, a good housekeeper and very bountiful to her servants.'

CATHERINE HOWARD (c.1525–1542)

Fifth Wife of Henry VIII

Among the queens of England there is no more pathetic story than that of Catherine Howard, fifth wife of Henry VIII. When she was barely sixteen she found herself Queen of England and less than eighteen months later on the executioner's block. Her early life had been unstable and promiscuous and, married to Henry, she soon became engulfed in a fraught situation with which she could only grapple helplessly and foolishly. Although she was not guiltless her execution was brutal and unnecessary.

Catherine came from aristocratic roots (niece of the Duke of Norfolk and first cousin to Anne Boleyn), but this did not ensure a happy and settled upbringing. Her mother died when she was a small child and her father, Lord Edmund Howard, a weak and ineffective character, married again twice, but achieved little more in life than fathering numerous children for whom he could not provide. At an early age Catherine was lodged in the household of her step-grandmother, Agnes Dowager Duchess of Norfolk, which might have been a blessing but proved to be a disaster, as the Duchess did not keep an orderly house, and Catherine found herself unloved and uncared for in the company of profligate young women from whom she picked up pernicious ways.[1] She also found herself bedevilled by sex-hungry male members of the Duchess's establishment who seemed free to play fast and loose.

At the age of fifteen Catherine became involved in an affair with her music teacher, not a major one as he was of too lowly estate to aspire to the hand of the niece of a duke, but one in which, nevertheless, as she later confessed, she suffered him 'at sundry times to handle and touch the secret parts of my body which neither became me with honesty to permit nor him to require.' A more

---

[1] She had learned, she later said, 'how women might meddle with a man and yet conceive no child'.

151

serious affair was with one Francis Dereham, a member of the Duke of Norfolk's household troop, a band of penurious gentry ready to spring to arms but with time on their hands. Catherine was later to confess that she and Dereham had full sex. 'He used me in such sort as a man doth his wife many and sundry times but how often I know not.' Whether or not there was a pre-contract of marriage (an engagement regarded in those days as binding) is doubtful, for Dereham too would hardly be considered an adequate match for a lady with Plantagenet blood in her veins. When in time the romance came to the notice of the Dowager Duchess she was so furious that she laid about her with her fists, and Dereham was forced to leave and take refuge for a time in Ireland.

Soon afterwards Catherine was appointed a maid of honour to Queen Anne (of Cleves), and while at court she came into contact with her cousin, Thomas Culpeper, a dashing and potent philanderer in the mould of Casanova, with whom she fell deeply in love. Later this was to have fatal consequences, but for the time being it was more momentous that the king had fallen in love with her. This had been contrived by Catherine's uncle, the Duke of Norfolk, who was at the head of a pro-Catholic group at court strongly averse to religious change. In opposition to them was a group headed by Thomas Cromwell, Henry VIII's chief minister, which was aiming for further Protestant reforms. The idea of Norfolk and other members of the Howard family was to bring Catherine to the attention of the king, knowing how susceptible he was to attractive young women. With careful coaching they hoped that she would so captivate Henry that he would make her his queen and as such she would be an invaluable pawn in the contest with their opponents. In this they were all too successful. Henry succumbed at once to Catherine's charms and this, no doubt, was one of the reasons for his great haste in pushing forward the annulment of his marriage to Anne. But there was one fatal fly in the ointment: what Norfolk did not know, or chose to ignore, was that, although Catherine was barely sixteen years old, she was a woman with a past, and if this should ever come to light the consequences would be terrifying.

At first, however, everything went in Norfolk's favour: within three days of his marriage to Anne being annulled Henry married Catherine. Already by then Cromwell had been condemned to death. No one, not even Wolsey, had served Henry so faithfully and so capably as Cromwell, but since the debacle of the marriage to Anne of Cleves, which he had strongly urged, his fate was sealed: a trumped up charge of treason and heresy was brought against him as was an absurd accusation that he was plotting to marry Henry's daughter, Mary, and make himself king. He had no trial and was given no opportunity to defend himself – condemned by an Act of Attainder passed by a servile Parliament.

That the storm which overhung Henry's marriage to Catherine broke sooner rather than later was due to Catherine's foolishness and naivety. But first there was a brief honeymoon period. Henry was utterly besotted by his young wife, lavishing her with gifts and gratifying her every whim. He seemed to be in a daze of happiness: a foreign ambassador reported that he had never seen him in such good spirits. And Catherine, laden with riches and honours (although as yet no coronation) was revelling in her role as queen. But it could not last.

In July of 1541 Henry with Catherine set out on a tour of northern England where there had been outbreaks of rebellion and Henry was determined that these should be crushed and the people overawed by the power of his presence. Before leaving he showed his mood by ordering the execution of some Yorkists of royal descent who might be considered to have claims to the throne. Among these was the seventy-year-old Margaret Countess of Salisbury (daughter of George Duke of Clarence), a lady of great distinction and virtue. She had committed no crime of any sort but was roughly dragged from the Tower and hacked to death by an inexperienced axeman – surely one of the most heinous crimes in English history.

Henry's progress through the north seemed to be all that was expected – orderly and intimidating. But beneath the surface trouble was brewing. For Catherine had been behaving recklessly. Her one-time lover, Francis Dereham, she appointed her secretary, and Thomas Culpeper was allowed to visit her in the watches of the night. Of course this did not go unnoticed and gave rise to gossip. At the same time down in London one John Lascelles, brother of one of Catherine's chamberwomen, had heard tales of goings-on involving Catherine in the household of the Duchess of Norfolk and, being strongly averse to her for religious reasons, determined that what he had heard should be made known to the King. To approach him direct on such a matter was out of the question, but he managed to gain access to Archbishop Cranmer and told everything to him. Cranmer, a timid man, also had qualms about a personal confrontation with Henry and instead wrote him a letter setting out what he had been told. This reached Henry on his return from the north on the day after he had held a public service of thanksgiving for his marriage to Catherine; and he was dazed by the revelations it contained. He could not believe that the wife he so adored could have deceived him so grossly. But he ordered an investigation which was carried out thoroughly and brutally with the ready use of torture by his Lord Chancellor, Thomas Wriothesley. Anyone who could throw light on the matter was rigorously examined including the elderly Duchess of Norfolk over whom the death penalty hung for misprision of treason, that is failure to inform or reveal commission of acts of treason. Her stepson, the third Duke of Norfolk and head of the Howard family, was also threatened as he had been instrumental in insinuating Catherine into Henry's attention, but he lost no time in denouncing his niece as a prostitute and abasing himself before Henry and pleading for forgiveness. As a result of the Lord Chancellor's investigations scandalous stories emerged, and not only of Catherine's conduct before marriage but afterwards too. And these could not have been more bitter and humiliating to Henry who was shown to have been duped into marrying one who was no virgin and may have been pre-contracted to another and since then had been often cuckolded. Henry's love for Catherine had been passionate but it was now turned into consuming hatred.

Dereham and Culpeper were soon dispatched, both, in spite of torture, maintaining their innocence; the former on the grounds that he had only been intimate with Catherine before her marriage to the King and therefore could not be guilty of adultery and treason, but he was condemned for 'concealing the evil demeanours of the Queen to the slander of the King and his succession'; Culpeper too denied that he had committed adultery with the queen and he could not be proved to have done so, so he was sentenced for 'intent to commit adultery'. Being of noble descent he was condemned to the comparatively merciful fate of decapitation whereas Dereham, probably the less guilty of the two, had to endure the full horrors of a traitor's death.[2]

Catherine herself was examined by Archbishop Cranmer who

---

[2] Hanging and then while still alive castration and disembowelment.

found her hysterical: 'in such lamentation and heaviness as I never saw no creature so that it would have pitied any man's heart in the world to have looked upon her'. The matter might have been settled quickly and relatively easily if it could be shown that there was a pre-contract of marriage between Catherine and Dereham. In that case her marriage to Henry would have been invalid and she could have been shunted off into the sidelines in disgrace but free from the charge of adultery and treason. But in her despair and frenzy Catherine could not see that this was her only hope (albeit slight) of survival, and she refused to admit to any pre-contract and insisted her marriage to Henry was valid. Later, when she had calmed down, she confessed to misdeeds before marriage and to misleading the King as to her chastity, but strongly denied adultery after marriage. And this was what Cranmer was bent on establishing. As one of the leading lights of the reformists he wanted to bring down the pro-Catholic Howard family, and for this it was necessary that Catherine should be convicted of treason and removed from the scene. But on this she remained firm. In January 1542, however, an Act of Attainder was passed by Parliament in which she was convicted of 'having led an abominable, base, carnal, voluptuous and vicious life before marriage like a common harlot with divers persons, maintaining however the outward appearance of chastity and honesty'. In the face of this Catherine did not attempt to defend herself. She would do no more than confess and bewail her sins and plead for the King's mercy, but this was not to be forthcoming. She was to die. As the charge of adultery was unproved she was condemned for 'violent presumption that she had committed adultery.'

On 10 February 1542 she was taken to the Tower where the grim realisation of her fate overcame her and, according to the governor of the Tower, 'she cried out and tormented herself miserably without ceasing'. Three days later she was beheaded (fortunately adeptly) in the comparative privacy of Tower Green on the same block as had served her cousin Anne Boleyn six years previously. Like her she died proclaiming her innocence and calling down blessings on her husband the King.

CATHERINE PARR (1512–1548)

Sixth Wife of Henry VIII

In looking for a sixth wife Henry VIII did not make the mistake again of choosing an attractive and salacious young girl of sixteen. This time he opted for a twice married widow of thirty-one – sensible, scholarly and virtuous. It was perhaps appropriate that Henry's final wife should be the Queen of England with most husbands – altogether four. It is customary to regard Catherine Parr as a gentle, solicitous character who ministered to Henry in his pain-ridden old age and whose great achievement was that she survived him, although not altogether easily.

Catherine's roots were in the north of England where her grandfather was a large landowner; but her upbringing had been in her mother's county of Northamptonshire. Her father, Sir Thomas Parr, died when she was five, leaving his widow, Lady Maud Parr, to provide for three young children which she did very competently, seeing to it that they were well educated and married advantageously. Catherine was wedded at the age of fourteen to Lord Borough of Gainsborough, a wealthy Lincolnshire landowner, some fifty years older than she and said to be in ill health and 'distracted of memory', who died two years later (the possibility of which may have been borne in mind by Lady Parr in arranging the marriage). Lady Parr herself died at nearly the same time so that Catherine at sixteen was left a widow to look after herself. When she was about twenty she had a proposal of marriage, which she accepted, from John Neville, Lord Latimer, a Yorkshire landowner, twice married before and only twenty years older than herself. She might then have settled down to a comparatively peaceful existence as chatelaine of a Yorkshire castle but this was not to be. In 1536 there was an uprising in northern England known as the Pilgrimage of Grace, in protest against recent religious changes, particularly the closing of the monasteries. This put Lord Latimer in a difficult situation: his first loyalties were to the King but Robert Aske, leader of the movement, coerced him into joining the rebellion. When negotiations between King and rebels occurred, Latimer went down to London to take part in them and later was able to persuade the King that he had only joined the rebellion under duress, and was granted a pardon. But he fell ill soon afterwards and died in 1543, leaving Catherine a wealthy, childless widow of thirty-one.

As such she was bound to attract attention from ambitious men on the make. Before the death of Latimer she had moved down to London and was spending time at court where her sister was in waiting to Catherine Howard. There she came in contact with one who was to be the great love of her life. Thomas Seymour, later Lord Sudeley, was a dashing, irresponsible adventurer of great good looks and charm but of not particularly high birth and said by a contemporary to be 'somewhat empty in matter'. Before coming to the executioner's block at the age of forty-three he had managed to pack a good deal into his life: brother of one queen (Jane Seymour), husband of another (Catherine Parr), and the aspiring lover of a future queen (Elizabeth). He was also, with few qualifications for the post, Lord Admiral of England. That Catherine wanted to marry him is certain, but she became aware that the king was casting eyes in her direction and then that he was considering her as his next wife. As a plain, unspectacular middle-aged woman this might seem improbable, but there were drawbacks to younger more attractive women. By then it had become treason to put forward a maid for the king's consideration who was not 'clean and pure', as also it was even to know of a maid's impurity and not reveal it. Suitable young maids, then, were few in Henry's court and in any case Henry was shying away from them. Safer by far would be a widow whose virginity could not be expected and whose behaviour would be more dependable, and for this role Catherine Parr was ideally suited, and when in time she became aware of the king's feelings towards her she had to make a momentous decision. Should she follow the call of true love and marry Seymour? Or should she yield to sense of duty and devote herself to the ageing and rapidly deteriorating monarch? Certainly at fifty-two he was no romantic figure – diseased, explosively tempered and enormously fat – 'so fat', wrote a contemporary, 'that such a man had never been seen. Three of the biggest men that could be found could get inside his doublet'. What Catherine's motives were in choosing Henry rather than Seymour cannot be known – whether they were worldly with hopes of advantages for herself and her family, or whether they were genuinely public spirited. Whichever, in view of the fates of her predecessors, it was a brave decision.

On 12 July 1543 the five-times married Henry married Catherine Parr at Hampton Court. It was not like some of the king's other marriages a secret affair, but neither was it a spectacular occasion. Previously he had married either for diplomatic reasons or for love; there was always the hope of children being born. This time he was seeking comfort and companionship and there was little likelihood of issue: Henry was then fifty-two and no children had been born to him for five years, and Catherine at thirty-one had had no children in the course of two marriages. It was not Catherine's looks that had attracted Henry; no one at the time ever described her as a beauty; but it was rather her character and intelligence, and Henry became genuinely fond of her, calling her 'his most dearly loved and most entirely beloved wife'. He was grateful for the care she took to relieve his maladies, and he appreciated the influence she had at court where the tone was markedly different from that under Catherine Howard – more elegant, more erudite and more pious. Catherine was not, however, prudish and solemn in the manner of Catherine of Aragon; she had a robust enjoyment of worldly pleasures such as dancing, fine clothes, music and the antics of jesters. Her love of people was evident and this was reciprocated. Her great achievement was establishing a warm and happy relationship with her three step-children and in reconciling the daughters with their father. She even evoked human feelings from the formidably precocious and priggish eight-year-old Prince Edward who wrote to her that she had 'the dearest place in his heart', while at the same time giving her moral uplift, impressing on her that 'the only true consolation is from Heaven and the only real love is the love of God'.

In nearly all ways Henry and Catherine were well suited, and that Henry had complete confidence in her was shown when in 1544 he led an army to invade France and Catherine was appointed regent while he was out of the country. There was, however, one area where dissent and danger might arise. Catherine was interested in the religious controversies of the time where her sympathies lay with the Protestant reformers. She would have liked to see the reforms already carried out extended further. But this was anathema

159

to Henry. He had made himself head of the Church instead of the Pope but otherwise Catholic doctrines were sacrosanct. He was quite prepared to have executed anyone denying his supremacy but he was just as ready to condemn to a gruesome death anyone professing heretical Protestant views. And so it behoved Catherine to tread carefully, and this she did not always do. She loved to discuss religious questions with Henry who, up to a point, encouraged her in this, but it was always on the basis of a teacher–pupil relationship; he did not like her to express her own views too freely and certainly did not expect to be contradicted. Catherine should have been aware of this and should also have been aware of the strong opposition she was stirring up among religious conservatives, fervently loyal to the Church of Rome. These, led by Stephen Gardiner Bishop of Winchester and Lord Chancellor Thomas Wriothesley, came to regard Catherine as a dangerous influence on the King and lost no opportunity to denigrate her, the former going so far as to warn Henry of 'the viper in his bosom'. And this Henry took to heart as he had been angered by Catherine's outspokenness and lack of subservience. 'Ye are become a doctor, Kate,' he told her 'to instruct us, as oftentime we have seen, and not to be instructed by us.' And he felt it was time teach her a lesson. How severe a lesson cannot be known, but he was persuaded to order her arrest and interrogation by the hard and sadistic Wriothesley, and for a time it looked as if she might be going to follow in the footsteps of her predecessors. But Catherine became aware of what was afoot and the effect on her was overwhelming. She suddenly realised the danger she was in and became hysterical. Rushing to the king she abased herself before him and poured out her belief that 'women by their first creation were made subject to men', and that 'women should do all their learning from their husbands', and that she herself 'had special reason to be taught by His Majesty who was a prince of such excellent learning and wisdom'. It seems that Henry was not immediately convinced by these protestations but when Catherine, perhaps disingenuously, went on to say that she had only engaged him in argument to take his mind off his physical sufferings, he relented, and when the Lord Chancellor arrived to carry out her arrest he was dismissed abruptly.

In December 1546 Henry fell seriously ill and it was evident to all around him that he was dying, although no one dared to say

160

so as it was treason to prophesy the death of a monarch. He died finally on 28 February 1547. No English king has ever been such a despot as Henry: he struck fear into all and to his dying day he was condemning to death those close to him for real or imagined offences. Yet in spite of his tyranny and the damage he had wrought he was always held in awe and respect. People could not but admire his dynamism and the ruthless way he achieved his ends. He was lamented for longer and more deeply than many lesser and better men.

Widowed for the third time Catherine found herself in exalted and opulent circumstances. In his will Henry had designated her as first lady in the land above his two daughters, and had lavished wealth on her in recognition of her 'great love, obedience, chastity of life and wisdom'; although she was not for some reason appointed to the Council of Regency. This was dominated at first by the uncle of the nine-year-old Edward VI, Edward Seymour, now Duke of Somerset and Protector of the Kingdom, who distanced himself from Catherine. She was, however, ardently pursued by his younger brother, Thomas. Before her marriage to Henry they had been in love and were intending to marry, but then they had prudently kept their distance as any liaison would have given rise to dangerous gossip. But with Catherine a widow Seymour lost no time in pressing his suit, and she was hustled into a secret marriage probably within four months of the death of Henry. When the marriage became known it was not popular in some quarters, it being felt to be an affront to the memory of Henry VIII for his widow to remarry so soon after his death. There was also considerable mistrust of Thomas Seymour who was believed to have had at one time matrimonial designs on both Princess Mary and Princess Elizabeth. Soon after his marriage to Catherine the latter came to live with them *en famille* and while there Seymour treated her with great familiarity and impropriety, romping rumbustiously and flirting brazenly. At first Catherine made no objection to this, but when she realised that it was more than mere horseplay, she took strong exception and Elizabeth had to go.

Catherine was to outlive Henry VIII by only eighteen months, but during that time – at the age of thirty-five and into her fourth marriage – she surprised everyone, not least herself, by becoming pregnant. On 31 August 1548 she gave birth to a daughter, Mary, but, like Jane Seymour ten years before, she died of puerperal fever soon afterwards. The child should have been a great heiress, but Catherine had left all her wealth to Thomas Seymour, who did not long survive her. His relations with his brother Somerset had long been strained: there was great jealousy between them and frequent quarrels. This came to a climax a year after Catherine's death when Thomas was indicted by his brother of 'covetous, ambitious and seditious behaviour', and was executed by Act of Attainder. This meant that all his property passed to the crown and the unfortunate baby Mary was left penniless. For a time she was cared for, rather grumpily, by Catherine Duchess of Suffolk, second wife of Henry VIII's brother-in-law; but then she vanished from the scene, perhaps a victim of one of the many mortal diseases to which children at that time were prone.

Catherine Parr had been a dutiful and beneficent queen. She deserved well of history and it was unfitting that her interment should be attended by so much disruption and desecration. For a hundred years her coffin lay peacefully if obscurely in the chapel of Sudeley Castle in Gloucestershire where she died, but during the Civil War the castle was ravaged by Roundhead troops and her tomb became lost to sight. A hundred years later, however, it was discovered by the new owner of Sudeley and opened up to reveal that her corpse was in a remarkable state of preservation. The coffin was laid aside but a few years later it was manhandled by a party of drunks and roughly buried upside down. It was not until 1837, nearly three hundred years after her death, that Catherine's remains were finally lodged in an appropriate resting place.

ANNE OF DENMARK (1574–1619)

Wife of James I

Anne of Denmark was not one of England's more renowned queens. She made no great impact on the times in which she lived and is not remembered for any particular achievements. She had no significant influence on her husband and was of little help in the difficulties which confronted him. But James was not an ideal husband – arrogant and cold hearted with unsavoury personal habits and overtly homoerotic. Some wives in these circumstances might have taken lovers but, as far as is known, Anne never did, and although at times perverse and foolish, she was not a serious troublemaker and bore James seven children.

Anne was the daughter of Frederick II of Denmark, an irascible, hyperactive character, for ever involving his country in unsuccessful wars and unnecessary troubles. His wife, Sophia, sturdy and practical, soon realised that life with their father was too disturbing for young children, and Anne and her elder sister, Elizabeth, were sent off to their grandparents in Germany where they were brought up lovingly but strictly.

At an early age both sisters were sought in marriage by many suitors including James VI of Scotland who claimed as of right the elder, but he proved a laggardly lover, according to the English ambassador 'a cold wooer and not hasty of marriage', and this was corroborated by James himself who wrote: 'God is my witness, I could have abstained longer than the weal of my country could have permitted had not my great delay bred in the breasts of many a great jealousy of my inability, as if I were barren stock.' As a result of such indifference Elizabeth was married to a German prince and James had to be content with the younger daughter. This, he felt, was *lèse-majesté* for a reigning monarch but he resigned himself to it as he had heard glowing reports of Anne, and the only other serious contender for his hand at that time was the sister of the French king, Henry IV, who was eight years older than he was and brought with her no dowry, of which at that time he was sorely in need. And so marriage to Anne was agreed and, as was then the custom, this first took place by proxy in the Danish capital, the Earl Marischal of Scotland standing in as bridegroom.

Ten days later Anne set out for Scotland escorted by thirteen warships, but almost at once the fleet ran into exceptionally stormy weather, and Anne became in danger not only from drowning but also from being crushed by a cannon that had broken loose and was running wild. Finally the Danish admiral was forced to turn back and seek refuge in Norway, then part of Denmark. When news of Anne's plight reached James, waiting anxiously in Scotland, he determined to brave the raging waters of the North Sea, join Anne in Norway and bring her to Scotland. The outward voyage was achieved quite easily and James reached Anne in Oslo where a second marriage ceremony took place. For this James put on as impressive a procession as he could manage which included a bizarre dance in the snow by naked negroes who, not surprisingly, died soon afterwards of pneumonia. By then winter was well advanced and, rather than face another turbulent sea crossing, James accepted an invitation from Anne's family to visit Copenhagen. This involved a long, rigorous, overland journey by sledge, but it was accomplished safely and was followed by joyous celebrations including yet another wedding service. Communication at these was a problem as the Danes spoke no English and the Scots no Danish and so conversation had to be in Latin in which not everyone was fluent except James who had a unique mastery of the language which he was not averse to showing off, on one occasion making a speech of three hours to doctors of theology for which, surely deservedly, he was presented with a silver cup. This visit, lasting four months, was a poignant occasion. James was delighted with Anne and it was, perhaps, the only time in his life when he experienced genuine (but not to be lasting) heterosexual emotions; and Anne loved and admired him. It was not until the end of April 1590 that they embarked on the voyage to Scotland which Anne did with great trepidation, her previous experience having filled her with a terror of the sea, so much so that she never visited Denmark again. This time the voyage went smoothly and the royal party reached Leith where an enthusiastic welcome awaited them, and a week later there were splendid scenes in Edinburgh for Anne's coronation which lasted seven hours and consisted mainly of sermons and other perorations in different languages. These must have been a sore trial for Anne but she endured them bravely and made a favourable impression on the crowds that lined the streets by her responsiveness.

Anne must have soon become aware, however, that Scotland at that time was no haven of peace and prosperity. Feuds and bloodshed there had always been, but since the coming of the Reformation these had been intensified by bitter religious strife. There were those, especially in the north of the country, who remained faithful to the Church of Rome. In the south Protestants were in a majority but were divided, Episcopalians favouring a church similar to that set up in England with bishops and the king at its head, and Presbyterians who wanted a more complete break with Rome and were more democratic, acknowledging no authority other than their General Council of Elders, abhorring all bishops and allowing the king no place in the governance of their church, or kirk as it was known.

James had been in the midst of these differences since boyhood. He was crowned king at the age of thirteen months following the deposition of his mother, Mary Queen of Scots and was brought up strictly in the household of the Regent of Scotland, the Earl of Mar. He had been intensively educated and crammed in a way most children would have found unbearable but he was exceptionally intelligent and developed into a considerable scholar. When he came to govern Scotland James was to need all his intelligence. The task of maintaining some sort of equilibrium between the warring factions was formidable, especially as his own position was far from secure. Without a standing army, which he could not afford, he was often at the mercy of overpowerful nobles who bullied and threatened him, and once at the age of sixteen he was kidnapped by one group and held captive for ten months. By steering a devious course, however, he had been able to survive and maintain his position, even to some extent to enhance it. He had had a particularly difficult time in 1587 after the execution of his mother in England. He had no warm feelings for her, having not seen her since he was a baby and having been brought up to regard her as a murderess and adulteress, but the execution of an ex-Queen of France and Scotland had caused outrage and he could not remain silent. He had, however, to be careful to say or do nothing which would give offence to Queen Elizabeth as this would impair his chances of succeeding her on the throne of England to which, as a great-grandson of Henry VII, he was the leading claimant and which he desperately wanted. For it was his life's ambition to escape from the internecine feuds of Scotland and the humiliating poverty of its court to the comparative peace and affluence of England. To this end he took every opportunity to curry favour with Elizabeth who could make or break his chances. But the great Queen was not deceived. 'That false Scottish urchin,' she once declared. 'What can be expected from the double dealing of an urchin as this?'

Anne too was looking forward to a life in England as it had not taken her long to realise that being Queen of Scotland was no bed of roses. It was a life of insecurity and harassment. Many of the plots and counterplots which surrounded her husband extended to her, as her favour was sought and she was drawn, perhaps too easily, into one faction or another. And many times she was in great physical danger. It was not long too before Anne became aware of James's shortcomings as a husband: his homosexual bent was always in evidence and they had few tastes in common. Anne was no intellectual and could muster little interest in the long scholarly dissertations James was for ever imposing on her. And life at court was deadly – either dour and oppressive or crude and licentious. For James was a man of bewildering contrasts – at one moment the academic discoursing learnedly, but at another a foul-mouthed sot, revelling in dirty stories and drinking himself under the table. In none of these activities would Anne participate. Her tastes were lighter and more salubrious: she loved dancing, music and dramatic productions but in these James had little interest. And so they had fallen out of love, and this must surely have been hastened by James's personal habits, some of which were obnoxious: he was unwashed and malodorous and his manners were gauche and uncouth especially at table where he would eat and drink voraciously and messily. Life with such a man, particularly sex life, could hardly have been pleasurable. It was no mean feat that Anne bore him seven children in seventeen years.

Other crosses too Anne had to bear, notably compulsory listening to interminable sermons from Presbyterian ministers who, as well as boring her to death, seemed to delight in criticising her and finding fault with her 'ungodly' lifestyle, particularly her love of fine clothes and dancing which one of them described as 'night waking and balling'. It was perhaps partly because of them that at some time in the 1590s Anne became a secret Roman Catholic. Certainly there was much in Anne's life that was frustrating and disagreeable, and overshadowing everything were financial straits. For Scotland was an impoverished country. Much of its land, though beautiful, was barren and infertile, communications were exiguous and foreign trade limited, being far outstripped by that of England. And nowhere was this poverty more evident than in life at court. Royal residences were bleak and tumbledown. At the time of James's wedding the English ambassador reported that not one of them was in a proper state of repair. Their furnishings too were bare and inadequate, James often having to borrow plate and cutlery for state occasions and sometimes even asking guests to bring their own food and drink. The situation was made worse than it need have been by both James and Anne having no money sense, spending recklessly and accumulating huge debts at exorbitant rates of interest.

During the thirteen years between their marriage and their accession to the throne of England the relationship between James and Anne deteriorated, and this became especially apparent when James was in trouble and Anne failed to give him the support he needed. During their first two years together James was plagued by a wild and dangerous enemy, Francis Hepburn, fifth Earl of Bothwell (nephew of Mary Queen of Scots' third husband), known as 'the wizard earl' because of his dabbling in witchcraft. Under sentence of death because of this, he had escaped from prison and for two years was a constant menace, living as an outlaw and making sudden raids to try and kidnap James and hold him to ransom. He attracted some followers in Scotland partly because of the support he gave the kirk and partly because of his charm and good looks, and it seems that Anne was not entirely immune from these, and did not have the abhorrence she might have had for her husband's arch-enemy.

In 1592 there was great outrage in Scotland at the murder of a handsome, popular Protestant lord, James Stuart Earl of Moray. His murderer was the Catholic George Gordon Earl of Huntly, charismatic but vicious and treacherous. There was a loud outcry for him to be brought to justice, but for some reason James let him off lightly. It seemed as if he might have a secret relationship with him possibly of an erotic nature, and there were those who thought James had colluded in Moray's murder. Among those who called for vengeance was Anne who was believed, with little evidence, to have been in love with Moray.[1]

Another incident in which the King and Queen were at odds was the mysterious Ruthven Affair. In 1600 James was staying in the house of John Ruthven third Earl of Gowrie in Perth. The Ruthvens had a history of disloyalty to the Stuarts: one had taken part in the murder of Rizzio, Mary Stuart's alleged lover, and another had been one of the group who had kidnapped James as a young man and held him captive, so James may well have been mistrustful of the family and during his visit he found himself alone in an upper chamber with the Earl's younger brother, a handsome youth known as the Master of Ruthven (described by a contemporary as 'a learned, sweet and artless young gentleman'). It seems they became involved in a scuffle and James cried out for help and his page rushed to the rescue and at James's behest killed the young man. Subsequently the Earl of Gowrie was also killed. James's story that he had been lured into the house and his life threatened was scarcely credible but it was accepted by many including a convention of clergy, and thanksgiving was offered in churches throughout the country for his safe deliverance. But there were many sceptics and these included Anne who bitterly resented being forced to give up her maid of honour, Beatrix Ruthven, sister of the murdered earl.

These instances of Anne's estrangement from James were significant but not critical. More serious was the action of James following the birth of his and Anne's first child, Prince Henry, when he insisted that the baby be taken from his mother and brought up by the Earl of Mar. This was in accordance with historical precedent, but Anne was outraged and vented her fury both on James and the Earl. But James was adamant: he had fears that unless his heir was well guarded he might become the centre of plots to replace him so that unscrupulous nobles could assume power during the child's minority (as had happened in his own case). It must be

---

[1] His death was commemorated in one of the most haunting of Scottish ballads, *The Bonnie Earl of Moray*:

> He was a braw gallant and he rode at the glove,
> And the bonnie Earl of Moray he was the Queen's love.
> Oh long will his ladye look from the Castle Doune
> Ere she see the Earl of Moray come soundin' through the toon.

doubtful that these fears were justified but James, who had lived in the midst of conspiracies all his life, was convinced they existed and held firm; and in doing so cast a permanent blight on his relationship with Anne.

Queen Elizabeth died on 24 March 1603 and James lost no time in leaving for England to claim his inheritance. The old Queen had never been willing to talk about her successor but her chief minister, Robert Cecil, later Lord Salisbury, had ensured that it would be James, as he could be relied on more than any other claimant to maintain the Protestant establishment. Anne did not accompany James, as she was pregnant and needed more time. She also seems to have thought that this would be a good opportunity to regain possession of Prince Henry, as the Earl of Mar was going with James to England. Her attempts to do so, however, were foiled owing to the obduracy of the Dowager Countess of Mar, and this threw Anne into such paroxysms of rage that she had a miscarriage and became seriously ill. When James heard of this he became alarmed, as to secure his position as King of England he needed a wife in good health with whom he was on good terms. So he ordered the Earl of Mar to return to Scotland and hand Prince Henry over. But Anne was not in an accommodating mood and refused to receive the Prince at the hands of the Earl of Mar whom she detested. Here too James gave way and detailed someone else for the task to which Anne was ready to agree, but at the same time she demanded and was granted the return to her service of Beatrix Ruthven. A notable victory for her.

Anne finally set out for England, accompanied by Prince Henry and a large entourage, two months after James, but she was still disposed to make difficulties. When James sent a number of English ladies and gentlemen to meet her with a view to being appointed to her court she refused to receive them, preferring to retain the ones she already had. But this was too much for James who sent her a sharp rebuke saying that 'he took her continued perversity very heinously.' On her progress south Anne was received royally everywhere. Fetes and feasts and other entertainments awaited her all the way. People with expectations of a place at court hastened to join her train. By the time she had reached Windsor she was accompanied by no less than 250 carriages and 5000 horsemen.

As expected Anne had a particularly warm reception in London. James was ready to overlook her recent tantrums as he needed her by his side especially for the coronation which had to be put off because of an outbreak of plague in the exceptionally hot summer. In this, as in all public ceremonies, Anne was at her best, smiling and waving graciously and obviously enjoying contact with the crowds who lined the streets, in contrast to James who disliked and despised them and showed it.

In politics Anne took no great part. Robert Cecil, who was the King's chief minister for the first nine years of his reign, tended to keep her at a distance, regarding her as 'weak and a tool in the hands of clever and unscrupulous persons'. She was also looked on askance by some because of her friendly feelings towards Spain, then regarded as England's foremost enemy, and for her Roman Catholic tendencies; these were not strong and were kept under wraps but it was noted that at the coronation service she would not take the sacraments according to the rites of the Church of England, and after the Gunpowder Plot Catholicism stirred up strong emotions.

On her way from Scotland Anne had been struck by the wealth she found in England, not only among the aristocracy but in humbler homes too; this was even greater than she expected and spurred her on to ever more lavish extravagance. James saw to it that she was provided generously with funds but she was soon heavily in debt. She spent large sums on clothes and jewellery, but her main expenditure was on court entertainments – recitals, plays (including those of Shakespeare in which he himself performed) but more especially masques – magnificent spectacles incorporating music, poetry, dance, drama and pageantry. On these Anne, with tacit support from James, spent recklessly, and with the help of two men of genius – the poet Ben Jonson and the painter and architect Inigo Jones – produced masques the like of which have never been surpassed. Between them they contrived brilliant scenes – moonlit lakes, sparkling caverns, roaring oceans, inhabited by gods and goddesses and legendary figures of romance, splendidly apparelled and declaiming heroically. Anne herself would often take part in these, sometimes arrayed in rich raiment and priceless jewellery but sometimes more scantily dressed than some thought proper. These productions were immensely popular and invitations to them were eagerly sought. James would attend some of them although they were not among his main interests – he would rather be in the hunting field – but he did not begrudge their tremendous cost.

170

At first, after her arrival in England, Fate smiled on Anne. Life became easier and more enjoyable. She was on better terms with James and her children were a delight to her. Her eldest son, Henry, was developing into a vigorous, gifted youth with wide interests and sound judgement. Her younger son, Charles, had been a frail baby with weak limbs and a speech impediment, but he was showing determination to overcome these handicaps; and her eldest daughter, Elizabeth, was showing signs of beauty and a strong character. There was too the exhilaration of a new environment and the company of talented people anxious to please and be of service.

But this exaltation was not to last. All too soon clouds began to gather. In 1606 when she was no more than thirty-two, Anne gave birth to her seventh child who, like the previous three, died almost immediately, causing her to decide that her child-bearing days were over and that henceforward she would lead a separate life from her husband. At the same time James's standing as a king and hers as queen were undermined by the appearance on the scene of one Robert Carr, a youth of striking good looks but little brainpower with whom James became totally besotted and on whom he proceeded to lavish not only honours and riches but positions of considerable responsibility. Nothing shows more clearly the ambiguities of James's character: a brilliant scholar but unable to see that such a person was incapable of holding high office and finding no indignity in making love to him in public. Anne had long been aware of her husband's proclivities and had come to tolerate them and, much as she disliked Carr, did not seek to oust him, and he was to remain in favour for seven years in which time he became first Viscount Rochester, then Earl of Somerset, and held a number of public offices including that of Lord Chamberlain.

Other troubles and tragedies were to crowd in on Anne. In 1612 she was devastated when Prince Henry at the age of eighteen died of typhoid fever. He had been growing in reputation – active, well intentioned and widely popular; the signs were that he would have been an admirable king. At the same time her daughter, Elizabeth, made what was to prove an ill-fated marriage to a Protestant prince of Germany, Frederick V, Elector of the Palatinate. James had been in favour of this union as it would balance that of his son to a Roman Catholic princess of Spain, but Anne had always been unhappy about it, thinking that her daughter should be wedded to no one less than a crowned head. For a brief time Frederick was to be King of Bohemia before being expelled, bringing to Elizabeth the sobriquet of 'The Winter Queen'.

Besides family troubles Anne could not but be affected by James's increasing difficulties in the political arena. From the death of Lord Salisbury in 1612 and the rise of Carr these had become critical: his debts continued to mount and his relations with Parliament to grow worse. Members were becoming increasingly perturbed by his financial irresponsibility and his policy of friendship with Spain; nor had they any sympathy for his oft proclaimed theory of the divine right of kings – that kings had been created by God and should be obeyed as if they were God. As a result each Parliament that was called became more vocal and more obstructive. Although not closely involved Anne did have strong views on certain subjects: she was in favour of peace with Spain and a Spanish marriage first for her elder and then for her younger son. She also wanted the penal laws against Roman Catholics to be mitigated; but although herself a Catholic, she did not press this too hard, feeling that it would raise a storm and do more harm than good.

The ascendancy of Robert Carr (Earl of Somerset) was to last longer than expected, but it was to end in a blaze of scandal when he and his wife, the one time Countess of Essex, were arraigned for murder in the Tower of London by the poisoning of Sir Thomas Overbury, who had once been Carr's close friend and mentor. At their trial they were induced to plead guilty, confident that the sentence of death would be commuted by the King, as indeed it was, but imprisonment in the Tower and the end of Carr's career could not be avoided.

Already, before Somerset's downfall, a new favourite had appeared on the scene. George Villiers (later Duke of Buckingham) like Somerset owed his advancement entirely to his good looks, but he was cleverer and even more ambitious and with a grace and charm that was to insinuate him into the love not only of James but also in time of Charles I. He had all the qualities James lacked – good looks, elegance and courage. It could not be expected that Anne would have any love for him, but she regarded him as an improvement on Somerset and accepted that she had to tolerate him.

From her early thirties Anne had been beset by ill health: first by gout and arthritis, later by dropsy and a haemorrhage of the lungs. In her last years she led a retiring life but was not entirely

172

quiescent. She still had influence. A shrewd assessment of her was made by the Venetian ambassador: 'Of a lively humour, rather good looking and still more gracious, particularly to those who fall in with her humour, but she is terrible proud and intolerable to those she dislikes.'

Among those for whom she felt pity and sought to help was the old Elizabethan sea dog, Sir Walter Raleigh. Early in James's reign he had been convicted unjustly of conspiring to dethrone James in favour of his cousin, Arabella Stuart. He had been condemned to death but James had shrunk from carrying out the sentence on one so popular. He was imprisoned in the Tower for fourteen years when he was allowed out to go and find a gold mine in South America, but there was a strict condition that he must not fall foul of the Spaniards. This, perhaps inevitably, he did and on his return James, who was in the midst of a difficult negotiation with Spain concerning the marriage of his son to the Infanta, yielded to the demands of the Spanish ambassador for his execution. In spite of differing strongly with him on some subjects, Anne had always had an admiration for Raleigh and used to visit him in the Tower where he was allowed to carry out scientific experiments and Anne believed that the cordials he gave her did her more good than the ministrations of the royal doctors (which, as these included sawing wood and applying the innards of newly killed chickens to affected parts, may well have been true). She had been appalled when James had granted Raleigh's estates to the Earl of Somerset and later did all she could to save his life, although unavailingly. Another person, of a very different sort, whom Anne tried to help was the Red Indian Princess Pocahontas who had saved the life of Captain John Smith, later president of Virginia, and had then married another English settler who deserted her and whom she followed to England in the vain hopes of being reunited with him. In spite of the Queen's solicitude, however, she was to die of cold before returning to America.

Anne died in 1619 at the age of forty-five. There was some confusion before her death partly because she could not be brought to make a will (and she had considerable property) and partly because of her religious status. She had been brought up a Lutheran and at some point had converted to Roman Catholicism but had shown no great zeal for the faith and had usually been ready to observe the outward forms of the Church of England. On her deathbed, the Archbishop of Canterbury had been concerned that she should declare her adherence to the established church, which she did but not clearly.

Anne has not always been treated kindly by posterity. D.H. Willson in his masterly biography of James I (Cape 1956) wrote of her that she was 'incurably frivolous and empty-headed. She possessed high spirits and a playful sprightliness, but these qualities were shallow and vacuous, and they must have easily palled. Her love for gaiety and dancing, for games, masques and pageants, was childish rather than courtly.' But this is surely a harsh judgement. Matrimonially she trod a thorny path which she may not have done unerringly but not disastrously. On the whole James was a considerate husband but not an easy or an attractive one. And not every wife would have been so forbearing and tolerant of her husband's homosexuality. Anne's attitude to the arts too is underrated; the poet Ben Jonson and the architect Inigo Jones owed much to her patronage. Certainly she was no intellectual nor was she devout; her religious beliefs did not run deep. But could not this be preferable to intolerant bigotry? And she did have merits. She was a good mother adored by her children and the tone of her court was higher than that of some queens; and her rapport with ordinary people was warm and sincere and was reciprocated; whenever she appeared in public she invariably had an enthusiastic reception.

When Anne died her body was embalmed and lay in state in a royal palace until enough money could be found for her funeral. When this did at length take place it was a grand one, and perhaps not altogether undeserved.

HENRIETTA MARIA (1609–1669)

Wife of Charles I

Apart from Margaret of Anjou no Queen Consort has had such an adventurous and dangerous life as Henrietta Maria. Like Margaret she is controversial. There are those who allege that she dominated a weak and wavering husband, and it was her influence more than any other that led to civil war and ultimate disaster. But to others she was a loyal and courageous wife totally dedicated to Charles for whom she was ready to make any sacrifice. Certainly she was a hawk rather than a dove and her advice was always full-blooded and sometimes misguided; but not all her husband's mistakes can be ascribed to her. Her sufferings on his behalf were gruelling and no one can doubt her sincerity when she wrote to him: 'There is nothing in the world, no trouble, which shall hinder me from serving you and loving you above everything in the world.'

Henrietta Maria was the daughter of one of France's most famous kings, Henry IV or Henry of Navarre as he was known. His great achievement was to bring some measure of unity to the country after years of civil and religious strife. He was a great warrior and an astute statesman, also a man of charm and humour. His religious views were pragmatic, changing from Catholic to Protestant (Huguenot) and then, when it was evident that he could only become King of France if he was a Catholic, changing back, remarking, so it was said, that 'Paris is worth a mass.' Henry was also a man of great promiscuity – with two wives, innumerable mistresses, six legitimate children and at least eight bastards. His first marriage had been loveless and childless, and his second was hardly romantic. Marie de Medici, massive and formidable, was the daughter of a Florentine banking family to whom Henry was deeply in debt; she was to bear him six children of whom Henrietta (as she will henceforth be known) was the youngest. Her safe delivery in 1609 seems to have made little impression on him; he was playing cards when the news was brought to him and he did

175

not consider it necessary to break off; the birth of a third daughter was no great matter and he had more important things on his mind. At the time he was about to go to war with Austria over who was to succeed to the German principality of Cleves. Before he set off Marie de Medici was insisting that she should have a formal (and somewhat belated) coronation so that in the event of his death she would have the principal right to the regency during his eldest son's minority. To this Henry agreed in spite of a prophecy that the ceremony would be followed immediately by his own decease, which did actually occur. For on the following day he was assassinated by a fanatical friar with an obsession to rid France of a heretical king.

Henrietta was six months old at the time of her father's death, and so her upbringing was to be entirely in the hands of her mother who, uneducated herself, saw no reason for her daughter to be subject to more than a narrow, strict Catholic regimen. When Henrietta was no more than ten her mother was already laying plans for a prestigious marriage. Charles Prince of Wales, heir to the throne of England, was always in her sights. Charming, handsome and of impeccable reputation, he would have been a splendid match for a younger daughter, but he was not for a time available as he was set on marriage to the Spanish Infanta, Donna Maria. In this he had the support of his father, James I and, perhaps more significantly of his favourite, the Marquess (as then he was) of Buckingham.

In pursuance of this, the young Prince Charles, accompanied by the Duke of Buckingham, made an unconventional journey to Spain, travelling across Europe incognito as Thomas and John Smith. The Spanish government was surprised at their arrival but received them courteously and entered into negotiations about a marriage treaty, but these soon ran into difficulties. At heart the King of Spain and the Infanta herself were uneasy about a marriage to a Protestant and demanded rigorous terms. In his eagerness Charles agreed to these and a betrothal was formally agreed, but was not to last. The strongly Protestant English Parliament would never agree to it, and soon after the Prince's return the betrothal was broken off. A few months later the two countries were at war.

The rupture with Spain meant that England was in need of an ally in Europe and the country most likely to support her was France, whose chief minister, Cardinal Richelieu, was seeking to

176

contain the power of Spain and Austria. And so the matter was raised of a marriage between Charles and Louis XIII's youngest sister, Henrietta. In 1624 a special 'wooing ambassador' was dispatched to France to pave the way for a betrothal. Lord Kensington (later Lord Holland) was ideally suited for this post – eloquent, romantic and a ladies' man of no mean repute, he had no difficulty in convincing Henrietta and her overpowering mother of Charles's virtues, notably his good looks and abstemiousness. At the same time he sent Charles and his father glowing accounts of Henrietta, describing her as 'the loveliest creature in France and the sweetest thing in nature ... for Beauty and Goodness an Angel.' But here Lord Kensington allowed himself to be carried away for Henrietta was no great beauty; vivacity and charm she might have had but not classical looks. The way was then set for a betrothal but hard bargaining lay ahead, for the French were to prove as intractable as the Spanish in drawing up a marriage treaty. They too envisaged England being converted to Catholicism; and stipulated that all Catholics in England should be set free; moreover that Henrietta should be accompanied by no less than twenty-eight priests, deacons and chaplains and that all her personal staff should be French Roman Catholics. It was also required that her children by the marriage should be in her sole charge until they were fourteen years of age. To all of this Charles was ready to agree and so was James I, although he had given his word to Parliament that the marriage treaty would contain nothing contrary to the laws of England. He well knew that some of the terms would cause outrage, and so these were contained in a secret document which in years ahead was to cause trouble.

In 1625, however, difficulties were sorted out and soon after the death of James I, Charles and Henrietta were married first by proxy outside the West Door of Notre Dame Cathedral, no heretics being allowed inside. Charles was to have been represented by the Duke of Buckingham but he had been delayed by obsequies for James I and his place was taken by the French Duke of Chevreuse who pronounced Charles's vows for him.

Soon afterwards Henrietta set out for England with a retinue of some 200 attendants. Her brother, the King of France, and her domineering mother accompanied her for part of the way, but did not complete the journey to the coast. In taking her leave Marie de Medici gave her daughter a long highly charged letter setting out the duties that lay ahead of her in England – how she must protect and succour all English Roman Catholics, how she must do everything in her power to convert the heretics, and in particular to pray daily that her husband the king might see the error of his ways and return to the faith for which his grandmother, Mary Queen of Scots, had been martyred. It was, then, as much a missionary as a bride that Henrietta arrived in England in the summer of 1625.

At the time she was no more than sixteen and the expectations of her were clearly unrealistic; in the fevered and embittered religious strife of that time she was always likely to do more harm than good. At first everything went wrong: she had an exceptionally rough crossing which prostrated her with seasickness and delayed her arrival so that Charles was not there to greet her and she was forced to find what comfort she could in the bleak and inhospitable portals of Dover Castle. When Charles arrived next morning there was awkwardness and constraint between them and discord about such minor matters as to who should ride in which coach on the drive to London and whether English or French courtiers should have precedence. Their arrival in London too was not what it might have been, as the city was racked with plague and it was necessary to proceed up river by barge rather than through brightly decorated but fever-infested streets.

These troubles were to continue for some time. Henrietta was ill at ease in England, showing little willingness to adapt to English ways or even to learn the language, and kept herself to her French entourage, refusing to include in her court any English men or women. And her relations with Charles remained cool and distant; understandably she resented his subservience to Buckingham whose attitude to her was disdainful and patronising. She was not prepared to be lectured on her duties as a queen by such a man. After a year the situation became so taut that Charles peremptorily ordered nearly all her French attendants to leave the country which caused her greater distress, and her position became even more lonely and vulnerable in the following year when England and France drifted into an unnecessary war.

But then suddenly the situation improved. In 1628 Buckingham was assassinated by a discontented army officer and, freed from his dominion, Charles discovered a love for Henrietta. Soon afterwards she became pregnant and, although the baby died immediately, she declared that in Charles's love she was the happiest of women. And in the following year another baby was born – a particularly sturdy one, the future Charles II – and six more in rapid succession.

If by 1629 Charles had found domestic bliss there was no respite for him on the political front. Relations with Parliament were as stormy as ever. Like his father he believed fervently in the divine right of kings, regarding Parliament as no more than an advisory body who should assent to his wishes as if they came from God. But more and more Parliament was countering these claims and asserting its right to have a say in government policy and the appointment of ministers. This it was able to do by keeping a tight control of the King's finances. For the King could no longer 'live of his own'. He could not do without grants from Parliament and this was especially the case in time of war when expenditure rocketed, and Parliament was not above urging the King into war so as to increase its hold on him. In the early years of his reign Charles under the aegis of Buckingham was too easily drawn into wars and so became desperate for Parliamentary grants which were usually withheld until 'grievances' had been redressed. And these included, among others, the 'popish' practices of Queen Henrietta who practised her religion openly and avowedly, letting into her services any Roman Catholic who might want to attend and not holding back from making converts. To a predominantly Puritan Parliament this was a matter of grave concern and was one of the reasons for increasingly acrimonious relations with the King. These came to a head in 1629 when Charles, as was his right, dissolved Parliament; but certain members used force to prevent the Speaker from leaving until certain resolutions had been passed denouncing the King's religious policy and his raising of unlawful taxes.

This high-handed and illegal act was followed by eleven years of Charles's so-called 'personal rule' when no Parliament was called. For Henrietta this was an interlude of calm and contentment – between the tension and discord of the first years and the calamities that were to follow. She lived in the love of her husband while her family increased steadily; she was also able to indulge her taste for magnificent masques as well as for more quirky entertainments involving dwarves and wild animals. Charles too had his delights, including hunting and playing tennis and above all collecting works of art in which he showed exceptional discernment, perhaps more than any other English monarch.

Although on the surface there might seem to be peace and prosperity, trouble was stirring. Charles could only survive by imposing taxes of dubious legality, notably Ship Money, and these caused deep resentment and lost him many friends.[1] His religious policy too was unpopular: the high Anglicanism practised by himself and his domineering Archbishop of Canterbury, William Laud, caused great offence to the Puritans as also did the licence allowed illegally to Henrietta and English Catholics. The number of the Queen's Catholic attendants was forever increasing and in 1636 a special Papist envoy was sent to England, officially to minister to English Catholics but also to work covertly for the restoration of the Roman Church. The official reception of such an envoy, the first since the Reformation, inevitably aroused suspicion and not only among Puritans. Even Archbishop Laud became uneasy. 'I conceive it most true,' he wrote at the time 'that the party of the Queen grows very strong, and I fear some consequences of it very much.' It must be doubtful that Henrietta ever sought the re-establishment of the Roman Catholic church; it is likely that she sought no more than freedom of worship and the abolition of penal laws, but she was always suspected of more sinister designs.

The end of Charles's 'personal rule' was heralded by the fateful decision of himself and Laud to impose on Scotland by law the use of the English prayer book. This stirred up a hornets' nest, for such a book was anathema to the Presbyterian Scots who rose in fury to resist it. In 1638 a National Covenant was drawn up signed by hundreds of thousands pledging themselves to 'defend the true reformed religion to the utmost of their power against the errors, corruption and all innovations which had no warrant in the word of God.' This great national movement Charles was unable to resist: not only did it become dominant in Scotland but an army of Covenanters then invaded England and Charles with only a scanty standing army was helpless in face of them, and it became necessary to pay them large subsidies to prevent them from invading further south. In this dire emergency Charles on the advice of his chief minister, the Earl of Strafford, felt he had no option but to call a Parliament. After eleven years there was doubt as to what

---

[1] Ship Money was originally imposed on the Cinque Ports for the upkeep of the navy but was extended by Charles to the rest of the country. John Hampden, a Buckinghamshire squire, refused to pay it and his trial became a *cause celèbre*.

would be the nature of such a body, but it soon proved as refractory as its predecessors; under a new leader, John Pym, a man of great determination and strength of character, it showed no inclination to let Charles 'off the hook' without redress of grievances. The so-called 'Short Parliament' was soon dissolved but its successor the 'Long Parliament' was to sit on and off for the next twenty years.

During the tumultuous period leading to civil war which saw, among other things, the dominance of Parliament, the execution of Strafford, frenzied negotiations with the Scots, a barbarous rebellion in Ireland and at times mob rule in London, Henrietta was in the thick of the action striving, like Lady Macbeth, to instil courage and resolution into a wavering husband and belabouring him with advice which was always vehement if often ill-conceived. Always she was in favour of a hard line and opposed to any concessions, and this was widely known so that there were death threats and talk of impeachment which prompted Charles into his rash and abortive attempt to arrest five leading members of Parliament. In this, as always, he hesitated but Henrietta was remorseless. 'Go, you poltroon,' she was said to have shouted at him. 'Go and pull those rogues out by the ears, or never see my face again.' It was not the first or last time she was to use such threats.

In the great crisis that was to engulf the English monarchy Charles was not the man for the part. A strong and ruthless tyrant might have prevailed, but Charles was not cast in that mould. As a child he had been a weakling, unable to walk properly for a long time, with a nervous stammer and woefully short of self-confidence. To some extent he had been able to overcome these disabilities but he was never a natural leader: he hesitated and prevaricated and was all too often under the domination of a stronger personality, not least his wife.

By 1642 civil war had become imminent. Both sides were preparing for it and no one more strenuously than Henrietta: she had been stirring up support wherever she could – from English Catholics, the King of France, the Pope – and these activities had been noticed so that she had come to be seen by the leaders of Parliament as the driving force behind the King and the chief barrier to an agreement with him. In February 1642 Parliament presented to the King a declaration that: 'Priests, Jesuits and Papists have powerful influence upon the Queen who is permitted to

181

intermeddle with great affairs of state.' They demanded the dismissal of all priests and Catholics from her employment which she refused. At the same time popular frenzy was being whipped up by wild reports that she was secretly plotting an invasion by French and Irish troops to overthrow Parliament. As a result her life became seriously endangered and Charles wanted her for the time being to seek safety abroad. This she was reluctant to do but for the sake of Charles's peace of mind she agreed. In the previous year her daughter, Princess Mary, had been married (at the age of six) to the son and heir of the Prince of Orange and he was urging that she be sent to Holland as soon as possible to become acquainted with Dutch ways and to learn the Dutch language. This was agreed and Henrietta decided to go with her but not so much with the idea of giving maternal support as in mustering military aid for her husband. She therefore took with her a quantity of crown jewels and plate to be turned into armaments. But this proved difficult: Dutch merchants were not convinced that the jewellery was hers to sell and so they drove a hard bargain. Arms dealers too were unaccommodating, realising the urgency of her needs; in the words of Henrietta 'keeping their foot on our throat'. And this was not the end of the story, as the problem then arose as to how the arms were to be transported to England; for this it was necessary to run the gauntlet of the English navy which had declared for Parliament and was ready to intercept any shipments. The amount of military supplies that reached England cannot be known, but it must be doubtful if it was significant.

Henrietta had arrived in Holland with a small but rather strange retinue which included her constant companion, Henry Jermyn (believed by some, probably erroneously, to be her lover) as well as her pet dwarf, Geoffrey Hudson, to keep her amused. She must have soon become aware that she was not welcome. She had been openly opposed to the marriage of her daughter and the Dutch royal family was embarrassed by her presence, while the stern Calvinist burghers of the States General felt little favour towards a Catholic queen, and there was much sympathy for the English Puritans and a wish not to antagonise the English Parliament which seemed to be gaining the upper hand at that time. During the year she was in Holland Henrietta kept in touch with Charles by letters in a pre-arranged code as there was danger of these falling into the hands of Parliament. The tone of her letters was always bracing and imperative, for ever urging him to remain firm and to take immediate and decisive action. 'You are beginning again your old game of yielding everything,' she chided him and stated bluntly that if he came to an agreement with parliamentary leaders without her consent she would not return to him but would withdraw to a nunnery.

In early 1643 Henrietta decided that, whatever the dangers, she must return to England; she was longing to see her children again and disturbing reports were reaching her of Charles coming to a negotiated settlement with the leaders of Parliament, and she felt she must be with him to strengthen his resolve. Besides, money for her personal expenses was running out and she was living close to penury. And so in February, to the relief of her Dutch hosts, she set sail with a small fleet, some carrying her entourage and some armaments. But her voyage, like most she undertook, ran into trouble. In order to avoid the Parliamentary navy it was deemed safest to land in the north of England, but when in sight of land the ships were caught in an exceptionally violent storm and because of contrary winds had to turn back. For nine days the Queen and her party were buffeted remorselessly and were lucky to escape with their lives. Back in Holland she might have been expected to spend some time in recuperation, but she insisted on setting out again at once on what was to be an epic odyssey during which she was nearly drowned, was bombarded by artillery, marched at the head of an army from York to Oxford, gave birth to a baby, narrowly avoided capture by enemy forces and then after another nightmarish sea crossing reached France and was installed in some state in Paris in the Louvre.

Henrietta's second crossing from Holland was mild and she was able to land safely on the Yorkshire coast near the village of Bridlington, but soon afterwards she came under fire in the cottage where she was staying from a Parliamentary ship which had been tracking her, and once again she came close to death.

Most of the north of England at that time was in the hands of the Royalists, and she was soon able to make contact with their commander, the Duke of Newcastle, in York. She was wanting to proceed southwards at once to join forces with Charles in Oxford, but this was not possible as enemy forces lay in between and she could not go without an adequate army to protect her and this was not immediately available as there were Parliamentary strongholds in the north, notably Leeds and Hull, which were still holding out and which had to be contained. And so it was not until 4 June that Henrietta was able to set out with a sizeable force and herself at its head. During the march she insisted on sharing the hardships and dangers of the soldiers under her and the journey was completed without having to give battle. On 12 July she met up with her husband in the village of Kineton near to the battlefield of Edgehill. From there they went on to Oxford where Henrietta was to stay for the next nine months, hospitably entertained by the University.

Great as was the king's joy at the arrival of his wife, this was not to be an unmixed blessing for the Royalist cause: her strong and abrasive views stirred up divisions in their ranks and her influence on the King was not altogether beneficial. In 1643 there was a possibility that he might come to terms with Parliament, but not while Henrietta was there. She remained as steadfast as ever in opposing all concessions and, as nearly always, Charles submitted to her. Henrietta might have stayed with Charles to the end, but it became necessary for her to leave as she found that she had become pregnant. Oxford by then was under threat of a siege and this she could not endure in her condition. And so in April 1644 she set out with a few companions (including the ever-present Jermyn and the dwarf Geoffrey Hudson) aiming westwards in the hope of finding a ship to take her to France. By June she had reached Exeter where she gave birth to a daughter, Henrietta Anne. She could not, however, afford to linger as Roundhead forces were closing in and so, leaving her new-born baby in the care of a trusted friend (Lady Anne Dalkeith) she moved on a few days later into Cornwall where enemy forces were searching for her. At one stage she found herself crouching in a ditch overhearing her pursuers talking among themselves about the rewards they might expect in the event of her capture.

Eventually, however, she was able to reach Falmouth where she boarded a Flemish ship to take her to France. But still her adventures were not at an end as a Parliamentary ship gave chase and opened fire and there was danger that her ship might be captured in which case she ordered the captain to blow the ship up rather than let her fall into the hands of the enemy. But this did not become necessary. The pursuit was shaken off and she and her party were able to scramble ashore on the coast of Brittany where they were at first regarded with some suspicion; but when it became known who she was – a princess of France and a daughter of the great Henry IV – she was given royal treatment. She was first taken off to a famous spa to recover her health which was indeed necessary as since she had left Oxford she had been racked with pain, partly because of her pregnancy and partly because of a seizure of paralysis. Someone who saw her just before she left England described her as 'the woefullest spectacle my eyes yet ever looked on.' At the time she was no more than thirty-five and few people expected her to live much longer. But as was to happen, twenty-five years of life lay ahead of her.

The French government at that time was headed by the Queen Dowager known as Anne of Austria who was acting as regent for her six-year-old son, Louis XIV; but effective power lay with her chief minister, Cardinal Mazarin who had succeeded Richelieu in 1642. Anne extended generous hospitality to her sister-in-law, providing her with a residence (the Louvre), courtiers and an ample income. She also provided the best medical care so that Henrietta's health began to revive, although it was never to be robust. As soon as she was able she was devoting all her energies to the relief of her husband, drumming up support from any likely quarter and cutting down her expenses to a minimum so as to send him as much money as possible. Since she left England his fortunes had declined disastrously: in 1644 a royalist army had been heavily defeated in the north of England at the battle of Marston Moor and in the following year the *coup de grâce* had been delivered at the battle of Naseby. For a time Charles continued to hold out, but in 1646 he left Oxford secretly and surrendered to the Scots between whom and the English Parliament differences were beginning to arise.

Henrietta was convinced that Charles could only be saved by an invasion of a foreign power, and this she was trying hard to bring about. France was her main hope but Mazarin, although sympathetic, would afford no practical help. There were other calls on French troops at that time and besides it suited French interests that England should be embroiled in civil war as it kept her out of European affairs and a possible alliance with France's main enemy, Spain. Henrietta also had hopes from Holland as her daughter, Mary, was wedded to the Prince of Orange, but he too was unable to do much. There was a possibility at one time that Irish troops might be brought over, backed by the Pope in return for terms

185

favourable to Roman Catholics, but agreement could not be reached on this. A more likely prospect was an invasion from Scotland. After the surrender of the King to their forces Scottish leaders had tried to drive a hard bargain, enjoining him to sign the National Covenant and to agree to the setting up of Presbyterianism in England, but on this Charles was obdurate; he would not agree to the abolition of the episcopacy. An impasse being reached, the Scots in consideration of a large sum of money handed Charles over to Parliament.

At the time a rift was growing ever wider between Parliament, which was primarily Presbyterian, and Cromwell's New Model Army whose members were of a more extreme form of Puritanism known as Independent. Now the civil war seemed to be over, Parliament wanted to disband the army, but the army was unwilling to go, especially as there were large arrears in their pay. More and more the army chiefs were asserting their authority. In 1647 a force was dispatched to take possession of the King and put him under the control of the army rather than that of Parliament; and in the following year a force under a Colonel Pride intercepted members arriving at the Houses of Parliament and only let through those deemed to be favourable to the interests of the army (known to history as 'Pride's Purge').

The army generals under Cromwell then tried to come to terms with Charles who seemed responsive and ready to make concessions, but all the time he was dissembling and carrying on secret correspondence with the Scots, English Royalists and with Henrietta who as always was urging him to stand firm and threatening not to return to England if he gave way too much. He also contrived to escape from custody in Hampton Court and fled to the Isle of Wight where he hoped to rally support, but this was not forthcoming and he was imprisoned in more severe conditions in Carisbrooke Castle. Exasperated by this double dealing Cromwell came to the conclusion that no pact with Charles was possible as he could not be relied on keep to his word, and furthermore that his secret dealings with foreign powers amounted to treason for which he should be brought to trial and if found guilty, put to death, and this was to be done openly; he was not to be assassinated secretly like Edward II and Richard II but executed in public for all to see and held up as a warning for all future kings and governors. And so a revolutionary tribunal was set up to try him and pass judgement.

This had no kind of legal or historical authority and from the first Charles refused to take any part in its proceedings and seemed unmoved by the sentence of death. The dignity and courage with which he faced his execution struck awe into all who witnessed it, and when his severed head was held up for the crowd to see there was, according to one present, 'such a groan as I never heard before and desire I may never hear again.' Far from being an end to the monarchy as the 'Saints' of Cromwell's army hoped, Charles's execution made certain its revival.

When the news of Charles's execution was broken to Henrietta she was so overcome that for a time she was unable to speak. She had never envisaged the possibility of such an act. In time, however, she was to recover and was devoting herself with her usual zeal to the fortunes of her eldest son, already regarded by Royalists as Charles II. But the following years were to be hard times for her. As well as the shock she had sustained her health continued poor (toxic rash, abscesses and insomnia among other afflictions) and she also found herself in the middle of a civil war in France known as the *Fronde* in which for a time Paris was overrun by rebels and she had to flee from the city, and her allowance went unpaid so that she was living in penury and having to sell her jewellery.

Meanwhile Cromwell and his 'Ironsides' were consolidating their position. In 1650 they defeated the Scots, by then their enemy, at the battle of Dunbar, and they then crossed to Ireland and wreaked terrible vengeance on Irish Catholic rebels massacring them mercilessly at Drogheda and Wexford. In 1651 Prince Charles, grasping at any straw, made a pact with the Scots whereby he pretended to convert to Presbyterianism, signed the National Covenant and led a Scottish army into England which at first had some success, reaching as far as Worcester, but then it was scattered by the Ironsides, and Charles, after a narrow and dramatic escape, arrived back in France, once again a penniless refugee.

By then Henrietta had been reunited with her other children apart from Princess Elizabeth who had died in England in 1650 and Princess Mary who was married to the Prince of Orange; but James Duke of York (later James II), Henry Duke of Gloucester and Henrietta Anne (she who was born in such hazardous circumstances in Exeter in 1642) had been able to leave England and join their mother. But they did not all bring her joy. Charles, whom she expected to have under her thumb, was tending to go his own way with little heed of her advice and with his own set of advisors led by Edward Hyde (later Lord Clarendon), a strong Protestant whom Henrietta particularly disliked, and in the disputes between them James, her second son, usually sided with his elder brother. Prince Henry of Gloucester, a bright and attractive youth of twelve, made a great impression when he arrived in Paris but then came under pressure from his mother to be brought up a Catholic which he resisted and Henrietta in a fury turned him out of the house so that he had to take refuge with his elder brothers. Only Henrietta Anne gave her mother no anguish, content with a Catholic upbringing and ready for the time being to accede to her mother's wishes.

In the physical and mental stress Henrietta suffered during these years she ever more sought comfort from religion. She had always spent much time in religious houses and in 1650 she founded one of her own, Chaillot in the outskirts of Paris in a house that had once seen some grandeur but had become run down and was reputed to be of ill fame. Her idea was that it should be for the benefit of women of gentle birth who might find it difficult to adjust to the full rigours of monastic life, but the nuns who were brought in as founder members found their surroundings inadequately austere and insisted on sleeping in the attics until other rooms had been refashioned.

Henrietta was always confident that one day her son Charles would return to the throne of his ancestors and she never ceased to strive for it. But as the 1650s unfolded prospects of this happening seemed as remote as ever. England remained firmly in the grips of a military dictatorship. In 1653 Cromwell was appointed Lord Protector with powers far exceeding any monarch. Already by then, as well as executing the King, he had abolished the House of Lords, disestablished the Church of England and dismissed judges. He had also attempted to reduce the House of Commons to a group of yes-men, but here he had not been entirely successful; in five years he had summoned four parliaments, some of which had been elected and some nominated, but they had all proved refractory in some way and had soon been dismissed. Britain had never before or since experienced such tyranny; for in addition to being deprived of their rights people were subjected to Puritan morality; all kinds of amusement were frowned on, drinking and gambling prohibited, alehouses and theatres closed, even maypoles cut down; bear baiting and cock fighting too were banned but not because of the suffering caused to the animals but of the enjoyment to the spectators. Never has there been such interference in the lives of ordinary people. Nearly all classes – Royalists, Presbyterians, Catholics, merchants, farmers – groaned under the yoke, but they were held down. Both at home and abroad the Ironsides, as the New Model Army had come to be called, seemed invincible.

Of course such a situation could not be permanent and change when it came was likely to be extreme. The restoration of the monarchy, however, did not come suddenly. It began with the death of Cromwell in September 1658. This was followed by an interlude in which his son, Richard, succeeded him as Lord Protector, but this did not last long as it soon became evident that he was incapable of stepping into his father's shoes. Then came a period in which the Army generals jostled for power and this was significant: so long as the Army was united, the country remained in its power, but once there were divisions in its ranks there was hope of liberation. In the end the general who prevailed over the others was the commander of the army in Scotland. General George Monk was a soldier of fortune who had fought on both sides during the Civil War on land and at sea. He was astute, pragmatic and unencumbered with too much religion. He believed in keeping his cards close to his chest and keeping his options open, but on 1 January 1660 he committed himself: contrary to the orders of the Central Council he led his army across the Coldstream into England and began his march on London. When he arrived opposition was dispersed and this humbly born man of Devon found himself master of the situation – in effect arbiter of the country's destiny. As always he proceeded cautiously, but he had become convinced during his march from Scotland that it was the overwhelming wish of most people to see an end to the rule of the so-called 'Saints' and a return to old ways including the restoration of the monarchy. But he did not hurry. The first step was to call a free Parliament which was named a Convention as it had not been summoned by a sovereign; and this body lost no time in proclaiming Charles II King and inviting him to return. And so on 25 May 1660 Charles landed in England and amid scenes of wildest rejoicing progressed to London.

Henrietta was of course overjoyed by this turn of events. Her great hopes had come to pass; her son was King of England, her days of penurious exile were over and she could hope that all her family would now be reunited 'and no longer vagabonds.' She did not, however, immediately join her son in London. She had other business to attend to, notably the betrothal of her youngest daughter, Henrietta Anne or *Minette* ('Little puss') as she was known whose matrimonial prospects had been greatly enhanced by her brother's enthronement. Before she had been of little account and had been turned down by several princes, but as sister of a reigning monarch she was of much greater consequence. She might even have landed Louis XIV but he had recently been wedded to an uninspiring Spanish princess, Maria Theresa. There was, however, his younger brother, Philippe, known as 'Monsieur' and soon to be created Duke of Orléans – a sullen, reclusive character of uncertain sexuality – but his mother, Anne of Austria, was strongly in favour of his marriage to Minette and he himself (for the moment) was said to be madly in love with her. Such a marriage would make Minette the third lady in France with the title of 'Madame' and so Henrietta too did all she could to promote it, and it was soon arranged.

1660 was not, however, to be altogether an *annus mirabilis* for Henrietta. In September her youngest son, Henry Duke of Gloucester, died of smallpox, and she was greatly upset, even though she had not become reconciled to him after expelling him from her household six years before. At the same time there was another disaster: her second son, James Duke of York, felt himself obliged to go through with a secret marriage to one of his mistresses, Anne Hyde, who had become pregnant by him. Henrietta was outraged by this; it was not just that her son was marrying a commoner but the daughter of Charles's hated minister, Edward Hyde, and for a time she vowed she would have no contact with her daughter-in-law.

It was not until November that Henrietta came to England. Her entry into London was marked by celebrations – bonfires were lit and church bells rung – although Samuel Pepys, diarist and clerk of the King's ships, wrote that these were somewhat low-key and his impression was that her return 'do please but very few,' and when later he was able to catch sight of her he wrote that she was 'a very little plain old woman and nothing in her presence in any respect nor garb than any other woman.' Henrietta had not intended to stay long in England as it was necessary for her to return to France to attend to the nuptials of Minette, but she was delayed by another family tragedy, the death in England of her eldest daughter, Mary, widow of the Prince of Orange.

Henrietta along with Minette at last took ship from Portsmouth at the end of December, but as so often her sea voyage was blighted with misfortune. No sooner had the ship set sail than a storm arose and in returning to port ran aground on a mudbank, and at the same time the unfortunate Minette was struck down with measles and for a time became seriously ill. At the end of January they set out again this time without misadventure and reached France where they were eagerly awaited especially by Monsieur, who still professed himself in love with Minette; and they were married on 30 March. Minette then made her debut in French court life where she was an immediate success, not so much for her beauty as for her charm and vivacity. 'Never was there a princess,' wrote a courtier at the time, 'so fascinating and so ready to please all who approached her.' Not least among these was Louis XIV who was amazed at her transformation from the skinny, unprepossessing child he had once known (dubbed by him as 'the bones of the Holy Innocents') into the well-rounded charmer she had become – such a contrast to his dull, phlegmatic wife, so much so that he paid her attentions that gave rise to gossip and jealousy.

Henrietta stayed in France for over a year and might have stayed longer: as a princess of royal blood and the mother of 'Madame', now after the death of Anne of Austria the second lady in the kingdom, she was accorded great honour. But it was necessary for her to return to England to settle her financial affairs and to obtain a suitable dowry for Minette. In London she was treated respectfully and generously. Denmark House, her residence in the Strand, which had fallen into decay during the Commonwealth, was refurbished and her parliamentary grant was such that she was able to live there in some state. Her court included, among others, Gentlemen of the Queen's Music, Master of the Queen's Games, twenty-four gentlemen-at-arms as her personal escort and twelve liveried bargemen. Also in attendance was her constant companion of many years, Henry Jermyn now Earl of St Albans, as comfortable and prosperous as ever. His official position was Chancellor but there were those who believed that he was also husband and that Henrietta had borne children by him. As Samuel Pepys wrote: 'How true God knows'. But it is improbable. Jermyn lived and died a Protestant and marriage to Henrietta would have required a Papal dispensation and there is no record of this ever having been granted.

Henrietta by then was fifty-three. She had long since lost her good looks but still had personality and charm, and the court she held was probably more cultured and certainly more savoury than that of her son, the King. She was to find too that there were few restrictions on her religious practices. There was still an undercurrent of hostility towards Catholics and the penal laws were still in place, but these were not always enforced, and Henrietta was able to keep a group of Capucin friars who celebrated Mass and even engaged in works of conversion.

One of Henrietta's purposes in returning to London had been to meet her new daughter-in-law, Catherine of Braganza, who had recently been married to Charles II, and with whom she was delighted – gentle, accommodating and a pious Roman Catholic. 'I am truly blessed in her,' she wrote. 'The best creature in the world who shows me the greatest goodwill.' With so much in her favour Henrietta might have been tempted to spend the rest of her life in England, but there were forces drawing her back to France, in particular to be with her youngest daughter again. Minette's marriage had not run smoothly. As many had expected Monsieur's devotion to her had not endured. He was said to have declared once that it had only lasted a fortnight; the general opinion was summed up by a courtier that 'the miracle of kindling the Prince's heart was reserved for no earthly woman.' Minette's health too was precarious. She had had several pregnancies, some of which had resulted in miscarriages and had given birth to two daughters but only one much-hoped for son who died tragically at the age of two.

In 1665, then, Henrietta resolved on a visit to France, leaving London just in time to avoid the worst of the Great Plague. She had only intended to be away for a short time, but she was not to return to England again. In France she found peace and contentment – at times in the convent she had founded at Chaillot and at others in her country house in the village of Colombes outside Paris. It was here in the summer of 1669 that she was taken seriously ill. The leading physicians in France were summoned to her bedside, and at first her condition was not deemed to be serious, caused by 'vapours rising to the head' which was only a temporary malaise, but one of the cures prescribed for her insomnia was some grains of laudanum (an opiate) which sent her into a deep sleep from which she did not awake.

On being told of her death Louis XIV ordered that she should have a state funeral and be buried beside her father, Henry of Navarre. At Chaillot there was another service with a deeply moving address by a bishop specially chosen by Minette who begged the congregation to join with him 'in honouring the memory of the most high, most excellent, most puissant princess, Henrietta-Marie, Queen of England, Scotland and Ireland, daughter of the French King Henry the Victorious, wife to King Charles the Martyr, mother of King Charles at present reigning in England, and aunt to his most Christian majesty Louis XIV.' The preacher, reputed to be the most famous in France, then recounted her life story:

You will see in a single life all the extremities of things human: happiness without bound as well as misery; the long and peaceful enjoyment of one of the most noble crowns in the universe; all that which can render birth and position most glorious heaped upon one head, and then exposed to the outrages of fortune; the good cause at first followed by good success, and then suddenly reverses and changes unprecedented... There is the lesson God gives to kings; thus does he show to the world the worthlessness of its pomp and grandeur.

CATHERINE OF BRAGANZA (1638–1705)

Wife of Charles II

Catherine of Braganza, the Portugese wife of Charles II, has generally been neglected by history. When noticed she has usually been pushed aside with a few condescending comments and little attempt to evaluate her role as Queen Consort. There has always been much greater interest in Charles's mistresses. As wife of one of the most libidinous monarchs her life was unsettled and often mortifying and she had every reason for quitting and returning to a calm and sequestered life in Portugal. But her love for Charles was such that she chose to stand by him, enduring the calumny and humiliation that came her way. At times in his reign Charles came within danger of losing his throne, and a thrustful and scheming wife might have been disastrous. Catherine, low-key and self-effacing, was a blessing which Charles himself always appreciated.

Catherine was the daughter of King John of Portugal, a retiring and infirm character under the domination of his wife who took charge of Catherine's upbringing which was secluded and narrow, her education consisting of little more than a grounding in Catholic doctrine. Of the ways of the world she was ignorant and had no experience. At an early age plans had been afoot for her to marry Prince Charles of England, but these had been interrupted by the Civil War and Charles's long exile, but when in 1660 he was restored to the throne negotiations were renewed. It might seem that a dim Portuguese princess of no great beauty, hidden away in Lisbon, a fervent Roman Catholic and dominated by a termagant mother, was an unsuitable choice as queen of England, but there was much in Catherine's favour. Although unworldly and unremarkable she was said to be docile and gentle, and for the lifestyle to which Charles at the age of thirty had become accustomed these were going to be essential qualities. But the main consideration was her dowry which was substantial – £350,000 in cash and important trading rights in the Mediterranean including the strategic port of Tangier and in the Far East including Bombay. In return Portugal would have English support in her wars with Spain and in suppressing the Barbary pirates who were a serious menace to her shipping.

Charles was soon won over to the idea in spite of some strong opposition: this came mainly from Spain whose ambassador in London spread it abroad that Catherine was 'deformed, in bad health and barren.' There was opposition too at home notably from Charles's chancellor, Lord Clarendon (once Edward Hyde) who thought it essential that the King's wife should be Protestant. Nevertheless, in 1661 a betrothal was agreed and this pleased no one more than Catherine. She had, of course, had no say in the matter; it had all been in the hands of her mother, but she had long looked on Charles as a romantic hero, and certainly he had had an exceptionally adventurous life. At the age of twelve he had been in the first battle of the Civil War at Edgehill and thereafter with the King's forces until their ultimate defeat. Then had come his taking up of arms first in the Channel Islands, then in France and then leading an invasion of England from Scotland followed by his defeat at Worcester and a thrilling escape out of the country. During his long years of exile he had been harried from place to place by European governments, anxious not to offend Cromwell and his Ironsides; but finally he had come into his own again and returned to England amid wild rejoicings. No woman could have been unaffected by such a story, certainly not Catherine, who was in love with Charles before meeting him.

On 25 April 1662 a fleet of fourteen men-of-war arrived in Lisbon to escort Catherine to England. It should have been a splendid occasion but for various reasons it was delayed and somewhat marred by the inability of the Portuguese government to pay Catherine's dowry in full so that the commander of the English fleet, Lord Sandwich, wondered whether he should return to England without her. But this was ruled out, and Catherine was borne through the tempestuous waters of the Bay of Biscay, desperately seasick, to England where she immediately collapsed with a fever. It was perhaps fortunate that Charles was not at hand to have his first sight of her in such a pitiful condition, and it was five days before he arrived by when Catherine had more or less recovered and was in a fit state to receive him which she did delightedly. Charles's reception of her was more reserved. 'Her face,' he wrote to Clarendon, 'is not so exact as to be called a beauty though her eyes are excellent good.' He seemed unperturbed by the non-payment of her dowry and insisted on marrying her the following day. Catherine was distressed that this was to be by the rites of the Church of England; for her the only true marriage service was that of the Church of Rome. About this Charles was sympathetic and agreed there should be two services – one Protestant, grand and well publicised, the other Catholic, quiet and inconspicuous.

Charles was at pains to ease Catherine's entry into English life. He realised how hard it might be coming from a pious, semi-monastic life to be plunged into the licentiousness of Restoration London. For the English were reacting strongly from Puritan severity. Everywhere moral standards were declining. The royal court in particular was notorious: drunkenness and debauchery were rife and Samuel Pepys wrote that it was 'governed by lust and women and rogues.' Certainly Catherine needed protection from these and Charles felt he must provide it. For the paradox of Charles was that although he was the most unfaithful of husbands, he was in other respects one of the kindest. He felt a tender and loving care for Catherine and wanted her to be happy, but there were certain matters on which he was unyielding. During his exile he had given full rein to his libido. Mistresses he had had in profusion and these he was not going to forsake now. Preeminent among them was Barbara Countess of Castlemaine (once Mrs Roger Palmer), a courtesan of considerable beauty and charm as well as formidable temper. She had had at least one child by Charles and had established a hold over him which she was determined should not be broken. At the time of his marriage, agitated and imminently pregnant with another child of his, she made a number of exorbitant demands to maintain her status. She asked for a residence near Hampton Court Palace where she could be readily visited, and this was granted her; she asked for increased financial support and this too was accorded; she then asked to be taken on as a lady-in-waiting to Catherine and to this too Charles was ready to agree, but here he had opposition. He thought Catherine did not know about his relationship with Barbara and blithely included her name with others for Catherine's consideration, but Catherine had been told all about Barbara and would have nothing to do with her. This might have been the end of the matter but Charles, usually pliant and easy going, for once dug his toes in and refused to take no for an answer. For a time Catherine was adamant, saying she would rather return to Portugal and enter a nunnery than agree to such a sinful arrangement. Charles was thus caught between two fires – innocence and indignation on one hand, sex and passion on the other, and it was the latter which prevailed, for Charles became uncharacteristically vindictive. He attempted to force Catherine's hand by sending away the large Portuguese entourage, over a hundred in number, which she had brought with her. This was a motley throng consisting among others of dishevelled and unwashed monks as well as gaunt intimidating ladies who looked on themselves as a kind of bodyguard for Catherine. Charles had always longed to be rid of them but out of consideration for Catherine had forborne to dismiss them, but now they were unceremoniously sent packing. He also tried to introduce Barbara to Catherine by stealth, presenting her under an unfamiliar name with a group of other ladies. At first Catherine was deceived, but when she was later enlightened she had to be carried away fainting. It seemed the impasse could not be broken, but then Catherine suddenly climbed down, apologising to Charles for any 'passion or peevishness' and assuring him of 'future obedience and duty'. The reason for this sudden change of heart may have been that her confessor urged on her that it was her duty to stay with Charles and work for his conversion to Catholicism. It may have been too that her mother-in-law, Henrietta Maria, to whom she was devoted, also applied pressure. But from then on, although coolly and uneasily, she acknowledged and accepted Barbara into her court.

Catherine was in some ways an admirable wife for Charles – discreet, undemanding and totally loyal. Her lifestyle was devout and correct and, besides her religious devotions, she occupied herself contentedly with such harmless matters as playing the harp, embroidery and writing letters. She made a favourable impression on Samuel Pepys who wrote of her 'good, modest, innocent looks', and on her mother-in-law, Henrietta Maria, who described her as 'saintly'. She also kept her distance from politics and politicians – 'without that meddling and activity in her nature which hath many times made those of that religion troublesome and restless' according to a contemporary diplomat. But in the country at large she was not always popular. She was no great beauty and not with a gracious and outgoing personality, and she incurred much blame unjustly. Her shyness and reserve were mistaken for haughtiness and she was thought by some to be extravagant, but this was demonstrably untrue: compared with the King's mistresses her dress was plain and well worn and the furnishings in her apartment modest, even austere. Of course this gave rise to the opposite allegation that she was mean and penurious, but this was equally untrue: she lived within her means which were not excessive and in times of financial crisis not always forthcoming.

Catherine was soon to find that it was not only towards Barbara that she had to show tolerance. There were others, less formidable, who also had to be taken into account. Of these the one who made the greatest impact was Frances Stuart whose story was a curious one. She was of exceptional beauty and a devoted friend of Charles's sister, the Duchess of Orléans (Minette) who dispatched her at the age of fifteen to her brother's court in London. Why she did so can only be surmised. In view of Charles's reputation it would hardly seem to have been in her best interests. It may be she thought that Frances might distract him from Barbara whom she detested and wanted to bring down. If this was her motive she had some success, as Charles, ever susceptible, fell deeply in love with Frances, perhaps more so than with any of his other attachments. But Barbara was to linger on for some time yet. The other consequences of Frances' presence were more unpredictable, for not only did she arouse no jealousy in Catherine but they became close friends. It seems that Catherine realised intuitively that Frances was not, like Charles's other women, covetous and grasping, nor was she cloying and passionate. To his dismay Charles was kept at bay by her and allowed no favours – a notable feat for a naive teenager. For different reasons Frances was well received by Barbara, whom she was intended to displace. At the time Barbara was having an affair with a young nobleman and wanted a temporary respite from Charles and calculated, mistakenly as it proved, that an unworldly girl of fifteen could fill the gap until such time as she was ready to come back. Of course when this ploy went astray she and Frances became bitter enemies.

Charles's love for Frances, La Belle Stuart as she became known, did not go unnoticed by those about court, and Frances' prestige rose accordingly, for it was believed by some that Charles might consider finding reasons for ending his marriage to Catherine and marrying Frances instead, especially if Catherine were to remain childless. But there they were wrong. Charles never had thoughts of divorcing Catherine. He was genuinely fond of her and grateful for her tenderness and tolerance. She might not stir up in him the erotic frenzy aroused by Barbara, but he knew at heart that she was the one woman in his life who was utterly devoted to him and loved him for himself and not for ulterior purposes.

The test of Charles's devotion came in 1663 when Catherine was struck down by puerperal fever and came close to death, and it was thought that Charles might take this calmly; but his concern was impassioned and genuine. He spent long hours beside her bedside, soothed her and nursed her and probably saved her life. In the care of the medical practitioners of that time she was subjected to every manner of quack remedy including the laying of dead pigeons on her feet and the shaving of her hair to be replaced by a cap which was supposed to have mystical qualities; and her sickroom was stifling and fetid and full of people serving no useful purpose. Taking charge, Charles ordered the room to be cleared, the windows to be thrown open and carcasses and other festering objects to be removed. More important he poured loving words into Catherine's ears, begged her to forgive him for his treatment of her and besought her to live for his sake. And Catherine began to recover but this was to take time. For some years her health was to be fragile – racked by migraine and weakened by further miscarriages. While she was in that condition London was smitten by one of the most ghastly disasters in her history. It had been waiting to happen for some time for the city then was one of the dirtiest, most disease-ridden and overcrowded in Europe.

Every year thousands of people died from diseases such as tuberculosis and smallpox, but in the early summer of 1665 (to be one of the hottest ever) the dreaded bubonic plague ravaged the city and every week hundreds and then thousands of Londoners died from it. In the face of such a calamity the local authorities seemed helpless. Most of the well-to-do citizens were bent on getting out of the city as soon as possible. It was open to the King to do the same but Charles stayed put and braced himself into action, seeing to it that basic practical measures were taken – disposal of refuse, sealing off infected houses and burial of the dead in deep enough graves. Catherine would have liked to stay with him and give support, but Charles was insistent that it was her bounden duty not to risk her life unnecessarily and she was sent off to the safety of Salisbury.

In the following year disaster struck again. On 2 September 1666 a fire broke out in a bakery in Pudding Lane. Efforts to put it out were unavailing and it was soon spreading over the City. Once again Charles was seen at his best. While others were concerned only in escaping and saving what property they could, he and his brother James plunged into the inferno and took control of the situation and saw to it that houses in the path of the fire were blown up so that a barrier was created to halt its progress. They also took their turn in firefighting with buckets of water and urging people to greater efforts. Charles would return to Whitehall at the end of the day, blackened with soot, holes burnt in his boots and his periwig scorched. The fire was to blaze for five days and the toll was terrible – 375 acres devastated, 13,200 houses and 87 churches destroyed. At the end people were bitter and resentful and looking for culprits: the French and Dutch, with whom England was at war at that time, were the main targets, but so too were Roman Catholics, and Catherine came in for much abuse and threats against her life. Yet another calamity awaited England in 1667. Because of impending national bankruptcy much of the navy had had to be laid up so that there was nothing to stop a Dutch fleet from sailing into the river Medway, setting fire to a number of warships at anchor and towing away the battleship *Royal Charles*, an unprecedented national disgrace.

During the years of these disasters Catherine suffered much anxiety and grief of which the most galling was her inability to bear live children, as one miscarriage followed another. But Charles was always soothing and kindly, taking the blame for these on himself for the way he treated her. He also encouraged her to share some of his special interests such as shipbuilding and scientific experiments. She had long since become resigned to his eclectic sex life and mistresses continued to come and go. Barbara Castlemaine was on the way out although she could never be completely excluded and was to remain as grasping and explosive as ever. Frances Stuart was still in favour although her relationship with Charles was set back (although not completely severed) when she secretly eloped with the Duke of Richmond and Lennox. Others who took Charles's fancy included actresses among whom was the notorious Nell Gwyn, 'pretty, witty Nell' as she was known. A child of the London streets – her father died in prison and her mother kept a brothel – she was no great beauty but of irrepressible high spirits and good humour and never pretended to be anything but what she was, referring to herself on occasions as 'the Protestant whore'. Charles loved her dearly and Catherine could not but be amused by her.

Certainly Catherine was endlessly forbearing. She realised that Charles's sexual appetites were such that she alone could not satisfy, and she was, no doubt, aware of his nickname of 'Old Rowley' (the name of a particularly prolific stallion), but she was convinced that her relationship with him was quite different from that of those she called his 'pretty little fools'. He had many light loves but only one wife. As a strict Catholic she could not but deplore these connections but felt that only by condoning them could she keep her marriage intact and work for the great objective of Charles's conversion to Catholicism. In 1670 there were signs that this might be imminent. In that year his greatly loved sister, Minette, came on a visit to England, charged by her brother-in-law, Louis XIV, to agree a treaty of alliance between England and France which she succeeded in doing in the Treaty of Dover.[1]

The open part of this treaty provided that in return for a large subsidy England would unite with France in a war against Holland. But the treaty also contained secret clauses to the effect that Charles at some point would announce his conversion to the Roman church and restore it to its former position in England, and Louis would support him in this with money and, if necessary, armed forces. Whether Catherine was aware of these ignominious conditions is not known nor, if she did, what she thought of them. Certainly she would have welcomed the conversion of Charles and the restoration of the Roman church, but it is surely unlikely that she would want to see this happen under duress from a foreign army. There must be doubt too that Charles ever had serious thoughts of putting the treaty into practice; he must have known what a storm it would have aroused, and was only stringing the French king along for the money he so desperately needed.

As far as Catherine was concerned the immediate effect of the Treaty of Dover lay not in its terms but in the coming to England of a new, powerful and sinister mistress for Charles. For Minette on her visit had brought with her in attendance a beautiful Breton maid of nineteen, Louise de Kéroualle, with whom Charles

---

[1] Her disagreeable and perverted husband, the Duke of Orléans, would only give his permission to the visit on condition that she went no further inland than Dover.

immediately fell in love and begged Minette to leave her behind. This, however, Minette felt could not then be done honourably but might be arranged in the future. It was not, however, to be achieved by her as within a few weeks she had died of peritonitis. But the matter was taken up by Louis XIV who saw great advantages in having a secret agent such as Louise in the court of the ever susceptible Charles. Louise was the only mistress of Charles whom Catherine cordially disliked. She felt at once that there was something pretentious and devious about her. Whether she suspected her of being a French spy is not known, but instinctively she felt a distrust of her that she did not feel towards any of Charles's other womenfolk – even Barbara Castlemaine. And it was not only by Catherine that Louise was disliked: her airs and graces and pro-French, pro-Catholic stance made her generally unpopular, and Nell Gwyn had a fine time mobbing her up. Charles, however, was not to be put off and when she gave birth to a son he set her up in Whitehall and created her Duchess of Portsmouth, which was too much for Catherine who moved out into Somerset House which had become hers since the death of her mother-in-law, Henrietta Maria. Charles made no objection to this and did not regard it as a formal separation and visited her frequently.

In being party to the Treaty of Dover Charles must have known what a dangerous game he was playing. His openly pro-French policy was not popular in the country and there were widespread suspicions about his Catholic sympathies; for these did exist and he could not altogether conceal them, and besides his wife, mother, brother and sister were all Catholics as also were two of his principal mistresses (Castlemaine and Portsmouth). Any suspicion of Catholic policies on his part always stirred up feverish opposition, and should the secret clauses of the Treaty of Dover ever leak out there would be uproar. And this was to happen.

It was initiated in 1678 by two scoundrels, Titus Oates and Israel Tonge who thought much money could be made by spreading abroad scare stories about a Popish plot to assassinate the King, replace him by the Duke of York and re-establish the Roman Catholic church. This they did by laying a deposition before a London Magistrate, Sir Edmund Berry Godfrey. Their accusations were fantastic and unsubstantiated and normally would have attracted little attention, but soon afterwards the magistrate was found murdered which resulted in an outbreak of hysteria and panic. It was immediately supposed that Roman Catholics were responsible in order to suppress Oates's accusations which became widely held to be true, and further stories were then circulated about murky Papist activities and an impending French invasion. For a time all Catholics went in fear of their lives and Oates, acclaimed as a hero, was ready for a fee to accuse innocent people and bear false witness against them, and a number of these were convicted of treason and condemned to horrific deaths. In this madness the insolence and mendacity of Oates knew no bounds: he even accused Catherine of taking part in a plot to kill her husband. On this, however, he was confronted directly by Charles who cross-examined him rigorously and exposed his lies, although this did not prevent Catherine from being abused and threatened by berserk crowds so that she was forced to leave York House and take refuge in Whitehall.

In time the frenzy died down and some sanity restored; and Charles was able to gain a signal victory over his political opponents who, led by the unscrupulous and embittered Lord Shaftesbury, had sought to make use of the Popish scare to pass an act of Parliament excluding the Catholic Duke of York from the throne and replacing him as heir with Charles's illegitimate son, the Protestant Duke of Monmouth. But on this issue Charles was adamant and by a combination of firmness and political dexterity was able to thwart their designs and to disgrace them so that they had to flee abroad; and his last years were the most peaceful and prosperous of his reign.

They were not, however, to be entirely free of troubles of which the most serious was the treacherous behaviour of his eldest natural son. James Duke of Monmouth had been born while Charles was in exile and having an affair with Lucy Walter, a woman of Welsh origins described by the diarist Evelyn as 'bold, brown, beautiful but insipid.' She had a number of lovers but the son born to her in 1649 was acknowledged by Charles to be his and he arranged for him to be cared for by another English exile, Lord Crofts. Soon after the Restoration James was brought to England where, although only thirteen, he made a vivid impression by his good looks and vitality. Pepys described him as 'the most skittish, leaping gallant that ever I saw.' Charles was delighted with him and heaped on him riches and honours including the dukedom of Monmouth and betrothal to one of the richest heiresses in the country. But his response to this was that of a spoiled child: the more he was given the more he wanted. His behaviour became ever more erratic as he found he could get away with murder.[2] And in time he aspired to be king and tried to make his father admit that he had been married to Lucy Walter so that he was his legitimate heir. This Charles strongly denied and in consequence Monmouth joined forces with Lord Shaftesbury in his efforts to exclude the Catholic James Duke of York from succession to the throne. He was paraded as 'The Protestant Duke' free of papistry who was being denied his birthright; and by his charm and bravura he attracted much support. In time the Exclusion Bill failed, Shaftesbury and his supporters disgraced and Monmouth sent into exile. He was soon to return, however, and become engaged in further subversive activities for which he should have been hunted down and brought to justice, but this Charles could not bring himself to do. Like King David of the Jews and his wayward son Absalom he was so besotted by him that he could not take drastic action. There were many reconciliations and promises by Monmouth to amend his ways, all of which he later had no compunction in breaking. Like many others Catherine too was beguiled by her stepson's winning ways and was always looking for excuses for his behaviour and pleading with Charles to be merciful, which he was all too ready to be. With his uncle, James II in the next reign, however, he was to get no mercy. After another unsuccessful rebellion he ended up on the executioner's block.

At the beginning of February 1685 Charles was suddenly struck by an apoplectic fit. His condition at first was not unduly serious and with a strong constitution and at no more than fifty-four he might have recovered, but a cluster of doctors closed in on him and started administering their fearsome cures – bleeding, blisters, purgatives and emetics – and his condition grew worse and gave rise to anxiety. A number of Anglican bishops then gathered round him, urging that he take the last rites of the Church of England; but these he resisted. During his lifetime his religious beliefs had never been clear, but now it became apparent that, such as they were, they were inclined to papacy, for when his brother James suggested bringing to him a Roman Catholic confessor, he agreed readily and one was smuggled into his sickroom and he took the

---

[2] Literally. His father once pardoned him for the murder of a night watchman.

205

last sacraments according to the Church of Rome. It seems that Catherine had no part in this but she must have been thankful; it was what she had always hoped and prayed for. At the time, however, her overwhelming feeling was one of grief at the thought of losing the husband she adored. For long hours she sat at his bedside, comforting him as best she could, but the stifling atmosphere of the overcrowded room was too much for her and she had to be carried away fainting. Later she sent word to Charles begging him to forgive her if she had ever offended him. 'Alas, poor soul!' replied Charles. 'She ask my pardon? I beg hers with all my heart.' Somehow Charles managed to survive the ministrations of the doctors for four days, apologising at one point with characteristic humour for being so long dying; but on Friday 6 February his suffering at last came to an end.

Charles's death left Catherine desolate. Life seemed purposeless without him. She was ready for death and would have been shocked if she could have known that twenty years of life still lay ahead of her. Her immediate thoughts were for returning to Portugal where her brother King Pedro was eager to welcome her, but for one reason or another she was prevented from leaving England for the time being. The new King, James II, had a great respect for her and was unwilling to let her go, and his second wife, Mary Beatrice of Modena, was devoted to her and needed her support. She and Catherine had much in common – a strict Catholic upbringing, then marriage to an older and unfaithful husband in an alien and unsympathetic country, and apparently after fourteen years unable to give birth to surviving children. But in 1687 Mary was pregnant again (for the sixth time) and the baby, if safely delivered, would be heir to the throne. At her *accouchement* Catherine was present and later signed a written statement to the effect that she had witnessed the birth of the baby, although this did not prevent the spread of the absurd story that it had been smuggled into Mary's bed in a warming pan.

Catherine was to observe from the sidelines all the events of the so-called 'Glorious Revolution' when James was deposed and replaced on the throne by his nephew and daughter, William of Orange and Mary. As a fellow Catholic she must have felt sympathy for his attempt to restore the Roman Church in England but it is likely that she was concerned by his heavy-handed tactics and compared them unfavourably with the deft and cautious policies

206

of her husband. James's expulsion from England might seem to have been the cue for Catherine too to go, but still she stayed on. She seemed bent on recovering from the exchequer all money due to her so that she could leave her staff properly provided for. William III, her nephew by marriage, taciturn and graceless, proved friendly and helpful, but Mary was openly hostile, sometimes offensively so. The reason for this is not clear, but it may be that she bore a grudge against her for being one of those who had forced her into an unhappy marriage.

It was not until 1692, seven years after Charles's death, that Catherine at last left England for Portugal. She was then a widow of fifty-three in frail health, and it might have been expected that the remainder of her life would be spent in gentle and reposeful retirement. But this was not to be. She arrived in Portugal to find she was a national heroine and was given a rapturous reception. The people of Portugal were grateful for the help given them by the English navy in their war with Spain and considered Catherine mainly responsible for this. They also admired the way she had held steadfastly to her Catholic faith in a strongly Protestant country and thought it mainly due to her that Charles had been converted to Rome, albeit on his deathbed. No one was more delighted to see her than her brother King Pedro whom she had not seen for thirty years. With him and his warm-hearted wife, Maria Sophia, she soon established rapport and not only on a personal level; Pedro also came to have a great admiration for her political judgement which had never before been in evidence. In England she had been completely overshadowed by Charles and had steered clear of politics, knowing full well that any suspicion of interference from her was liable to stir up storms. But in Portugal there was no such animosity, and when later King Pedro's health broke down and he had to go into temporary retirement he had no hesitation in nominating her as Queen Regent, a position she held with distinction, presiding over a successful war with Spain and the conclusion of an honourable peace treaty. Who could have foreseen this from the shy, retiring, somewhat unprepossessing figure she had cut as Queen Consort of England?

In her last years Catherine was saddened by the death in exile of her brother-in-law James II, and was outraged when her niece by marriage, Princess Anne (later Queen Anne), let it be known that she did not believe that James's son (later to be known as

'The Old Pretender') whose birth Catherine had witnessed, was the true daughter of Mary Beatrice of Modena. Catherine died in 1705 at the age of sixty-six at the height of her popularity and fame. She was greatly mourned in Portugal. In England her death was taken more calmly.

ANNE, DUCHESS OF YORK (1637–1671)

First Wife of James II

Anne, Duchess of York, was married to James II for eleven years before he became king. The marriage was not popular partly because it was a 'shotgun' affair, James having made Anne pregnant during his exile on the Continent, partly because she was a commoner and partly because she was not blessed with either charm or good looks. Her position then as wife to the heir to the throne was prejudiced. She was aware of being looked down on and in consequence gave herself exaggerated royal airs which were resented and ridiculed. But James, although never a remotely faithful husband, treated her with respect and she was to bear him seven children, only two of whom, Mary and Anne, were to survive into adulthood and in time to become queens of England.

Anne was the daughter of Sir Edward Hyde (later Lord Clarendon), chief minister of Charles II during his exile and for the first six years of his reign in England. He was a man of wisdom and ability but arrogant and abrasive and with too keen a sense of his own worth. In his memoirs he could solemnly describe himself as 'a man without blemish and believed to be without temptation.' His only daughter, Anne, accompanied him into exile and in 1654 at the age of seventeen was appointed a maid of honour to Charles's sister, Mary Princess of Orange in whose court she attracted the roving eye of Charles's younger brother, James Duke of York. At the time James, rootless and impecunious, was earning his living as a professional soldier in the army of France where he had won for himself a reputation for courage and leadership. Handsome and full-blooded he also had a reputation as a lady-killer. During the bleak years of his exile he had sought consolation in numerous transitory love affairs but in 1659, when he was twenty-six, he found himself seriously in love with Anne who responded to his advances and became pregnant by him, whereupon he made a solemn and for the time being secret compact to marry her. Such

209

an engagement between a prince of royal blood and a commoner (for Sir Edward was no aristocrat) would always have been looked at askance by some but James at the time an outcast and a younger son, carried little weight in royal circles and a marriage to Anne might not have stirred up too much opposition.

In the following year, however, his position was transformed when his brother Charles was restored to the throne of England and he became heir to the throne. When his engagement to Anne became known there was a chorus of disapproval. Charles was angry that he had been kept in the dark about the matter, and it did not suit him to be related by marriage to his chief minister. Other members of the royal family too were displeased. Princess Mary took it amiss that she would now be of inferior status to her former maid of honour while James's younger brother, Prince Richard of Gloucester, let it be known that he had always disliked Anne and that 'she carried about with her the smell of her father's green bag'. Stronger in disapproval, predictably, was Henrietta Maria, the Queen Dowager, who was appalled that her son should be marrying a commoner and the daughter of an old enemy of hers. Of Anne's pregnancy she took the gloomiest view: 'God grant,' she said, 'that it may be by him. A girl who would abandon herself to a prince would abandon herself to another.' And she made haste to come to England intent on breaking the engagement off. The greatest fury of all, however, came from Anne's father. On hearing of what had happened Sir Edward became beside himself with rage. Madly he blustered that he would rather have his daughter James's whore than his wife, and that he would turn her out of his house as a strumpet to shift for herself and would never see her again. He even raved that she should be sent to the Tower and executed. It is not altogether clear why Sir Edward felt so outraged. No doubt he thought the family honour had been tarnished by his daughter conceiving a child out of wedlock, but there must have been more to it than that. It may be he felt that his preeminent position had been compromised and that his enemies would accuse him of an evil and treasonable plot to insinuate himself into the royal family.

It seems that at one point James may have wavered in face of such opposition and he may even have lent an ear to a malevolent scheme propounded by some of his boon companions to blacken Anne's name by alleging that she slept around and that any of them could be the father of her child, and James was therefore under no obligation to her; but it would be out of character for James to comply with such a ploy. In the end it was the authority of Charles which settled the matter. He took the view that what was done could not be undone and the best must be made of the situation, and in the end even Henrietta Maria relented and, albeit grudgingly, accepted Anne into the family. The formal marriage of James and Anne could not have been more low-key and unromantic – in the dead of night in a private chapel with only two witnesses, one of whom was Anne's maid. Her baby was born seven weeks later.

The marriage, which lasted eleven years, was hardly idyllic. James made no pretence at being faithful, taking to himself mistresses as and when they came, outstripping in this field even his brother Charles. Anne too did not altogether stay on the level, having a brief, although none too passionate, dalliance with her Master of Horse. James was hardly in a position to take a high moral tone about this but, according to a contemporary, he saw to it that the man was 'put out of court with much precipitation.' Nevertheless he and Anne remained fond of each other as seven children were born to them.

It has been seen that Anne, aware of her middle class origins and determined to live up to her new rank, became haughty and overbearing. Pepys called her 'the proudest woman in the world' and a contemporary diplomat, with some sarcasm, wrote: 'She upholds with as much courage, cleverness and energy the dignity to which she has been called as if she were of the blood of kings.' Few people at that time regarded her as a beauty. Pepys, no mean judge, described her as 'a plain woman like her mother', but conceded that she had a 'most fine white and fat hand'. And James, while admiring her, made little effort to contain his love life which remained as promiscuous as ever, also somewhat bizarre. Many were surprised by the objects of his desire, who were not at all beautiful. Gilbert Burnet, a bishop with a taste for gossip, wrote in his memoirs that 'James was perpetually in one amour or another without being very nice in his choice.' And one of his mistresses, Catherine Sedley, once remarked 'We are none of us handsome and if we have wit, he has not enough himself to find it out.' King Charles summed the matter up succinctly, saying that his brother's mistresses must be a form of penance.[1]

---

[1] No other English monarch equals James's paternity – seven children by his first wife, eight by his second and at least four illegitimates.

Anne died in 1671 at the age of thirty-four. It is not known for certain what was the cause of her death, but it seems likely that overeating had something to do with it. She was not greatly lamented. Apart from her arrogance and extravagant ways her conversion to Roman Catholicism in her last years aroused suspicion and hostility. As Duchess of York, however, she had on the whole conducted herself with prudence and was allowed to have had wit and vivacity. Bishop Burnet wrote of her that 'she had great knowledge and a lively sense of things'.

MARY BEATRICE OF MODENA (1658–1718)

Second Wife of James II

On the death of his first wife James, then Duke of York, thought it necessary to remarry as soon as possible. He was heir to the throne and as it was becoming increasingly apparent that Catherine of Braganza would be childless, it was up to him to provide for the next generation. He did have two daughters, Mary and Anne, but he should, he thought, have a son for a smooth succession. Left to himself he would have been willing to marry one of his English loves, Lady Belasyse, but Charles II would have none of it, telling him somewhat harshly that he had made a fool of himself once and must not do so again, and this time should marry someone of royal rank. And so the Earl of Peterborough was despatched to look round the courts of Europe for a suitable candidate who was required to be good looking, free from family complications and preferably Protestant. But such a paragon was not immediately to be found. The Protestant princesses of Germany were either plain or had termagant mothers or around them there was a whiff of scandal. In Italy, however, there was one of great beauty and untarnished reputation. About Mary Beatrice d'Este, sister of the Duke of Modena, a small principality in northern Italy, Lord Peterborough became lyrical: 'Her complexion is of the last degree of fairness, her hair black as jet, so are her eyebrows and her eyes, but the latter so full of light and sweetness, as they did dazzle and charm too. There seemed given to them by nature a power to kill and a power to save.' But there were drawbacks. Mary Beatrice was only fifteen and a devout Roman Catholic whose hope was for a religious life in a convent, and she was appalled at the thought of marrying a man twenty-five years older than herself and heir to the throne in a Protestant country of which she had scarcely heard. But of course the decision did not rest with her but with her domineering mother who saw considerable political advantages in such a match, and so the

213

marriage went ahead with great immediacy. She was first married by proxy in Modena, the fifty-year-old Lord Peterborough standing in for the bridegroom, and then sent straight off to England where on landing in Dover she was met by James and after the quickest and most unceremonious of wedding services was bedded the same night.

Mary Beatrice arrived in England in 1673. It was not one of the more glorious moments in the country's history. The year before Charles II had signed the secret treaty of Dover with Louis XIV and in pursuance of his policy of restoring the Roman church had issued a Declaration of Indulgence giving freedom of worship to all Christian denominations. This was done without the consent of Parliament and caused an uproar as suspicion was growing that Charles II had ulterior motives. In consequence he was compelled to withdraw the Declaration and at the same time to agree to a Test Act requiring all holders of public offices to take Communion according to the rites of the Church of England. Anti-Catholic feeling in the country was running high, at times fanatically so; all the great disasters occurring then – the Great Plague, the Great Fire, the unsuccessful war against the Dutch – were being attributed to Papist machinations, and rumours were abroad of foreign invasions and sinister conspiracies, to come to a head five years later with the infamous Popish Plot fabricated by the villainous Titus Oates.

In this fraught atmosphere James's marriage to Mary Beatrice was not popular and Parliament tried to prevent it – unsuccessfully as it was too late. Charles II was already encompassed by Catholics (mother, brother, sister and two principal mistresses) and the arrival of another into the family circle was not welcome. Mary Beatrice was admired for her grace and youthful charm, and it was generally agreed that she was an improvement on her plain and haughty predecessor, but because of her religion she was not trusted and came in for much ill-feeling, and it was not considered safe for her to have the chapel she had been promised where she could worship publicly according to Catholic rites.

Mary Beatrice also had to adapt to the personal ways of her husband which were openly licentious. Paramours abounded in his court, notably Arabella Churchill, sister of the future Duke of Marlborough, a lady of no great beauty but who had held James in thrall for several years and borne him two sons (later the Duke of Berwick and the second Duke of Albemarle).[1] As a strict Catholic Mary could not but be shocked by her husband's infidelity and did not accept it as meekly as Catherine of Braganza, but her relationship with him was sustained by a strong religious bond. It is not known for certain exactly when James converted to Catholicism, as for long it was kept secret on the orders of Charles II. What must be certain is that by his conversion his life became doomed. Before, if not loved, he was an admired military and naval commander and respected for his bluffness and straightforwardness. Afterwards he became an object of suspicion and abuse whom many wanted to keep off the throne and whose conduct as king resulted in his being deposed within three years. By the time of his second marriage Catholicism dominated his life. Mary Beatrice said of him: 'He is firm and steady in our holy religion.' James always admitted the sinfulness of his ways and was constantly vowing to amend them, but always failing to do so. Like many another he combined deep piety with unbridled promiscuity. In old age he confessed piteously. 'I must own with shame and confusion I let myself go too much to the love of women which but for too long got the better of me. I have paid dear for it.'

Another great sorrow of Mary Beatrice was the loss of all the children she bore, five in all who were either still-born or died in infancy. Sadly she was to sum up her life in this period: 'I only knew happiness in England from the age of fifteen to twenty; but during those five years I was always having children and lost them all, so judge that happiness.' At the end of those five years the lives of James and Mary Beatrice became enveloped in crisis with the hysteria that swept the country following revelations concerning the Popish Plot.

In all his lies and accusations Titus Oates never went so far as to say that James was taking part in the plot; he was no more than a figurehead to be put on the throne by the conspirators when the time came. But although innocent, James and Mary Beatrice drew a lot of fire and this was intensified by the discovery of correspondence carried on by her secretary, Edward Coleman. Among all Oates's falsehoods this was one charge that had some

---

[1] James was said to have become enamoured of Arabella when she became dismounted in the hunting field and the disarray of her clothes revealed limbs which he found irresistible.

semblance of truth. Coleman had indeed been carrying on an indiscreet and at times treasonable correspondence mainly with fellow Jesuits abroad concerning ways in which the Roman church might be restored in England. Some of these letters were found stuffed up a chimney and were highly incriminating. To what extent James was aware of them cannot be known for certain; it seems unlikely he was entirely ignorant of them, especially as some of Coleman's ideas he later put into practice. Coleman, however, did not betray him and faced up to a horrendous death without saying a word.

The frenzy that erupted over the 'Popish Plot' was to last for three years and came to a head when Lord Shaftesbury and his followers (who had come to be known as Whigs) introduced a bill into Parliament excluding James from succession to the throne. But this Charles, often flexible and yielding, determined to resist, and his policy for doing so was astute and deceptive – in essence giving his opponents enough rope and waiting for them to hang themselves. This, however, needed patience and guile, two qualities lacking in James, and Charles decided that for the time being it would be better if James and Mary Beatrice were out of the way. And so they were sent into exile first to Holland, which they did not enjoy, and then to Scotland where, somewhat to their surprise, they were treated more kindly than in England, and they were able to lead safe and contented lives, James spending much time hunting and playing the new game of 'goffe' (golf) and Mary interesting herself in concerts and theatricals.

Meanwhile in England Charles's policy was paying off. The Whigs were becoming rash and intemperate and there was a strong reaction against them. At the same time Louis XIV for ulterior purposes (mainly English neutrality in his war with the Dutch) resumed paying Charles subsidies so that for the last years of his reign he was able to rule without Parliament. And James was able to return amid general acclamation, and there was no more action to exclude him from the throne, and when Charles died three years later his accession took place peacefully and with little opposition.

Few would have foretold the strength of James's position at the outset of his reign. The country was at peace, its finances flourishing and the Parliament summoned by James proved loyal and accommodating, voting him large sums of money for life which along with subsidies received from Louis XIV were ample for his needs. His personal reputation in the country also stood high: his candour and sincerity were appreciated and compared favourably with the dissimulation of his brother, as also was the moral tone of his court which was remarked on by several contemporaries as being more respectable. Not that James's personal conduct was any less lascivious than his brother's, if anything rather more so but not so blatant and cynical.

But amid all the goodwill and prosperity there was danger. A percipient observer might have seen trouble ahead. James's honesty was all very well, but he had dangerous failings: he was obstinate and unimaginative and woefully autocratic; opposition infuriated him, contrary opinions he brushed aside, and he resented people who argued with him and stood up to him. Basically he was unfitted to be a monarch in the complex and sensitive conditions which prevailed at that time. He lacked the necessary insight and political skills with the result that within three years his position had been eroded and he became a fugitive from his kingdom.

All went well at first. In his opening speech to the Privy Council he was reasonable and conciliatory, declaring that he would 'go as far as any man in preserving the nation in all its just rights and liberties'. Soon afterwards two rebellions – one in Scotland led by the Earl of Argyll and one in south-west England led by the Duke of Monmouth – were easily overcome. But trouble was to arise in the second year of his reign when he set about relieving the plight of his fellow Roman Catholics. If this had been done with tact and discretion something might have been achieved, but James's methods were too forceful and direct. He claimed the right to 'dispense' with laws whenever it suited him and this he did to appoint Catholics to public offices from which they were banned by the Test Act. Fears grew that he was planning a Catholic takeover of the government. In the next year he went even further and on his own authority without reference to Parliament issued a Declaration of Indulgence which gave all Christian denominations freedom to worship as they chose; at a stroke all recusancy laws, including the Test Act, were abolished, prisoners of conscience were set free and noone was to be punished for his beliefs. On the face of it this was an enlightened measure which should have been greeted with rejoicing, but in the event it pleased hardly anyone and caused an uproar. The Church of England was outraged that its privileged position was being undermined; the Protestant Non-Conformists were appalled that Papists were being given complete freedom and would rather do without their own than agree to it; and Roman Catholics too were uneasy, fearing that it would draw on them even greater hostility and suspicion than existed already. What has never been clear, and historians today are divided on the subject, is whether James was genuine in his proclaimed belief in liberty of conscience or whether he was masking a plan for a Catholic restoration. Dissembling was foreign to his nature, but he may have had a simple and, as it proved, an erroneous belief that the Non-Conformists would cooperate with him in bringing down the Church of England and he would turn against them later.

What James most needed at this time was someone he trusted completely who would calm him and restrain him. The person most able to do this should have been Mary Beatrice but she did not do so. It is doubtful if she ever had great influence on him in political matters, but she would not have advocated caution. Her Catholic ardour was just as great as his and ever since her arrival in England she had looked for the reconversion of the country to Rome. Although she had come in for criticism and suspicion, in her early days she had not been generally unpopular. Her ways were gentle and attractive and people had been drawn to her. On becoming queen, however, she seems to have undergone something of a sea change. Gone were the grace and charm and instead had come hardness and bad temper. Some of her old intimates had become estranged from her, notably her stepdaughter Princess Anne who had a sharp tongue when roused and wrote scathingly to her sister Mary in Holland:

> One thing I must say of the Queen which is that she is the most hated in the world of all sorts of people, for everybody believes that she presses the King to be more violent than he would be himself; which is not unlikely, for she is a very great bigot in her way, and we may see that she hates all Protestants. All ladies of quality say she is proud, that they don't care to come oftener than they must needs, just out of mere duty; and indeed, she has not so great court as she used to have. She pretends to have a great deal of kindness for me, but I doubt it is not real, for I never see proofs of it, but rather the contrary.

A change in Mary Beatrice was also noted by a doggerel writer of the time:

When Duchess she was gentle, mild and civil;
When Queen she proved a raging, furious devil.

This new side to Mary's character became particularly evident at the time of Monmouth's rebellion. After it had been defeated his supporters were rounded up and shown no mercy: many were hanged and many more transported into slavery in the West Indies. It was an opportunity for a compassionate queen to intercede and plead for mercy at least for the minor culprits. But Mary Beatrice held back. On the contrary she was not above making money out of their plight by accepting bribes and profiteering from their sale as slaves.

It must be doubtful that James's downfall was due significantly to the influence of his wife but, unwittingly, it was certainly expedited by her. In September 1687, while on a visit to the West Country, they visited the shrine of St Winefrede where there was a well which was reputed to have miraculous qualities. There they prayed earnestly for the birth of a son and St Winifrede responded: within a matter of weeks Mary Beatrice was pregnant. As she had not been in that condition for five years James was convinced that this was due to divine intervention and he was equally certain that the child would be a boy. To others the news came as a shock. The prospect of a male Catholic heir was something they dreaded. When the birth of the baby occurred on 20 June 1688 witnessed by more than thirty people, it did indeed turn out to be a boy. At the time James was arousing indignation by his pro-Catholic measures. Many were now convinced that James was bent on a Catholic restoration which could not be tolerated, but they were held back from open rebellion by the thought that James was an old man (actually fifty-five) and unlikely to live much longer, and would be succeeded by his Protestant daughter, Mary Princess of Orange. With the birth of a son, however, there was the prospect of a permanent line of Catholic kings. It was this that gave rise to the fantastic notion that the baby, allegedly born of Mary Beatrice, was in fact not hers but another that had been smuggled into her bed in a warming pan,[2] and many were to believe this story including James's two daughters, Mary and Anne, perhaps influenced by the fact that they were being superseded in the line of succession. Such a tale would have rescued the Protestant establishment from a critical situation, but it was not sustainable. It was realised that more had to be done, and soon afterwards an invitation signed by a number of prominent men was sent to James's nephew and son-in-law, William Prince of Orange, to invade England in order to preserve the Anglican church and traditional English liberties.

It is not necessary here to recount in detail the events that followed the landing of William at Torbay on 5 November, the defection of James's two daughters and most of his army led by John Churchill (later Duke of Marlborough), the flight of Mary Beatrice followed by that of James himself, and the offer of the throne to William and Mary jointly.

The flight of Mary Beatrice was attended by some difficulty at first, but as soon as she was in France a royal reception awaited her. Louis XIV for his own reasons wanted to establish the fugitive family in state, as their great enemy, William of Orange, was also his, and he wanted to attract to them as much support as possible. And so they were lodged in the magnificent palace of St Germain-en-Laye and were provided with ample funds. Louis also gave backing to James's attempts to regain his throne, but these were doomed to failure: an expedition to Ireland ended with defeat at the battle of the Boyne and a fleet intended for the invasion of England was destroyed at the battle of La Hogue. By then it had become apparent that James was no longer the great military commander he had once been. He had grown apathetic and weak willed and obsessed with religion. He engaged in rigorous fasting and painful penances and brooded morbidly on death. In being restored to his kingdom he seemed to have lost interest. One great consolation he had in his declining years was the birth of a daughter, Louisa Maria, whom he loved dearly, declaring joyfully 'I have

---

[2] There were, however, certain aspects of this wild story that gave it verisimilitude. Mary Beatrice had seemed to be barren for five years and she was very secretive about her pregnancy, resisting all intimacy on the part of Princess Anne and others close to her. Also the birth was premature and unexpected and not all the witnesses were there who should have been. Most of the leading Protestants, including the Archbishop of Canterbury, were absent. And, unlike all Mary Beatrice's previous children, Prince James Francis was to survive infancy and live into old age.

now a daughter who has never sinned against me.' He called her 'La Consolotrice'.

Unlike her husband Mary Beatrice was militant, stirring up trouble for William wherever she could. The French king was supportive, but as he became more involved in his continental wars he had less resources for a campaign against England and Holland, and at the treaty of Ryswick in 1697 he acknowledged William as King of England. At the same time James continued to lose all worldly ambition and lapsed into senility.

In 1701 James fainted while in chapel and from then on his health declined rapidly. Louis showed immediate concern and arranged for him to take a cure in the waters at Bourbon, but these did little lasting good and it was evident that he was dying. Louis visited him frequently and tried to rouse him by announcing, contrary to the treaty of Ryswick, that he regarded him as the rightful King of England and after his death would acknowledge his son as such. But nothing could arrest James's decline. In his last days he became ever more devout and supine – a very different figure from the harsh autocrat he had once been – forever pleading for atonement of his sins and pouring out forgiveness on those who had wronged him; and there was indeed much to forgive as few monarchs have been so brazenly betrayed by those nearest to him. He died on 16 September, his last wish being that he should have a simple funeral and a headstone bearing on it only his name and title as King of England. But this was not granted him, Louis insisting on a ceremony with full regal pomp, and his body was embalmed and put away safely so that one day it might be transferred to the Henry VII chapel in Westminster Abbey. But this was not to be.

Mary Beatrice was to have a widowhood of seventeen years. During that time she continued to be treated with great generosity and respect by the kings of France. She was allowed to stay on at the château of Saint-Germain which was to become the centre of activity for the Jacobites – those who regarded William III as a usurper and James II as the rightful king and after him his son, James Francis Edward, whom they proclaimed James III. At the time of his father's death he was only thirteen and Mary Beatrice was recognised as Regent with royal powers.

The Jacobite movement was to persist with varying degrees of fortune for nearly fifty years. It attracted a mixed bag of supporters

– on the one hand the honest and conscientious whose belief in hereditary monarchy and the divine right of kings could not be compromised, and on the other ambitious politicians with their eyes on the main chance and those who had fallen on hard times and sought to repair their fortunes with a change of dynasty. Mary Beatrice took many of these into Saint-Germain where they became a serious incubus with their petty quarrels, jealousies, importunities and disorderly behaviour. She did what she could for them but her own resources were to become severely strained. As the fortunes of war turned against Louis XIV his allowance to her was not always paid regularly and there was little hope of the money due to her from England being paid while the country was at war with France. At times she could not afford the barest necessities.

It was a great relief to Mary Beatrice to spend much time in the convent at Chaillot founded by her mother-in-law, Henrietta Maria, during her exile in France. Devotional life she loved dearly, more than her agitated existence at Saint-Germain, but she felt an obligation to rally as much support as possible for her son. Since coming of age James Francis, who had become known in France as the Chevalier de Saint George (and in England as the Old Pretender), had been actively engaged in schemes to press his claims to the English throne and these might well have prevailed and would almost certainly have done so if he had been willing to renounce his Roman Catholic faith and become a Protestant but this he would never do, influenced, no doubt, by his mother who had once declared that 'sooner than see him give up his faith she would see him dead at her feet'.

These were troubled years for Mary Beatrice. Almost always there was some besetting anxiety. James Francis was in constant danger not only because of his involvement in Jacobite plots but also because he fought with the French army against the English under Marlborough, notably in the battles of Oudenarde and Malplaquet where he was distinguished by his bravery. 1712 was a particularly agonising year when both James and his sister Louise Mary (La Consolatrice) were struck down by smallpox. The former was to survive but not the latter which was a grievous blow to her mother to whom of all people she was the closest. In 1714 there was further disaster when Louis XIV after a succession of military defeats was compelled in the treaty of Utrecht to renounce James and ban him from living in France. And then in 1715 came a major Jacobite rebellion in Scotland when a reward of £100,000 was offered for the capture of James dead or alive. In the event James arrived too late to take part in the rebellion which by then had petered out. Soon afterwards Mary Beatrice's health began to deteriorate seriously. Gout and cancer were among her afflictions. She died suddenly from inflammation of the lungs in 1718.

During her life of sixty years Mary Beatrice had had much to endure: a turbulent life in England with much undeserved abuse and suspicion because of her religion; the infidelities of her husband; the loss of five children in infancy and another in the prime of life; and then the dethronement of James and thirty years (half of her life) in exile, facing up to much harassment and misfortune. But during this time she softened from the sharp-tempered, rapacious woman she had once been and became noted for her piety and charity. There were many to whom she had given help, and at her death there were those who regarded her as a saint.

MARY II (1662–1694)

Queen of England and Wife of William III

Mary II is unique in English history in having been both a Queen Regnant and a Queen Consort, occupying the throne jointly with her husband, William III. This special arrangement had been necessary in order to bring about the so-called 'Glorious Revolution' of 1688, a revolution that was different from others in that it was bloodless, unaccompanied by bitter class warfare and resulting in no immediate social change but, nevertheless, of lasting constitutional importance.

Mary's role in it was passive but crucial. Her husband was always the dominant partner but without the support she gave to him and the Protestant religion rather than to her father, James II and the Catholic church, the revolution could not have occurred in the way that it did.

Mary was the elder daughter of James II and his first wife, Anne Duchess of York. Like most Stuart princesses she had an unsettled and tragic childhood. She and her sister Anne were the only survivors of a family of seven, and her mother died when she was nine. Her father by then had been converted to Catholicism, as too had her mother shortly before her death, but her uncle, Charles II, saw to it that she and Anne were placed in a Protestant family to be brought up as Anglicans, a faith to which both of them became strongly devoted. They continued to have contact with their father who treated them with love and kindness and did not attempt to impose his new-found faith on them. Two years later he married Mary Beatrice of Modena, only four years older than Mary, who became a close friend of both sisters. Mary was a lively, intelligent child with no great intellectual interests and her education was simple and unexacting – music, needlework, poetic drama but also a grounding in the doctrines of the Church of England. By nature she was sensitive and emotional, longing to love and be loved, and this led to a rather peculiar correspondence she carried on with a girl nine years older than herself, Frances Apsley, in which she imagined herself a lovesick heroine of romance and expressed herself in extravagantly passionate terms, beginning her letters 'dear husband' and ending them 'loving wife' and in the course of them describing herself as 'your humbel [*sic*] servant to kiss the ground where you go, to be your dog in a string, your fish in a net, your bird in a cage, your humbel trout'. Such language inevitably gave rise to suspicions of lesbianism, but there can be little doubt that her feelings were innocent, no more than a schoolgirl crush.

In 1677 when she was fifteen and those letters were in full flow, she seemed to be giving no thoughts to marriage, but others were giving the matter great consideration. By then all the children of her aunt by marriage, Queen Catherine (of Braganza) had died in infancy as too had those of her stepmother, Mary Beatrice of Modena, so she was the heiress apparent after her father, James II, and her marriage was therefore of national importance.

In 1677 Charles II's pro-French, pro-Catholic proclivities were causing mounting unrest. Puritans in particular were becoming increasingly outspoken and it was felt that something should be done to placate them and one way of doing this was by wedding Mary to a Protestant prince. Of these the outstanding candidate was Prince William of Orange, stadtholder of the Dutch republic and a grandson of Charles I and therefore Mary's first cousin. He was a man of exceptional ability and strength of character and was destined to have a crucial role in English history, but he was hardly a romantic figure – twelve years older than Mary, undersized (five inches shorter than she), humpbacked, asthmatic and pockmarked from smallpox; he was also of a dour and morose disposition and seemed to prefer the company of men to that of women. Mary was horrified at the thought of marriage to him, not least because he was a mere prince and not a crowned head, and she was not backward in making her views known, but she was overruled; duty had to come first. William too was not attracted by such a marriage; he had little love for England, certainly not for his uncle, Charles II, whom (with some reason) he regarded as louche and irresponsible. But at the same time he realised that an alliance with England was essential if he was to achieve his lifelong ambition of thwarting the aggressive intentions of Louis XIV and cutting him down to size.

In 1677, therefore, he made enquiries about Princess Mary and was assured by the English ambassador in the Hague that she was 'modest, pious and healthy', and that his engagement to her might be acceptable, and so he visited England to put his suit before her father and uncle. At the time they were at Newmarket for the races, a sport which the puritanical William thought frivolous, and the meeting between them was uneasy. James, who had been hoping for a Catholic husband for his daughter, was aloof, and Charles was cynical and apt to be facetious; but he knew that the marriage would be popular and, after some wrangling about terms, gave his consent to it. The wedding, which occurred immediately, could hardly have been less romantic – in Mary's bedroom and attended by close family only. Mary was in tears throughout and William formal and stony faced, and the atmosphere was not elevated by the king who was in ribald mood, proclaiming when seeing the couple to bed: 'Now, nephew, to your work. St George for England!'

Afterwards nothing went smoothly. William in a hurry to get back to Holland, showed scant courtesy let alone love; and there were endless delays owing to storms in the Channel and contrary winds. When eventually the newly weds set sail they travelled in separate ships and, because of the weather, had to land in a remote fishing village in Holland and then walk some four miles in icy conditions before finally reaching the Hague.

It seemed probable that Mary like her mother-in-law (also her aunt), Mary Stuart, would find life in Holland intolerable; but such was not the case. She soon became attuned to Dutch ways – the neat trim gardens, clean tidy streets, and courteous and decorous court life in contrast to the licentious conviviality of that of her uncle. She also soon learned to love her husband whom she found a different person in Holland to the one she had known in England – more relaxed and attentive and even, sometimes, warm-hearted. She soon settled down to a contented and unexacting routine – reading, gardening, entertaining and seeing to the refurbishment of royal palaces. As might be expected of two such different characters all did not run smoothly. William was away from her for long periods on public business from which she was excluded, also with his army on the battlefield which Mary dreaded but William relished. It had always been evident that he preferred the cameraderie and excitement of life in camp to the formality and decorum of life at court. He loved to live dangerously, and his favourite occupation, which was not shared by Mary, was hunting wild animals. And even when he was at home life was not perfect as he formed an attachment with one of Mary's maids of honour, Elizabeth Villiers, a lady of no great beauty – according to John Evelyn she 'squinted like a dragon' – but sympathetic and intelligent and William enjoyed her company although the extent of their liaison cannot be known. But the affair was carried on with discretion unlike the blatant prurience of Charles II and James II. And Mary was not neglected: William grew to be fond of her and they had interests in common, notably art and gardening, which they shared happily. Mary's main anxieties during her first years of marriage were ill-health and childlessness. She was constantly beset by fevers and other ailments and it became apparent in time after a number of miscarriages that, like so many Stuart princesses, she was unable to bear children.

During the eleven years between his marriage and his invasion of England in 1688 William kept a watchful eye on the tumultuous affairs of that country – the Popish Plot, the Exclusion Bill, the escapades of the Duke of Monmouth and the shifty policy of King Charles, accepting bribes from Louis XIV so that he could rule without Parliament. William noted all of these but they only interested him in so far as they affected his wars with France. The contention for supremacy between King and Parliament concerned him not because of the principle involved but because Parliament was basically opposed to Louis XIV and his imperial designs while Charles was sympathetic to them. Nor did he have strong views on the disputes between Papist and Protestant. He had been brought up a Calvinist but was not deeply religious; he was anti-Catholic but this owed less to theology than to the devout Catholicism of Louis XIV.

Charles II died suddenly on 16 February 1685 and was succeeded by James II who still had no legitimate male issue and so Mary came one stage nearer the English throne. But this she did not welcome: she had no wish to exchange her quiet orderly life in Holland for the hurly-burly of the political scene in England. And William too had misgivings: while welcoming the opportunity of engaging England more closely in the war against France, he was not prepared to accept that his wife should be the sovereign power with himself in attendance on her. For a time Mary did not realise how strong were his feelings on this matter, but when she was apprised of them by Bishop Burnet (always ready to 'put his oar in') she immediately made it known to William that he needed to have no fears on this score. 'A husband,' she told him, 'should never be obedient to his wife. Such was contrary to God's law.' This clarification came as a great relief to William and was important because thereafter he was more ready to intervene in English affairs.

The accession of James II had occurred peacefully and at first there was reason to hope that he would act reasonably, but by the end of 1686 he was setting in motion plans for the restoration of the Roman church. For the Declaration of Indulgence he issued, granting religious freedom to all, he attempted to get the support of William, but William would not be drawn; he might approve of religious toleration but if he supported the Declaration he would antagonise Parliament and so jeopardise the accession of himself and Mary to the throne. James also made an attempt to convert Mary to Catholicism. In a letter he told her how he had once been a strong Anglican but had then become convinced of 'the infallibility of the Roman faith to undermine which would destroy the whole foundation of true Christianity'. But Mary was not persuaded. She had studied the matter in depth and replied astutely: 'One does not need to read much history to find out that not all the popes have been guided by the Holy Spirit. Must they still be considered successors of St Peter when their lives contrasted so blatantly with his doctrine?'

In 1687 all James's actions were calculated to stir up strong opposition especially from the monarchy's most loyal supporters: the appointment of Roman Catholics to commands in the army and offices of state; the stationing of a large menacing standing army just outside London on Hounslow Heath; the arrest of seven bishops for protesting against the Declaration of Indulgence. All of these strained passive obedience, doctrine of faithful Tories, to the limits, but the last straw came with the birth of a son, James Francis to Mary Beatrice of Modena in 1688 with the prospect of a line of Catholic kings stretching out indefinitely. Even the staunchest Tories then became convinced that James had to be deposed which could only be done with foreign help and the man most capable of affording this was William of Orange.

And so the invitation, signed by some of the greatest names in the country, was sent to him to come to rescue traditional English liberties and the English church and to ensure the Protestant succession. William had no great interest in English liberties or the English church, but he was deeply concerned about the succession of his wife. So far he had been acting with caution, giving no

229

support to the rebellions of Monmouth and Argyll and doing nothing to provoke his father-in-law, but with the birth of Prince James Francis he decided he could remain inactive no longer and he must take an army into England. The risks of doing so were formidable. It might provoke an invasion of Holland by Louis XIV; he would have to run the gauntlet of the English navy; and his army would be outnumbered by that of James by at least two to one; without massive support in England he would be lost, and the fate of Monmouth's rebellion was a terrible precedent.

Nevertheless, he resolved to go. When he set out, with a fleet of more than two hundred ships, he was undecided whether to land in the north of England or in the south-west. In the event because of a strong wind from the east (known later as the 'Protestant Wind') he decided on the latter and landed in Torbay on 5 November 1688. At first English support was slow in coming in and William had thoughts of returning to Holland, but then it came with a rush – all of James's army, his chief ministers and his daughter Anne. James himself was but a shadow of the great commander he had once been, vacillating and indecisive, and he then made the fatal error of fleeing abroad. If he had stood his ground he might have retained his crown, as William as yet had made no claim to it, but in his absence William found himself master of the country without a shot being fired.

The crucial question then arose: what to do next. Should James remain as king under certain conditions? Should Mary be appointed regent on his behalf? By his flight could he be considered to have abdicated in which case the throne was vacant? His legal hereditary heir was his baby son, Prince James Francis, but he would certainly be brought up a Roman Catholic. The favoured candidate was Mary but she let it be known that she was only prepared to accept the throne jointly with her husband, William, and he made it plain that he was not willing to become his wife's 'gentleman usher' nor regent. He was willing to become joint sovereign with Mary but only on condition that if she predeceased him he would remain king for life to the exclusion of Mary's younger sister, Anne. Otherwise he and Mary would return to Holland. Faced with this intractability Parliament felt obliged to agree. This was of fundamental significance; it is not perhaps too much to describe it as epoch-making. For what had happened was that the throne had been declared vacant and Parliament had appointed a sovereign who was not the heir by right of birth. The logical conclusion of this was that Parliament was the ultimate power in the land, and the idea that kings were appointed by God and had divine rights could no longer be sustained. This was a bitter pill for faithful monarchists and for a long time yet the Jacobite movement was to have its supporters and at times came near to success. But the principle established in 1688 was not to be overturned.

During William's invasion of England Mary back in Holland had been suffering agonies of anxiety. She and William had had an emotional farewell during which William urged her to marry again if he should not come back and she had replied that she could never love anyone but him. Then there had been a wait of three weeks before she heard any news of how the expedition had fared. During this time as well as great suspense she had also had feelings of remorse. In the clash between her Catholic father and Protestant husband she had decided that her first loyalty lay with the latter and the preservation of the Church of England. But she could not but feel guilty about betraying her father who had always treated her well, and this had been exacerbated by a letter he had written appealing for her loyalty:

And though I know you are a good wife, and ought to be so, yet for the same reason I must believe you would be still as good a daughter to a father that has always loved you so tenderly, and that has ever done the least thing to make you doubt it.

And Mary Beatrice of Modena, to whom she had always been close, added her voice saying that she could not imagine that Mary would come over to England with her husband at the head of an invading force: 'I don't believe you could have such a thought against the worst of fathers, much less perform it against the best, that has always been kind to you, and I believe has loved you better than all the rest of his children.'

But Mary hardened her heart and never wavered in support of her husband. A fleet arrived in 1689 to take her to England which she regarded with mixed feelings. She had come to love Holland and was very happy there, far happier, she feared, than she would ever be as Queen of England. She was given a rousing reception, however, when she landed; people were eager to get a glimpse of their beautiful and youthful Queen, so much more prepossessing than her taciturn middle-aged husband. She came in for high praise but also some criticism. William had told her that in her first public appearance she should be smiling and cheerful and, as always, she complied, but there were those who thought that she overdid this and that out of consideration for her deposed father she should have been more sombre. John Evelyn wrote in his diary:

> It was believed that both, especially the Princess, should have shew'ed some seeming reluctance at least of assuming her father's Crown and made some apology, testifying by her regret that he should by his mismanagement, necessitate the nation to so extraordinary a proceeding ... but nothing of all this appear'd; she came into Whitehall laughing and jolly as to a wedding, so as to seem quite transported.

And the redoubtable Sarah Churchill wrote:

> For, whatever necessity there was of deposing King James, he was still her father, who had been so lately driven from that chamber, and that bed and if she felt no tenderness, I thought she should at least have looked grave, or even pensively sad, at so melancholy a reverse of his fortune.

Mary was sensitive to this criticism and told Bishop Burnet that she was 'merely obeying directions and acting a part which was not very natural to her'.

Mary's arrival in England came as a relief to William who was in need of support. He had never found relations with English people easy and they were becoming ever more strained. People resented his aloofness and the favouritism he was showing towards his Dutch friends, while William was angered by the attitude of some Englishmen who treated him with disdain and showed no gratitude for what he had achieved on their behalf. His temper was not improved by ill-health: the English climate and the smoke-polluted air of London did not agree with him and tuned up his asthma, and at times he seemed to have had thoughts of calling the whole adventure off and returning to Holland. Mary's charm and affability, however, made a great difference as also did her superior birthright which eased the consciences of would-be Jacobites.

Still there were many who would always regard William and Mary as usurpers; these included four hundred clergymen ('non-jurors') who were prepared to be expelled from their livings rather than swear allegiance to them.

William and Mary were crowned joint sovereigns on 11 April 1689. The occasion was one that William could hardly take seriously, describing it as 'a comedy and full of foolish old Papist ceremonies.' At about the same time James with a small army, provided for him by Louis XIV, landed in Ireland and overran most of the country. A force of mixed nationalities was despatched against him from England, but at first there was deadlock. In the following year William decided to go over himself and defeated James's army at the battle of the Boyne. While he was away Mary was left as regent in England, nominally at the head of a ruling council. This she found oppressive. She wrote at the time: 'I must hear of business which being a thing I am so new in and so unfit for, does but break my brains the more and not ease my heart.' Her cares were intensified by anxiety for the safety of both her husband and her father. It grieved her sorely to think of them confronting each other in battle and the possibility of one killing or capturing the other.

There were dangers too at home – the ever-present one of a Jacobite rebellion also of a French invasion which became more likely after an Anglo-Dutch fleet was defeated at the battle of Beachy Head and control of the English Channel passed for the time being to France. Certainly Mary was delighted at the safe return of William, although he was soon to be off again, this time to attend a congress of powers lining up for war with France. In the following years after war had been declared Mary had to become accustomed to her husband's prolonged absences. These were bleak times for her, left with ministers many of whom were unsympathetic and some of whom were secretly disloyal with Jacobite sympathies. Later she wrote in despair: 'I was very much neglected, little respected, censured of all, commended by none.'

What Mary needed while William was away was someone close to her in whom she could confide and pour out her troubles; but this she did not have. The obvious person was her sister Anne but at that time they were barely on speaking terms. Anne might seem stolid and amenable but she could also be petulant and obstinate. There had been disputes about money and state apartments and, more particularly, about her husband. Prince George of Denmark was generally thought to be ineffective and dim-witted, although amiable and harmless. His great wish was for a command in either the army or the navy, but this was vetoed by William who had a low opinion of him and treated him with scant respect which was strongly resented by Anne who loved her husband dearly, and her anger overflowed on to her sister. Later there was further ill-feeling when for flagrant disloyalty Marlborough was disgraced and Anne refused to part with his wife, Sarah, who was a member of her household and to whom she was devoted.

Mary might also have been close to her aunt by marriage, the Dowager Queen Catherine (of Braganza), but she was a devout Catholic and her sympathies lay more with James than with William, and she kept her distance. Mary's unhappiness during William's absences abroad were exacerbated by rumours spread by Jacobites bent on breaking up their marriage. Most of these were untrue but some had the ring of truth. It was undeniable that sometimes William spent more time abroad than he needed to have done, usually hunting with male companions. It was also the case that he was associating again with Elizabeth Villiers, a platonic friendship maybe but one that could not but cause Mary jealousy. Many times she must have looked back with longing on her life in Holland. 'I shall always remember,' she wrote, 'the tranquillity I enjoyed there and that I shall never find here.' Some comfort she found in charitable works, notably in the conversion of Greenwich Palace into a hospital for seamen and, further afield in the foundation of William and Mary College in Virginia. There was also a Puritanical streak in Mary which impelled her to take a stand against the vice and immorality she saw around her. She ordained that drunkenness and profanity be punished severely and the Sabbath strictly observed including such matters as the banning of hackney coaches and the baking of puddings and pies.

During the time William spent in England he always seemed restless and uneasy as well as in ill-health. He never felt at home there nor did he become attuned to the rough ways of English party politics. At first he had assumed that the Whigs, who had been mainly responsible for bringing him and Mary to the throne, would be his natural allies, but he was to discover that they had republican instincts and were always seeking to erode the prerogatives of the crown, whereas it was the Tories who, in spite of Jacobite sympathies, were the true supporters of the monarchy. He also soon became aware that most politicians of both parties were of dubious loyalty. They were not convinced that William and Mary were there to stay and that there might not one day be a Jacobite restoration, and so they hedged their bets by keeping in secret communication with the court at Saint-Germain just in case. Much as William might deplore this he considered that except in the most blatant cases he had to turn a blind eye to it, but it meant that there was never complete trust between himself and his ministers.

By the end of 1694 it became evident that Mary's health, always frail, had taken a serious turn for the worse, and just before Christmas there appeared fatal spots which betokened smallpox. Doctors applied their usual remedies (potions, hot irons, bleeding etc), but a few days later they despaired of her life and on 28 December, after what the Archbishop of Canterbury described as 'two or three strugglings of nature'; she died. She had approached death calmly and even seemed to relish it. Cares had been weighing heavily on her lately – Jacobite plots and smear campaigns, William's wars and their lack of success, the untrustworthiness of ministers, her quarrel with Anne, feelings of guilt about her father – she was finding these insupportable. She was only thirty-two but she had lost her looks, put on weight and become world weary. She told the Archbishop of Canterbury that she had little fear of dying and had prepared herself calmly and methodically and had nothing then to do but look up to God and to submit to his will. She could be satisfied that her life's work had been well done. With few intellectual gifts and no strong compelling personality she had performed a difficult and thorny role fittingly and had suffered much for it. She deserves a place in English history.

William was devastated by Mary's death. Seemingly so cold and impassive, he broke down completely and wept uncontrollably. For days he shut himself up alone in his room, numbed and unable to speak or attend to business. He even thought of abandoning all military ventures. 'I am more than ever unfit to command,' he said. He was to recover in time but he never ceased to mourn for Mary and looked on her death as a punishment from God and vowed to amend his life and break off 'all bad practices whatever', in particular his relationship with Elizabeth Villiers.

It was not only William who mourned. There was widespread grief. For once the people of England put aside their many divisions and, as Evelyn recorded, 'there was never so universal mourning'. Mary had expressed a wish that her funeral ceremonies should be 'simple and inexpensive' but in the event they were on an almost unprecedented scale. Everywhere was decked out in black cloth and purple velvet, people queued all day to pass by her lying in state, and her funeral was attended by both Houses of Parliament, the Lord Mayor and city aldermen and all the greatest in the land. There were many suggestions for a suitable memorial to her, but William was in no doubt that the one she would most have appreciated was the completion of her project to convert Greenwich Palace into a hospital for seamen, and Sir Christopher Wren was put in charge of this.

FURTHER READING

NORMAN

Appleby, John, *Troubled Reign of King Stephen* (Bell, 1969)

Ashley, Maurice, *The Life and Times of William I* (Weidenfeld & Nicolson, 1973)

Green, Judith, *Henry I* (Cambridge, 2006)

Huneycutt, Lois, *Matilda of Scotland* (Boydell, 2003)

Slocombe, George, *William the Conqueror* (Hutchinson, 1959)

Strickland, Agnes, *Lives of the Queens of England* (Colburn, 1840)

PLANTAGENET

Ashley, Maurice, *The Life and Times of King John* (Weidenfeld & Nicolson, 1972)

Baldwin, David, *Elizabeth Woodville* (Sutton, 2002)

Bevan, Bryan, *Edward III* (Rubicon, 1992)

Bevan, Bryan, *Henry IV* (Rubicon, 1994)

Bevan, Bryan, *Richard II* (Rubicon, 1990)

Bingham, Caroline, *The Life and Times of Edward II* (Weidenfeld & Nicolson, 1973)

Carpenter, D.A., *The Reign of Henry III* (Hambledon, 1996)

Erlanger, Philippe, *Margaret of Anjou* (Elek, 1970)

Gillingham, John, *The Life and Times of Richard I* (Weidenfeld & Nicolson, 1973)

Haswell, J., *The Ardent Queen* (Davies, 1976)

Hennings, Margaret, *England under Henry III* (Longmans Green, 1924)

Lloyd, Alan, *King John* (David & Charles, 1973)

Meade, Marion, *Eleanor of Aquitaine* (Muller, 1978)

Owen, D.D.R., *Eleanor of Aquitaine* (Blackwell, 1993)

Packe, M., *King Edward III* (Routledge Paul, 1983)
Pernoud, Regine, *Eleanor of Aquitaine* (Collins, 1967)
Prestwich, Michael, *Edward I* (Methuen, 1988)
Salzman, Louis Francis, *Edward I* (Constable, 1968)
Seward, Desmond, *Henry V* (Sidgwick & Jackson, 1987)
Strickland, Agnes, *Lives of the Queens of England* (Colburn, 1840)
Tuchman, Barbara, *A Distant Mirror* (Ballantine, 1979)
Tuck, Anthony, *Crown and Nobility 1272–1461* (Blackwell, 1986)
Weir, Alison, *Eleanor of Aquitaine* (Ballantine, 2000)
Weir, Alison, *Isabella – She Wolf of France* (Cape, 2005)

TUDOR

Fraser, Antonia, *Six Wives of Henry VIII* (Weidenfeld & Nicolson, 1992)
Ives, Eric, *Life and Death of Anne Boleyn* (Blackwell, 2004)
Lacey, Robert, *Life and Times of Henry VIII* (Weidenfeld & Nicolson, 1972)
Weir, Alison, *Six Wives of Henry VIII* (Bodley Head, 1991)

STUART

Bevan, Bryan, *King William III* (Rubicon, 1997)
Bone, Quentin, *Henrietta Maria, Queen of the Cavaliers* (Peter Owen, 1973)
Elsna, Hebe, *Catherine of Braganza* (Hale, 1967)
Falkus, Christopher, *Life and Times of Charles II* (Weidenfeld & Nicolson, 1972)
Fea, Allan, *James II and His Wives* (Methuen, 1908)
Fraser, Antonia, *King James I of England* (Weidenfeld & Nicolson, 1974)
Hamilton, Elizabeth, *Henrietta Maria* (Hamish Hamilton, 1976)
Hibbert, Christopher, *Charles I* (Weidenfeld & Nicolson, 1968)
Highham, Florence May Grier, *Charles I* (Hamish Hamilton, 1932)
Kiste Van der, John, *William and Mary* (Sutton, 2003)
Miller, John, *The Life and Times of William and Mary* (Weidenfeld & Nicolson, 1974)
Oman, Carola, *Henrietta Maria* (Hodder & Stoughton, 1936)

Palmer, Tony, *Charles II – Portrait of an Age* (Cassell, 1979)

Plowden, Alison, *Henrietta Maria – Charles I's Indomitable Queen* (Sutton, 2001)

Turner, Francis Charles, *James II* (Eyre & Spottiswoode, 1948)

Williams, Ethel Carleton, *Anne of Denmark* (Longman, 1970)

Willson, David Harris, *King James VI and I* (Jonathan Cape, 1956)

INDEX

241